Deleuze, Digital Media and Thought

Plateaus – New Directions in Deleuze Studies

'It's not a matter of bringing all sorts of things together under a single concept but rather of relating each concept to variables that explain its mutations.'
Gilles Deleuze, *Negotiations*

Series Editors
Ian Buchanan, University of Wollongong
Claire Colebrook, Penn State University

Editorial Advisory Board
Keith Ansell Pearson, Ronald Bogue, Constantin V. Boundas, Rosi Braidotti, Eugene Holland, Gregg Lambert, Dorothea Olkowski, Paul Patton, Daniel Smith, James Williams

Titles available in the series
Christian Kerslake, *Immanence and the Vertigo of Philosophy: From Kant to Deleuze*
Jean-Clet Martin, *Variations: The Philosophy of Gilles Deleuze*, translated by Constantin V. Boundas and Susan Dyrkton
Simone Bignall, *Postcolonial Agency: Critique and Constructivism*
Miguel de Beistegui, *Immanence – Deleuze and Philosophy*
Jean-Jacques Lecercle, *Badiou and Deleuze Read Literature*
Ronald Bogue, *Deleuzian Fabulation and the Scars of History*
Sean Bowden, *The Priority of Events: Deleuze's Logic of Sense*
Craig Lundy, *History and Becoming: Deleuze's Philosophy of Creativity*
Aidan Tynan, *Deleuze's Literary Clinic: Criticism and the Politics of Symptoms*
Thomas Nail, *Returning to Revolution: Deleuze, Guattari and Zapatismo*
François Zourabichvili, *Deleuze: A Philosophy of the Event* with *The Vocabulary of Deleuze* edited by Gregg Lambert and Daniel W. Smith, translated by Kieran Aarons
Frida Beckman, *Between Desire and Pleasure: A Deleuzian Theory of Sexuality*
Nadine Boljkovac, *Untimely Affects: Gilles Deleuze and an Ethics of Cinema*
Daniela Voss, *Conditions of Thought: Deleuze and Transcendental Ideas*
Daniel Barber, *Deleuze and the Naming of God: Post-Secularism and the Future of Immanence*
F. LeRon Shults, *Iconoclastic Theology: Gilles Deleuze and the Secretion of Atheism*
Janae Sholtz, *The Invention of a People: Heidegger and Deleuze on Art and the Political*
Marco Altamirano, *Time, Technology and Environment: An Essay on the Philosophy of Nature*
Sean McQueen, *Deleuze and Baudrillard: From Cyberpunk to Biopunk*
Ridvan Askin, *Narrative and Becoming*
Marc Rölli, *Gilles Deleuze's Transcendental Empiricism: From Tradition to Difference*, translated by Peter Hertz-Ohmes
Guillaume Collett, *The Psychoanalysis of Sense: Deleuze and the Lacanian School*
Ryan J. Johnson, *The Deleuze-Lucretius Encounter*
Allan James Thomas, *Deleuze, Cinema and the Thought of the World*
Cheri Lynne Carr, *Deleuze's Kantian Ethos: Critique as a Way of Life*
Alex Tissandier, *Affirming Divergence: Deleuze's Reading of Leibniz*
Barbara Glowczewski, *Indigenising Anthropology with Guattari and Deleuze*
Koichiro Kokubun, *The Principles of Deleuzian Philosophy*, translated by Wren Nishina
Felice Cimatti, *Unbecoming Human: Philosophy of Animality After Deleuze*, translated by Fabio Gironi
Ryan J. Johnson, *Deleuze, A Stoic*
Jane Newland, *Deleuze in Children's Literature*
D. J. S. Cross, *Deleuze and the Problem of Affect*
Laurent de Sutter, *Deleuze's Philosophy of Law*, translated by Nils F. Schott
Andrew M. Jampol-Petzinger, *Deleuze, Kierkegaard and the Ethics of Selfhood*
Nir Kedem, *A Deleuzian Critique of Queer Thought: Overcoming Sexuality*
Timothy Deane-Freeman, *Deleuze, Digital Media and Thought*

Forthcoming volumes
Axel Cherniavsky, *Deleuze and the Creation of Concepts: Philosophy and Methodology*, translated by Taylor Adkins
Sean Bowden, *Expression, Action and Agency in Deleuze: Willing Events*
Justin Litaker, *Deleuze and Guattari's Political Economy*

Visit the Plateaus website at edinburghuniversitypress.com/series/plat

DELEUZE, DIGITAL MEDIA AND THOUGHT

Timothy Deane-Freeman

EDINBURGH
University Press

Edinburgh University Press is one of the leading university presses in the UK. We publish academic books and journals in our selected subject areas across the humanities and social sciences, combining cutting-edge scholarship with high editorial and production values to produce academic works of lasting importance. For more information visit our website: edinburghuniversitypress.com

© Tim Deane-Freeman, 2024, 2025

Edinburgh University Press Ltd
13 Infirmary Street
Edinburgh EH1 1LT

First published in hardback by Edinburgh University Press 2024

Typeset in 11/13 Sabon LT Pro
by Cheshire Typesetting Ltd, Cuddington, Cheshire

A CIP record for this book is available from the British Library

ISBN 978 1 3995 1725 6 (hardback)
ISBN 978 1 3995 1726 3 (paperback)
ISBN 978 1 3995 1727 0 (webready PDF)
ISBN 978 1 3995 1728 7 (epub)

The right of Timothy Deane-Freeman to be identified as the author of this work has been asserted in accordance with the Copyright, Designs and Patents Act 1988, and the Copyright and Related Rights Regulations 2003 (SI No. 2498).

Contents

Acknowledgements	vi
Abbreviations	vii
Introduction: An Art of the Unseen	1
1 Where is the Outside?	18
2 The Image and the Out-of-Field	40
3 A Politics of the Out-of-Field	74
4 The Digital Image	105
5 Cybernetic Information	134
6 *Inland Empire*	164
7 Art and the Digital	199
Conclusion: The Digital Outside	231
Bibliography	239
Index	254

Acknowledgements

Every book contains a multitude, and this one couldn't have been realised without the kindness, criticism and encouragement of the following friends and colleagues, whom I list in no particular order: Robert Sinnerbrink, Ronald Bogue, Dork Zabunyan, Jeanne Etelain, Daniela Voss, Zoé Texereau, George Duke, Timothy Laurie, Vince Le, Kirk Turner, Amy Mead, Liam Kenny, Noirin van de Berg, my parents Chris and Judy, Tim Neal, Meg McCamley, Matt Sharpe, Jack Reynolds, Romi Graham and Tilly. I am particularly indebted to Sean Bowden and Anne Sauvagnargues, for their patient and enlightened supervision of the doctoral research from which this book emerged, and to Max Lowdin, for some incisive critical remarks at a crucial stage. I am also very grateful to Claire Colebrook and Ian Buchanan for including my work in the Plateaus Series, and to Sarah Foyle and the team at Edinburgh University Press for their help and patience.

A substantial portion of Chapter 3 appeared in the article 'An Unthinkable Cinema: Deleuze's Mutant Politics of Film', *Philosophy & Social Criticism*, 49(8) (2023), pp. 930–49. I gratefully acknowledge the permission of the journal editors to republish this material.

Abbreviations

CC   Deleuze, Gilles, *Essays Critical and Clinical*, trans. D. W. Smith and M. A. Greco (Minneapolis, MN: University of Minnesota Press, 1997)

CI   Deleuze, Gilles, *Cinema I: The Movement-Image*, trans. H. Tomlinson and B. Habberjam (London: Bloomsbury, 2013)

CII   Deleuze, Gilles, *Cinema II: The Time-Image*, trans. H. Tomlinson and R. Galeta (London: Bloomsbury, 2013)

DR   Deleuze, Gilles, *Difference and Repetition*, trans. P. Patton (New York: Columbia University Press, 1994)

I   Simondon, Gilbert, *Individuation in Light of Notions of Form and Information*, trans. T. Adkins (Minneapolis, MN: University of Minnesota Press, 2020)

MM   Bergson, Henri, *Matter and Memory*, trans. N. M. Paul and W. S. Palmer (New York: Zone Books, 2005)

N   Deleuze, Gilles, *Negotiations, 1972–1990*, trans. M. Joughin (New York: Columbia University Press, 1995)

PS   Deleuze, Gilles, 'Postscript on the Societies of Control', *October*, 59 (winter 1992), pp. 3–7.

Introduction: An Art of the Unseen

This book aims to place the philosophy of Gilles Deleuze in dialogue with contemporary digital media, and is animated by a conviction that this move might help us to better understand both digital media and Deleuze's thought. While Deleuze himself wrote relatively little about the digital, my claim is that his work nevertheless offers us a valuable set of concepts for thinking through the explosive proliferation of digital images that characterises twenty-first-century life. In particular, I argue that his two-volume study of cinema – *Cinema I: The Movement-Image*, and *Cinema II: The Time-Image* – can help us to grasp the complex ways in which digital images both provoke and problematise our thinking. These images *make us think*, in the simultaneously troubling and optimistic senses of that phrase, and I believe that Deleuze's work is particularly useful in drawing out this tension. In this context, I turn to the difficult concept of the 'outside' (*dehors*), which Deleuze takes up from the literary philosophy of Maurice Blanchot, redeploying this idea to help us think through digital image cultures.

The 'outside' emerges from one of Deleuze's keenest intuitions about film: that it is the site of unique experiments with the unseen. In order to understand this apparently paradoxical claim, we might think first of a simple example from Chaplin. In *A Woman of Paris* (1923), a train arrives at the platform, but all we see are the shadows and luminosity of its windows, traced across the waiting woman's face. We don't actually see the train – it doesn't, indeed, exist – yet its implied or virtual presence determines the very content of the image. In this way, through an exercise in *framing*, the image is constituted as much by what is 'outside' the frame as that which we see articulated before us in movement and in gesture. Of course, we might object that this device is found in other artforms. Painting has long used similar methods for projecting an 'out-of-frame', such as often implicates the spectator.[1] But cinema's capacities for the expression of both movement and time afford it unique powers in this space. By putting its images in motion – or rather by composing images *from* motion – cinema likewise renders this 'unseen' kinetic, causing it to become dynamic, fluid and multiple.

We might think of the gradually accumulating horror of Danny's tricycle rides in Kubrick's *The Shining* (1980). Here, the camera follows Danny from behind as he explores the labyrinthine hallways of the Overlook Hotel. We know already that the hotel is cursed, and that Danny's psychic powers destine him to first encounter its horrors. As such, his slowly unfurling trajectories are infused with a terror of anticipation; as Danny and the camera turn each corner, we know it's only a matter of time before he confronts a gruesome – but as yet unseen – vision. Here, in a perfectly cinematic structure, the 'unseen' becomes temporal, cumulative, evolving qualitatively; implicated with, yet irreducible to, the strictures of narrativity.

And these operations are not unique to horror in the strict sense. Resnais and Robbe-Grillet's *Last Year at Marienbad* (1961) uses disjunctive editing to create an 'irrational' environment in which the settings composed through shot and counter-shot make no sense in terms of subjective experience, in which characters speak without making a sound, and disembodied voices float over scenes with no clear relation to the visual image. The horror of Resnais' hotel is not one of ghosts or psychopaths, but of the shifting, uncertain functions of perception itself, which here ceases to serve coherent action or narrative, instead opening onto a vista of irrational and inexplicable movements of space and of time. Here, the unseen becomes the *unthought*, the *unthinkable*, a multiplicity of space-times which exist beyond the perceptual and cognitive habits of the human subject, in a function which in turn confronts us with the interests and contingency of these very habits.

And it's this play with that which is 'outside' both conditioned perception and habitual mentation that Deleuze sees as marking a uniquely cinematic contribution to philosophy. Something in the cinematic image *forces us to think*, and this – in keeping with a broader Deleuzian account of noesis – always indicates a movement beyond what thought has hitherto been in order to produce the unforeseen, singular and new. In this context, writes Deleuze, cinema 'expresses a new relation between thought and seeing, or between thought and the light source, which constantly sets the thought outside itself, outside knowledge, outside action' (*CII*, 182). Keith Ansell-Pearson has described Deleuze's philosophy more generally as a thought of the 'outside', a thought which intends to 'philosophise in the most radical manner conceivable, doing violence to the mind by breaking

Introduction

both with the natural bent of the intellect and with habits of scientific praxis'.[2] And it is indeed pursuant to this kind of philosophy that Deleuze turns to cinema, taking its unique relations with the 'outside' of the image as the vehicle for a profound 'deterritorialisation' of thought.

The present study, however, is dedicated to a problem which emerges at the close of Deleuze's work on film, and to a series of technical, political and aesthetic developments which have taken place in the years since he was writing. Digitisation – the translation, not just of cinema, but of almost every media form, into chains of discrete symbols for transmission, storage and distribution through computing and telephonic networks – has fundamentally altered the way images are produced, consumed and thought. Cinema, once *the* moving image, has abdicated its central position in screen culture, first to television, and subsequently to computers, tablets, smartphones and beyond, in an evolution effected by the immense efficiencies of digital encoding. The so-called 'digital revolution', indeed, was already so tangible an event when Deleuze was working on the cinema volumes in the 1980s that he was able to write, with no small prescience, 'the life or the afterlife of cinema depends on its internal struggle with informatics' (*CII*, 277) in an enigmatic ellipsis to these works.

L'informatique – rendered the slightly more obtrusive 'informatics' in English – is a term Deleuze uses in discussing 'the electronic image [...] the tele and video image, the numerical image coming into being' (*CII*, 272).[3] The term first emerged from the work of computer scientist Philippe Dreyfus,[4] and is a portmanteau of the words *information* and *automatique* – a coupling clearly at the forefront of Deleuze's thinking, given that he uses it in discussing a new configuration of social power linked to 'automata of computation and thought, automata with controls and feedback' (*CII*, 272). While Deleuze says relatively little about these new images, his brief remarks are intriguing, and comprise the starting point for the present work:

> The electronic image, that is the tele and video image, the numerical image coming into being, had either to transform cinema or to replace it, to mark its death. We do not claim to be producing an analysis of the new images, which would be beyond our aims, but only to indicate certain effects whose relation to the cinematographic image remains to be determined. The new images no longer have any outside (out-of-field), any more than they are internalised in a whole; rather, they have a right side

and a reverse, reversible and non-superimposable, like a power to turn back on themselves. They are the object of a perpetual reorganization, in which a new image can arise at any point whatever of the preceding image [...] And the screen itself, even if it keeps a vertical position by convention, no longer seems to refer to the human posture, like a window or a painting, but rather constitutes a table of information, an opaque surface on which are inscribed 'data', information replacing nature, and the brain-city, the third eye, replacing the eyes of nature. (*CII*, 272–3)

This strange passage is striking not just because it so thoroughly anticipates certain phenomenal and aesthetic dimensions of the twenty-first-century image. What Deleuze expresses here, albeit obliquely, is the fundamental philosophical challenge that the digital image presents. Deleuze suggests that these new images no longer have an 'outside', and while his English translators may have taken liberties here (Deleuze uses the word *extériorité*, rather than *dehors*), I believe that this claim nevertheless articulates, *avant la lettre*, a key problem of thinking with and through digital image technics.

While the cinematic image clearly has a limit – not only do spectators leave the cinema, but the cinematic frame itself delineates specific images, as such implicating the limits of our thought – the digital image of the twenty-first century seems increasingly to refuse externality, referring endlessly to further, networked images, in a ceaseless flow that characterises twenty-first-century life. Not only do we carry a mini-cinema with us in our pockets, but its limpid surface refracts a stream of interconnected and immersive image-worlds, which will become, in one digital mogul's estimation, 'the primary way that we live our lives and spend our time' in an imminently foreseeable future.[5] We can trace this development right across the ecology of digital images, from immersive, 'open world' video games to the nested pages of online and URL environments. The paradigm case is *virtual reality*, which eschews the explicit delineation of pictorial framing in order to pursue a multidimensional image-space. This development is simultaneously technical and aesthetic, linked to new possibilities for the composition of images and an attendant sense of how images ought to be experienced. In this context, as Gregory Flaxman has written, 'the off-screen is presented not as an aesthetic limit or philosophical problem but as a technological obstacle that we are sure to overcome', in a development with consequences for the Deleuzian account of thought.[6]

Indeed if, since antiquity,[7] philosophy has privileged a singular, albeit complex, relationship between the visible and the knowable,

Introduction

with the unseen thus analogous to that which we have not yet thought – then this evolution has implications for our 'image of thought', given that it smuggles an aspiration to *total visibility*, a desire to 'show it all' expressed in media as diverse as satellite imaging, pornography and MRIs. Central to this development is *information*, which 'replaces nature', inasmuch as it opens up the possibility of a total representational space. If everything – from Afghan wilderness to brain activity – might be imaged in its multiple dimensions by chains of digital code, then the world itself appears to lack an outside, and is as such potentially subject to the same reticular operations of 'control'.

The theme of control emerges across a series of Deleuze's later works, and is intimately related to these new image *techniques*. What Deleuze calls 'societies of control' are in the process of overtaking Foucault's disciplinary societies, replacing centralised and static forms of power with a-centred and dynamic mechanisms that are infinitely more efficient. These societies use information technologies in order to effect control in the cybernetic sense – of feedback loops and deutero-learning, which are used to maintain certain carefully selected variables. The image technologies of control societies, from dating apps to facial recognition software, thus work through a kind of flexible mechanism, 'learning' from the objects which they image in order to produce ever more efficient and targeted results. Commensurate with these technologies is a notion of thought itself as 'information processing', emerging from cybernetics, but now hegemonic across various strains of psychology, neuroscience and philosophy of mind.[8]

From a Deleuzian perspective, we might say that the problem with this approach – as both political technique and an image of mentation – is that it seems to lack an *outside*, and an account of how the unthought or non-actual might simultaneously displace and provoke our thinking. And while Deleuze ultimately remains agnostic as to the future of the informatic image, a number of remarks in his later works suggest a growing pessimism. 'A work of art does not contain the least bit of information', he suggested in a 1987 lecture, 'in contrast, there is a fundamental affinity between a work of art and an act of resistance.'[9] Or again, with Félix Guattari:

> The most shameful moment came when computer science, marketing, design, and advertising, all the disciplines of communication, seized hold of the word concept and said: "This is our concern, we are the creative

ones, we are the *ideas men*! We are the friends of the concept, we put it in our computers." Information and creativity, concept and enterprise: there is already an abundant bibliography.[10]

And while there has been relatively little scholarship linking these disparate critical salvos, we might well conclude that for Deleuze, the terms *information, computing* and *communication* signify grave dangers to the 'thought from outside' which is perhaps his primary philosophical objective.

Deleuze is not alone in suggesting that these new techniques of the image pose grave dangers to thought, in both its conception and its practice. Indeed, his later work is in some ways contiguous with a significant body of critical literature characterising digital technologies as deleterious to human noetic capacities, from Nicholas Carr[11] to Bernard Stiegler,[12] 'Bifo' Berardi[13] and Jean-François Lyotard.[14] While the story comes in various forms and levels of sophistication, in broad outline it runs thus: the ubiquity of digital technologies menaces our capacities for singular and resistant forms of thought, alongside those for solidarity, communicative reason and memory, in a development commensurate with a globalised economy plunging towards catastrophe. And indeed, I make no objection to the general outline of that thesis in this book. My work is also, however, animated by a conviction that Deleuze opens up stranger and more difficult paths, perhaps helping us to conceive of the digital image as that which *forces us to think*, in the affirmative sense that he will give this phrase.

It surprises no one today, after all, to say that digital media manipulate our sense of self, monitor or control us. And as such, these claims perhaps betray the proper spirit of Deleuze's philosophy, replicating an orthodoxy which serves to sadden nobody.[15] These charges, it should be noted, also bear a striking resemblance to that thesis regarding cinema – consistently rejected by Deleuze – according to which it is simply distraction or ideology, the apparatus by which hegemonic powers interpolate particular subjects and forms of subjugation. Part of what makes Deleuze so rich an interlocutor in our thinking on the evolution of the image, indeed, is his rejection of any such simplistic *telos*, and his hostility to stories both of historical progress and cultural decline. 'There is no need to ask which is the toughest or most tolerable regime', he writes in his 'Post-Script on the Societies of Control', 'for it's within each of them that liberating and enslaving forces confront one another [...] There is no need to

Introduction

fear or hope, but only to look for new weapons' (*PS*, 4). And indeed, this book, in its own modest way, constitutes a search for weapons, philosophical and otherwise, which might help us to think with and through the digital image cultures we inhabit.

How do digital images make us think? What does the 'outside' of thought look like, when the image no longer seems to have one? These questions lie at the heart of this book, and animate its attempt to articulate a uniquely *digital outside*: a problematic inner limit to both digital media and contemporary thought. In answering them, we must move beyond the letter of Deleuze's philosophy, taking in both the wellsprings of his concepts and exploring developments in the image in the years since he was writing. We must turn to cybernetics and information theory, eschewing a broadly visual conception of the outside and exploring the materiality of information itself.

Information, we must note before proceeding, is perhaps as ambiguous and contested a term as 'reality', 'being' or 'truth'. Indeed Claude Shannon, the mathematician and electrical engineer often cited as the 'father of information theory', was dubious that so general a concept could ever '*satisfactorily account for the numerous possible applications of this general field*'.[16] Without lapsing into lengthy definitions here, we might say that while a concept *like* information as a kind of immaterial or quasi-material operative principle *in-forming* matter has been present in philosophy since at least Aristotle's hylomorphism, the popular sense of the term today is invariably what Luciano Floridi describes as 'semantic',[17] equating information with something like 'facts', specifically those that might inform our courses of action. The term adopted a new and rigorously technical sense in the mid-twentieth century, however, following its use in telecommunications engineering. Here, information becomes a statistical designation, untethered from semantic meaning, and referring to the measure of a communication system's capacity for the transmission of (a fundamentally variable) content.

In their 1949 text *The Mathematical Theory of Communication* (henceforth the MTC), Shannon and his colleague Warren Weaver thus posit information in *quantitative* terms, as emerging from a probability space.[18] Information, in this context, refers to the quantity of uncertainty that is removed from an *informee's* understanding of a situation which, nevertheless, requires an initial level of uncertainty in order for information to be transmitted. And what information technologies predicated upon the MTC therefore aspire to is a maximisation of this initial 'data deficit' (the maximum possibility for messages) such that the amount of information (or reduction of data deficit) might be likewise maximal. We will return in detail to this model in the relevant chapter. For now, it suffices to say that information technologies based on the MTC are thus conceived as fundamentally 'neutral' *vis-à-vis* semantic questions of meaning or content. It doesn't matter what message I send, but rather *how much* information a particular message or communication system is able to accommodate.

But this apparent neutrality is rendered problematic by *noise*, the 'Augustinian Evil' which Norbert Wiener claims communication systems must always struggle against.[19] Noise, in terms of the MTC, is unwanted data in an information system, which information engineering thus strives to reduce and mitigate. But it is also potential information, according to the strictly a-semantic sense that information theory gives this term. The only means of distinguishing 'wanted' from 'unwanted' data, or noise from information, is by applying pre-determined semantic or intentional criteria, in a move that problematises information theory's ostensible neutrality. In this way, implicit communicative ideals of clarity and efficiency contaminate what is perhaps information theory's richest *philosophical* contribution, a concept of information as a-signifying and processual – irreducible to any particular intentionality or semantics. By conceiving of it in this way, early theorists like Shannon open the way for a philosophical model of information which might include noise, with information no longer conceived in terms of predetermined signals, but rather as a differential and differentiating *process of individuation*. And such, indeed, is the conception of Deleuze's contemporary Gilbert Simondon, whose philosophy of information we will also need to treat.

If information theory aspires, but ultimately fails, to escape from predetermined semantic criteria, then perhaps it can also learn from the case of art, where openness to non-intentionality and deliberate disorder of established semantic systems is a norm – at least under the auspices of modernism. And in the latter part of this book I try to theorise an 'informatic art', which might deploy a-signifying noise in order to articulate the limits of digital technics. In the works of David Lynch, among others, I identify a *digital outside*, constituted through a strategic deployment of noisy digital materials, and helping us to reconceive of information as that which forces us into the creative individuation of thought. I claim that such projects are perhaps commensurate with a broader emancipatory impulse, which,

Introduction

albeit ambiguous and fundamentally vulnerable, the likes of Walter Benjamin and Félix Guattari have identified in mass media cultures generally.

But before turning to these latter claims, we must sketch out the concept of the outside itself, our task in Chapter 1. Here, I map the outside across a series of related projects, establishing its significance throughout Deleuze's *oeuvre*. We begin with Maurice Blanchot, who claims the outside as the impersonal core of literature, the place at which the author no longer says 'I', and where literature begins to 'speak itself'. It is subsequently taken up by Foucault, who identifies the outside as the 'hiding place of all being', a 'silent rumbling' beneath, yet immanent to, the interested fabrications of discourse. After treating these two thinkers I proceed – albeit wary of the problems attendant to reading Deleuzian concepts as interchangeable across his works – to briefly explicate Deleuze's critique, in *Difference and Repetition*, of a 'dogmatic image of thought', establishing it as part of the same noetic project which will subsequently orient his outside. Deleuze's critique of this dogmatic image – a conservative and reactionary model of thought as recognition – provides the clearest distillation of his project to move philosophy away from its prejudices and habitudes towards a creative practice of 'encounters'. In this context, Deleuze posits thought as emerging from a simultaneous encounter with both the unthought and with thinking's inner limit – a refractory experience of provocation and constraint, which causes our noetic faculties to become differentially productive, provoked by their contact with what he calls a pure 'being of the sensible'.

In Chapter 2 I extend the Deleuzian critique of habitual thought into his work on cinema. We have seen that thought emerges from an encounter with the radically unthought, and in Deleuze's work on cinema this unthought is articulated in terms of the outside. Contrary, however, to the literary outside of Blanchot and Foucault, the cinematic outside emerges from film's unique capacity for 'framing'. This chapter will thus explore the means by which framing expresses a problematic relation between thought and the 'whole', eschewing our habitual modes of thinking, what Deleuze here calls, borrowing Bergson's term, the 'sensory-motor schema'. And in the temporally charged post-war cinema, Deleuze claims that this 'openness' of the image attains a new power. In post-war cinema – the desolate facticity of Italian neo-realism, the irrational temporalities of the French New Wave, the vague wanderings of New Hollywood – the 'whole' is replaced with an 'outside', no longer guarantor of the image's meaning, but of a fundamental incomprehensibility with which it is in contact. As such, this chapter closes by tracing the historical account which forms the axis of the two cinema volumes – the decline of the various sensory-motor 'action images' and the rise of a pure cinematic 'time-image' – a transition, albeit not 'historical' in any ordinary sense, which is nevertheless grounded squarely in concrete social and political circumstances. In this context, Deleuze claims that the cinematic image begins to form crystals and circuitries between the virtual and actual, drawing to the surface unthought temporal forces in a catalytic imbrication of 'truth', 'falsehood', 'dream' and 'reality', a state of affairs I explore through a brief discussion of Chris Marker's *La Jetée* (1962).

Chapter 3 turns to the political implications of the outside, and as such prepares the ground for the critical engagement with control societies that I mount in the latter part of the book. While the political status of Deleuze's work is far from a settled question – with Slavoj Žižek and Alain Badiou, for instance, both arguing that no positive or programmatic 'politics' can be derived from Deleuze's thought – I tend rather to follow Paola Marrati, who argues that the two cinema volumes constitute a major expression of Deleuze's political philosophy.[20] I defend this claim by explicating the key concept of 'belief in the world', as it emerges throughout *The Time-Image*, suggesting that cinema, in Deleuze's estimation, demonstrates the link between humans and their world, but only insofar as both terms – humans, world – are understood as fluid and fundamentally 'problematic' – a position influenced by Deleuze's idiosyncratic readings of Spinoza, Nietzsche and Marx. I also argue that Deleuze's cinematic philosophy accords with a Marxist inflection that we might trace right throughout his and Guattari's thought, and a conviction that the forces of resistance to capitalism must be conceived as immanent to capitalism itself.

In Chapter 4, explication of Deleuze's concepts gives way to a constructive movement squarely focused on defining – and problematising – the digital. Here, I take up Gregory Flaxman's argument that contemporary digital media, paradigmatically for his purposes a big-budget cinematic work like James Cameron's *Avatar* (2009), consecrate a series of operations which close philosophically valuable openings onto the outside, doing so in several interconnected ways: first, through a proliferation of the cinematic frame such that we are denied a literal 'outside' of the contemporary mass media image; second, through an overdetermination of capital in the

Introduction

image, which squeezes out potentialities for error and obscurity; and finally, through the embrace of a film-making practice which treats cinematic images as 'information' or 'data', eschewing all indexical relations to an external reality. Contrary to Flaxman, and in keeping with a profound mechanism of affirmation which I claim animates Deleuze's thought, I argue that it is by exploring these very processes that we might locate the digital image's own outside.

In this context, I briefly introduce what Luciano Floridi designates the 'informational turn' in contemporary philosophy, a paradigm which has seen various thinkers, drawing on information theory, philosophise with, about and against information in the late twentieth and early twenty-first centuries. I recapitulate Deleuze's critique of information in the closing stages of *The Time-Image*, as well as in his 'Postscript on the Societies of Control' and the lecture 'What is the Creative Act?', arguing that Deleuze, following a broader trend in French post-phenomenological thought, may have erred in equivocating semantic and technical concepts of information, as such limiting his thought. Technical and cybernetic accounts of information, I suggest, offer fertile connectives with the type of philosophy Deleuze advocates.

In Chapter 5, I introduce Shannon's mathematical theory of communication. Here, I argue that Shannon's strictly technical approach to information, as a probabilistic measure of uncertainty and subsequent reduction of data deficit, may resonate with Deleuze's thought in helpful and underexplored ways. I continue with a brief discussion of the ways in which the particular technical problems to which information theory responds, however, inadvertently reinscribe semantic dimensions that the theory is eager to avoid. I argue that the impossibility of any information transmission without some form of noise, and the difficulty with which information theory can distinguish 'useful' and 'unwanted' information without bringing any pre-established semantic systems to bear, points us to the possibility of a uniquely digital outside. In this context, I briefly introduce Simondon's ontogenetic account of information, as the operative element whereby concrete individuals are fundamentally open to variation, a consequence of their emergence from pre-individual 'metastable states'. This approach, I argue, helps us to conceive of informatic noise as fundamentally productive – irreducible to any given operation of control.

Chapter 6 returns to our overarching question. Is it possible to think of contemporary, digital media which do in fact present us with an outside? Which approach, in Gregory Flaxman's words, 'the point where and when we dispense with presuppositions and define thought itself as a problem?'[21] Such media would need to deploy informatic noise in such a way as produces 'unthinkable' perceptual events, as such calling the communicative logic of the digital itself into question. And David Lynch's *Inland Empire* (2006), I claim, does just that. Through a consistent foregrounding of the noise of its digital materiality, through its return to the cinematic 'index' in the form of an excoriating lead performance, through its profound criticism of Hollywood and the determinations of capital in the image, and through its presentation of loops of a-chronological and chaotic temporality, *Inland Empire* constitutes a film profoundly open to the Deleuzian outside, albeit on its own, uniquely digital, terms.

Inland Empire, however, occupies a strange position in the contemporary ecology of images, given its status as a feature-length, *auteur* production in the twentieth-century style. While it *reflects* the multiplicity of contemporary digital images, it remains in many ways a 'time-image' in the classical sense, composed with distinctly bourgeois aesthetic intent. In Chapter 7, I therefore extend my analysis of the digital outside into an account of both the televisual image and what Guattari calls 'post-media societies', and a world in which aesthetic production is perhaps no longer the privileged terrain of rare, 'genius' creators. Through a discussion of the televisual image in general, and the digi-televisual in Lynch's *Twin Peaks: The Return*, I pursue a new form of aesthetic production which overspills the world of art, deploying digital techniques in order to produce 'formal compounds' between the human being and the forces of the outside, in a potentially revolutionary constellation of becomings.

This is not, of course, a unique project, and scholarship dedicated to the complex relationship between Deleuze and so-called 'new technologies' abounds. A number of collections, including *Deleuze and New Technology*, edited by Mark Poster and David Savat, *Deleuze and the Contemporary World*, edited by Ian Buchanan and Adrian Parr, and *Control Culture: Foucault and Deleuze after Discipline*, edited by Frida Beckman, treat Deleuze's thought in the context of the digital 'revolution'. In addition, single- or dual-author studies focusing on pertinent aspects of Deleuze's philosophy in contemporary, digital contexts include those of Alexander Galloway – *Protocol: How Control Exists After Decentralization* and *The Exploit: A*

Introduction

Theory of Networks written with Eugene Thacker – David Savat and Tauel Harper's co-authored *Media after Deleuze*, and in a work dealing with themes perhaps most explicitly linked to my own, Kane Faucher's *Metastasis and Metastability: A Deleuzian Approach to Information*. This list is far from exhaustive, and indeed these works have all provided insights and exegeses that have informed my own research.

At the same time, given the centrality of the cinematic image to my analysis, I must here acknowledge the constellation of works dedicated to Deleuze's two cinema volumes. After a period of initial neglect in the Anglophone world,[22] since the early 2000s there has been an explosion of scholarship dedicated to the two Deleuzian cinema books, including the collections *The Brain is the Screen*, edited by Gregory Flaxman, *Deleuze and the Schizoanalysis of Cinema*, edited by Ian Buchanan and Patricia MacCormack, *Afterimages of Gilles Deleuze's Film Philosophy*, edited by D. N. Rodowick, and a spring 1997 edition of *Iris* dedicated to 'Gilles Deleuze, Philosopher of Cinema', also edited by Rodowick. In addition, there have been numerous monographs published, which can roughly be divided into two categories: explanatory works which clarify and comment upon Deleuze's cinematic 'taxonomy', and 'extensions' or 'redeployments' which put Deleuze's cinematic concepts to work in regions beyond their initial scope.

In this first category we might place Felicity Colman's *Deleuze and Cinema: The Film Concepts*, Ronald Bogue's *Deleuze on Cinema*, Richard Rushton's *Cinema After Deleuze*, David Deamer's *Deleuze's Cinema Books: Three Introductions to the Taxonomy of Images*, and Allan James Thomas's *Deleuze, Cinema and the Thought of the World*. These works have all provided me with rich insights into Deleuze's difficult cinematic philosophy. It is important to note, however, that despite occasional references, none of these works deals systematically with Deleuze's critique of information, nor with the 'digitisation' of cinema in depth. Colman, for instance, suggests that Deleuze's concepts generally work interchangeably regardless of the digital or analogue status of the image.[23] Bogue closes with a brief and thoughtful meditation on the televisual image, but ultimately concludes that 'television, computers and information technology in general provide external conditions of possibility for creativity in the cinema ... but internal, properly cinematic concerns are finally what guide directors in their invention of new images'.[24] Rushton makes similar remarks, arguing that the philosophical apparatus of the movement-and-time images are sufficient to give an account of cinema in its more contemporary guises.[25] For Deamer and Thomas, neither digitisation, nor information, are central terms, and are not dealt with in any extensive way.

Finally, I must here acknowledge the work of both D. N. Rodowick and Patricia Pisters, each of whom treats many of the same problems as the present volume. Rodowick, particularly in *The Virtual Life of Film*, is interested in the 'end of cinema' at the hands of digital media, and the implications digital media might have for film theory itself. Pisters meanwhile, in *The Neuro-Image: A Deleuzian Film-Philosophy of Digital Screen Culture*, links Deleuze's work to contemporary research in neuroscience and cognition conceived in the 4EA mould,[26] exploring this connection through digital image cultures. I have benefited immensely from their work, alongside that of Gregory Flaxman, to which I will return in depth. My own approach, however, differs in its focus on information theory and cybernetics, such that I believe it complements, rather than competes against, their works.

In closing, I'd like to situate this intervention in what I take to be its broader philosophical, or rather meta-philosophical context, which is the problem of thinking with and through technology. When Gilbert Simondon writes:

> The most powerful cause of alienation in the contemporary world resides in [a] misunderstanding of the machine, which is not an alienation caused by the machine, but by the non-knowledge of its nature and its essence, by way of its absence from the world of significations, and its omission from the table of values and concepts that make up culture...[27]

he in a sense articulates the central problem of this book. If philosophy, as Bernard Stiegler has likewise argued,[28] is in some sense founded upon its disavowal of *technē*, then our present crises, both epistemic and ecological, call for us to mediate this schism. Now that the destructive reach of human technology is global in its scale and microscopic in its applications, we philosophers can no longer afford to be inattentive to technical knowledges and realities, retreating into a privileged and apparently immaculate 'humanism'. We must think with and through techniques, including those of the digital image, in order to be adequate to the catastrophes that increasingly surround us. The present work, in its own modest way, contributes to this project.

Introduction

Notes

1 Michel Foucault's analyses of painting constitute a rich discussion of these functions, and of their philosophical implications. In his well-known treatment of Velázquez's *Las Meninas*, for instance, he posits the painting as indicative of a new *episteme*, and a modern representational schema which centres upon the fact of representation itself. As he writes: 'we are looking at a picture in which the painter is in turn looking out at us. A mere confrontation, eyes catching one another's glance, direct looks superimposing themselves one upon another as they cross. And yet this slender line of reciprocal visibility embraces a whole complex network of uncertainties, exchanges, and feints.' M. Foucault, *The Order of Things: An Archaeology of the Human Sciences* (Abingdon: Routledge, 2005), p. 5. See also M. Foucault, *Manet and the Object of Painting*, trans. M. Barr (London: Tate Publishing, 2009).
2 K. Ansell-Pearson, *Deleuze and Philosophy: The Difference Engineer* (London: Routledge, 2002), p. 2.
3 As Gregory Flaxman has noted, the oddness of this latter designation – of 'numerical images' rather than 'digital images' – reflects the fact that this terminology did not yet exist when the cinema books were first translated into English in 1989. See G. Flaxman, 'Cinema in the Age of Control', in F. Beckman (ed.), *Control Culture: Foucault and Deleuze after Discipline* (Edinburgh: Edinburgh University Press, 2018), p. 123.
4 See J. Gammack, V. Hobbs and D. Pigott, *The Book of Informatics* (Melbourne: Thompson, 2007), p. 2.
5 L. Fridman, interview with Mark Zuckerberg, 'Mark Zuckerberg: Meta, Instagram and the Metaverse', *Lex Fridman Podcast*, 27 Febrary 2022, https://www.youtube.com/watch?v=5zOHSysMmH0.
6 G. Flaxman, 'Out of Field: The Future of Film Studies', *Angelaki: Journal of the Theoretical Humanities*, 17(4) (2012), p. 128.
7 For a compelling account of the central role of visual perception in approaches to thought throughout ancient philosophy, see V. Fóti, *Vision's Invisibles: Philosophical Explorations* (New York: State University of New York Press, 2003).
8 As Gregory Bateson enthuses, referring to Norbert Wiener's initial work on information feedback systems during the Second World War, 'In World War II it was discovered what sort of complexity entails mind. And, since that discovery, we know that: wherever in the Universe we encounter that sort of complexity, we are dealing with mental phenomena. It's as materialistic as that.' Quoted in D. Belgrad, *The Culture of Feedback: Ecological Thinking in Seventies America* (Chicago: University of Chicago Press, 2019).

9 G. Deleuze, *Two Regimes of Madness, Texts and Interviews 1975–1995*, ed. D. Lapoujade, trans. A. Hodges and M. Taormina (New York: Semiotext(e), 2006), p. 322.
10 G. Deleuze and F. Guattari, *What is Philosophy?*, trans. H. Tomlinson and G. Burchill (London: Verso, 1994), p. 10.
11 Journalist Nicholas Carr provides a neuro-scientifically informed account of the recent changes wrought upon human consciousness in his 2010 bestseller *The Shallows*, drawing out the ways in which the human brain has become increasingly distraction-prone, and less oriented towards depth-thinking and complex problem-solving with the advent of information technology. See N. Carr, *The Shallows: What the Internet is Doing to Our Brains* (New York: W.W. Norton, 2010).
12 Stiegler, across various works, criticises a form of reason unable to properly (and politically) think its fundament in technics, which is thus 'essentially precarious', especially in the face of malevolent forces of marketisation. See B. Stiegler, *States of Shock: Stupidity and Knowledge in the Twenty-first Century*, trans. D. Ross (Cambridge: Polity, 2015).
13 See F. Berardi, *The Uprising: On Poetry and Finance* (Los Angeles: Semiotext(e) Interventions, 2012).
14 For a thorough reconstruction of Lyotard's critique of information – as smuggling a reductive and homogenising metaphysics – as well as a thoughtful discussion of the ways in which Lyotard might have got information theory wrong, see A. Woodward, *Lyotard and the Inhuman Condition: Reflections on Nihilism, Information and Art* (Edinburgh: Edinburgh University Press, 2016), ch. 2.
15 In his influential 1962 study of Nietzsche, Deleuze outlines the task of philosophy thus: 'It serves no established power. The use of philosophy is to sadden. A philosophy that saddens no one, that annoys no one, is not a philosophy. It is useful for harming stupidity, for turning stupidity into something shameful.' G. Deleuze, *Nietzsche and Philosophy*, trans. H. Tomlinson (London: Continuum, 2002), p. 106.
16 Quoted in L. Floridi, *The Philosophy of Information* (Oxford: Oxford University Press, 2011), p. 81.
17 See ibid., chs. 4–5.
18 C. Shannon and W. Weaver, *The Mathematical Theory of Communication* (Urbana, IL: University of Illinois Press, 1964), p. 8.
19 N. Wiener, *The Human Use of Human Beings: Cybernetics and Society* (London: Free Association Books, 1989), p. 34.
20 See P. Marrati, *Gilles Deleuze: Cinema and Philosophy*, trans. A. Hartz (Baltimore, MD: Johns Hopkins University Press, 2008).
21 Flaxman, 'Out of Field', p. 128.
22 D. N. Rodowick, 'Introduction: What Does Time Express?', in D. N. Rodowick (ed.), *Afterimages of Deleuze's Film Philosophy* (Minneapolis, MN: University of Minnesota Press, 2010), p. xiv.

Introduction

23 F. Colman, *Deleuze and Cinema: The Film Concepts* (Oxford: Berg, 2001), p. 6.
24 R. Bogue, *Deleuze on Cinema* (New York: Routledge, 2003), p. 196.
25 R. Rushton, *Cinema after Deleuze* (London: Continuum, 2012), p. 120.
26 A movement within the field of cognitive science that seeks to identify cognition not as a process which takes place within the circumscribed space of the brain, but as 'embodied, embedded, enactive, and extended'. P. Pisters, *The Neuro-Image: A Deleuzian Film-Philosophy of Digital Screen Culture* (Stanford, CA: Stanford University Press, 2012), p. 76.
27 G. Simondon, *On the Mode of Existence of Technical Objects*, trans. C. Malaspina and J. Rogove (Minneapolis, MN: Univocal, 2017), p. 16.
28 As Stiegler writes, at the beginning of the first volume of *Technics and Time*: 'At the beginning of its history philosophy separates *tekhnē* from *épistēmē*, a distinction that had not yet been made in Homeric times. The separation is determined by a political context, one in which the philosopher accuses the Sophist of instrumentalising the *logos* as rhetoric and logography, that is, as both an instrument of power and a renunciation of knowledge. It is in the inheritance of this conflict – in which the philosophical *épistēmē* is pitched against sophistic *tekhnē*, whereby all technical knowledge is devalued – that the essence of technical entities in general is conceived.' From this foundational rupture, in other words, we inherit 'two knowledges': on the one hand, a pure, formal and abstract knowledge of ideas, and on the other, a secondary and degraded knowledge of *techniques* and *technical realities*. A humanistic disavowal of this latter knowledge and its implications, Stiegler argues, is one of the chief causes of the catastrophic failure of rational, symbolic and noetic institutions today. B. Stiegler, *Technics and Time, 1: The Fault of Epimetheus*, trans. R. Beardsworth and G. Collins (Stanford, CA: Stanford University Press, 1998).

1
Where is the Outside?

Before we can turn to an engagement with information and digital media, we must introduce the concept of the outside itself, which, as we saw in the introduction, is perhaps one of Deleuze's most important theoretical instruments. Of course, the theme of exteriority or openness is far from unique to Deleuze, and forms a key motif in the work of Nietzsche, Bataille, Merleau-Ponty and Marx, to name a few.[1] Deleuze's own deployment of the concept of the outside, however, in the context of his work on cinema, must be read in terms of his engagement with Maurice Blanchot and Michel Foucault, each of whom develops the idea in different ways. What unites their interventions is a notion of the outside as grounded in the materiality of language, a language no longer spoken by any particular subject, but which is rather the *very condition* of subjects, in a model which is thus eminently political.

In this chapter, I trace these interventions into Deleuze's own account, which I link to his discussion of thought and temporality in *Difference and Repetition*. Indeed, in asking, 'Where is the outside?', we risk fundamentally misrecognising the concept, given its profoundly temporal character. The outside is not a particular place, so much as it is a particular *process*, a dislocation of habit which is characteristic of the temporal event which for Deleuze constitutes a subject. In this sense, the outside is also the *future* – that which irrupts upon a set of habitual contractions and calls forth an *author* or an *agent*, opening Deleuze's metaphysics onto a fundamentally ethical terrain. It is this process, as we will see, which is menaced by digital image technics, through their algorithmic habituation of thought. We will return to this critique in a subsequent chapter, but first, to Blanchot and Foucault, and the outside they discover at the very heart of literature.

The Literary Outside

Deleuze's references to the outside, indeed, begin with Maurice Blanchot's study of literature, an infrequent but important touchstone throughout the former's *oeuvre*. Blanchot, across a series of works,[2] returns ceaselessly to the 'question of literature', attempting to identify the idiosyncratic conditions of its very possibility. Eschewing a systematic response to this 'question', in favour of a project staging literature's profound indeterminacy, Blanchot ultimately offers less a definition than a thoroughgoing problematisation, writing, 'let us suppose that literature begins at the moment when literature becomes a question', in a distinctly Heideggerian moment.[3]

Blanchot's work takes place in frequent dialogue with Heidegger, and with the central Heideggerian determination to think *being*, albeit with a distinct emphasis which will eschew the latter's themes of authenticity and unconcealment. Blanchot's exploration of literature, indeed, is a response to some of the same historical problems which condition Heidegger's thinking on art. For Blanchot, the radical 'otherness' of literature is linked to the conditions of art in late modernity; shuddering into the same modes of self-referentiality and crisis which instigate Heidegger's aesthetic investigations.[4] But whereas Heidegger seeks to return to art a revelatory and foundational role such as the various twentieth-century 'isms' seemed to have abandoned, for Blanchot, the fact that art appears increasingly uninterested in a representational 'truth' allows it, for the first time, to pose the question of its own idiosyncratic being. Blanchot thus commences *The Space of Literature* with a restaging of the 'hermeneutic circle' as it appears in Heidegger's 'The Origin of the Work of Art', claiming that 'the writer belongs to the work, but what belongs to him is only a book...'[5] And while we may recall that for Heidegger, this intractable relation of artist and work points us to the 'feast of thought'[6] which abides in our constant movement between these terms, Blanchot is interested in the fundamental *impossibility* of any such relation.

This impossibility, indeed, emerges in Blanchot's earliest works, dedicated to the question of literature's materiality. In the 1943 collection *Faux Pas*, Blanchot rejects any understanding of literary language based on communication, whereby sentences and words are simply a means of expressing the inner life of a subject (an author's beliefs, thoughts, feelings, and so on). For Blanchot, as the example of poetry suggests, the materiality of literary language takes on an autonomy which resists the uses of any given subject. As he explains:

> We understand very well that the poet rejects daily language, if habit and the determinations of ordinary life have the effect of removing all material

reality from this language. We also understand that the poet wants to restore language as its own value, that he seeks to make it visible, that he separates it from all that annuls it. That said, if it is true that poetry must occupy itself with everything in words that serves no purpose, to be attentive to images, to meter, to rhythm, to the contour of syllables, it remains for us to wonder what this resurrection of language that wants to exist as such strives toward.[7]

The very materiality of language, in other words, its overabundance of meaning, constitutes a central function of poetry and literature, which as such resist the transparent communication of 'information'. These forms express an agency proper to *language itself*, over and above any meaning which an author might have intended. In this context, as Ulrich Haase and William Large summarise nicely, 'literature becomes what it is, rather than merely a carrier for something external, like the thoughts of an author or the meaning of a culture'.[8] Or, in Blanchot's terms (emphasis added): 'language doesn't speak anymore, but *is*. It devotes itself to the pure passivity of being.'[9]

The implications of this approach thus exceed literary technique, or the subsequent 'death of the author' at the hands of Roland Barthes. In *The Space of Literature*, Blanchot sets about crafting a philosophy of the negative as inherited (via Kojève) from Hegel, in which the delineations of both subjectivity and identity fall away before the negating power of pure language. Thus, for Blanchot, it is only in the context of an impersonal displacement, a destruction of self on the part of the author, who enters into the negative space of language, that literature can come to pass. As he writes:

> The writer ... gives up saying "I." Kafka remarks, with surprise, with enchantment, that he has entered into literature as soon as he can substitute "He" for "I." This is true, but the transformation is much more profound. The writer belongs to a language which no one speaks, which is addressed to no one, which has no centre, and which reveals nothing. He may believe that he affirms himself in this language, but what he affirms is altogether deprived of self.[10]

In effect, the writer is affirming *literature itself*, as a pure or suprasubjective process, a process which defines the author but over which she herself can have no dominion. As Blanchot explains, in this 'space of literature': 'I am not there; no one is there, but the impersonal is: *the outside*, as that which prevents, precedes, and dissolves the possibility of any personal relation' (emphasis added).[11]

Where is the Outside?

The nebulous, shifting nature of Blanchot's project determines that we should be neither glib nor definitive in evoking this literary 'outside'. Certainly, we should not read it as a spatial category, nor reducible to a simpler figure like the 'unknown' or the 'unarticulated'. For Blanchot, the outside constitutes the formlessness of *pure being*, unfettered by the subject and its presuppositions. In his words, it is:

> a region which cannot be brought to light, not because it hides some secret alien to any revelation or even because it is radically obscure, but because it transforms everything which has access to it, even light, into anonymous, impersonal being, the Nontrue, the Nonreal yet always there.[12]

As a perfectly present region which is nevertheless 'unreal' and 'untrue' – working to transform all means of access through its ceaseless deformations – we may already detect a resonance with the concept of the virtual, such as Deleuze inherits from Bergson. We will return to this relation in the following chapter. For now, it suffices to say that not unlike the virtual, Blanchot's outside can be said to be both 'Nontrue' and 'Nonreal' (although, of course Deleuze is adamant that the virtual *is real*) to the extent that it constitutes an exteriority to interested discursive practices which produce and depend upon these very categories.

In positing the outside as beyond both the subject and its 'reality', literature, in Blanchot's estimation, therefore renders the concept of truth itself problematic, given the historical dependence of truth upon these very conditions. Once we find ourselves in the presence of a language without addressee, without ends or ideals, abiding in the inhuman materiality of its own being, the categories of truth and falsehood reveal themselves as the partial and interested contingencies they are. Dedicating his discussion to one of Kafka's many 'exiles', Blanchot explains:

> He is in the outside itself – a realm absolutely bereft of intimacy where beings seem absent and where everything one thinks one grasps slips away. The tragic difficulty of the undertaking is that in this world of exclusion and radical separation, everything is false and inauthentic as soon as one examines it, everything lacks as soon as one seeks support from it, but nevertheless the depth of this absence is always given anew as an indubitable, absolute presence.[13]

Exiled to the outside, to the negative space of being, all 'positive' fabrications thus reveal themselves as contingency and appearance – the productions of a given subjectivity. This negativity is not, however – in the spirit of Hegel – a device for the resolution of contradiction, the advance of a self-knowing *Geist*. Blanchot seeks rather to *reside* in the negative, to posit contradictions *without resolution*, an approach commensurate with the various impasses an 'absolute' knowledge had arrived at in the twentieth century, with its collapse into irrationality and bloodshed. In this context, as Leslie Hill explains, 'Hegel's dialectic of spirit is rewritten by Blanchot as a series of discontinuous and incompatible demands rather than a progressive ascent towards absolute knowledge.'[14]

As I've already suggested, we must therefore be wary of thinking the outside in terms of simple exteriority. The outside is outside, but it is also the *very core* of literature, the most radical interior of the literary space. It constitutes the contradiction without resolution which forces the author into an impossible task, in a model Blanchot likewise traces into thought. In this context, in *The Book to Come*, Blanchot turns to Artaud's correspondence with the editor Jacques Rivière, of equal importance to Deleuze. Artaud, responding to the rejection of his poems by Rivière's journal, attempted to explain the mute suffering that was their condition. 'I myself speak [...] of a kind of cold suffering without images', he writes, 'without feeling, like the indescribable shock of abortions.'[15] And Blanchot identifies in this crisis of Artaud, the fact that he has not 'yet *begun* to think', a profound intimacy with the pure negativity of being, such as must be reduced and falsified each time we seek to represent it.

Artaud, by virtue of the unique coordinates of his schizophrenia, finds himself in too direct a contact with this negativity to ever fully consecrate a representation, be it 'thought' or 'image'. In Blanchot's words:

> It is as if he has touched, despite himself and by a pathetic mistake, whence his cries come, the point at which thinking is always unable to think: it "uncan" [*impouvoir*], to use his word, which is like the essential part of his thinking, but which makes it an extremely painful lack, a failing that immediately shines from this centre and, consuming the physical substance of what he thinks, divides itself on all levels into a number of particular impossibilities.[16]

Artaud's inability to think, in other words, the *impossibility* of his thought, propels him into the direct and painful presence of the pure negative – the outside – 'the giant murmuring upon which language opens',[17] which is itself the paradoxical condition of thought.

Where is the Outside?

According to this model, thinking is no longer habitual 'cognition', but rather an extreme and violent encounter with its own fundamental incapacity. Untethered from knowledge, it emerges as a profound power of negation, dividing and dissolving all possible relations. As Blanchot explains, taking a path similar to that which Deleuze will later follow:

> When we read these pages, we learn what we do not manage to know: the act of thinking can only be deeply shocking; what is to be thought about is in thought that which turns away from it and inexhaustibly exhausts itself in it; suffering and thinking are secretly linked... Might it be that extreme thought and extreme suffering open onto the same horizon? Might suffering be, finally, thinking?[18]

And while Deleuze, as we shall see, eschews the image of suffering in favour of a mechanism for the posing of problems and the formation of ideas,[19] avoiding equally the negative in his immanent conception of becoming, this vocabulary of the 'failure' or 'shock' which characterises thinking will remain one of his core motifs.[20]

This problematisation of truth and the subject, both sketched as the outgrowths of a negative fundament of which they are contingencies, subsequently provides Michel Foucault with a model via which he might restage his 'archaeological' investigation of discourse. Foucault takes up Blanchot's philosophy in one of his strangest texts, 'Maurice Blanchot: The Thought from Outside', in which he explicitly purposes the outside to elude philosophical tendencies towards stability and dualism, particularly those animating the subject/object schism. Thus, claims Foucault:

> If the only site for language is indeed the solitary sovereignty of "I speak" then in principle nothing can limit it – not the one to whom it is addressed, not the truth of what it says, not the values or systems of representation it utilises. In short, it is no longer discourse and the communication of meaning, but a spreading forth of language in its raw state, an unfolding of pure exteriority.[21]

Again, in terms which will prove prescient to our subsequent critique of 'communication' in the context of informatic images, we see a supra-subjective, indeed *inhuman* aspect of language, according to which 'representation' becomes always already interested and impersonal. In the presence of such a language, claims Foucault, we encounter a form of thought which is radically exterior to the subject and its interests, derived from 'neither truth nor time, neither eternity nor man', but rather 'the always outdone form of the outside'.[22]

Such a thought, in Foucault's hands, and in keeping with his longstanding philosophical objectives, becomes a means of drawing out politicised functions of abstraction and of law which operate within language, or more broadly in the Foucauldian corpus, discourse. It also constitutes a strangely metaphysical moment for Foucault, given his general reticence to speculate beyond textual and discursive analyses. This 'pure exteriority' gives us a sense of those mysterious forces that he will elsewhere suggest serve to displace a given episteme, given that he here allows for both a language and a thought in excess of any particular *dispositif*. As he writes:

> For a long time it was thought that language had mastery over time, that it acted both as the future bond of the promise and as memory and narrative; it was thought to be prophecy and history; it was also thought that in its sovereignty it could bring to light the eternal and visible body of truth; it was thought that its essence resided in the form of words or in the breath that made them vibrate. In fact, it is only a formless rumbling, a streaming; its power resides in its dissimulation.[23]

In the thought of/from outside – the French article *du* allows us to say both – Foucault thus sketches a kind of impersonal discourse untethered from the 'body' of truth, a pure exteriority which might be pressed into the service of the localised, singular and resistant becomings to which he would increasingly dedicate his work. It is in these enigmatic terms that Foucault closes 'The Thought from Outside', writing that through such a language, no longer indexed to truth or falsehood, 'every single existence receives, through the simple assertion "I speak," the threatening promise of its own disappearance, its future appearance'.[24]

'Every single existence', under Foucault's pen, become the dispossessed and marginal subjects of his 'archaeology': the mad, the sick, prisoners, women, homosexuals. In problematising the universality of discourses which have effected their marginalisation – religious truths identifying spaces of sin and penitence, scientific and medical truths delineating spaces of perversion, confinement and pathology – Foucault seeks, across his *oeuvre*, to identify the terms by which such existences might reassert themselves according to new and counter-hegemonic participations in discourse, drawing on forces from 'outside' dominant images of the human. And indeed, it is this notion of the outside as that which overspills and problematises a particular image of the human being which Deleuze takes up in his work during the 1980s.

Where is the Outside?

In an appendix to his book on Foucault, Deleuze evokes just this theme, connecting the outside to the Nietzschean figure of the 'overman'. Through contact with the outside, conceived as those technical, biological and linguistic forces in excess of the human as it has hitherto been defined, Deleuze claims that we might elide the repressive dimensions of that very concept. As he writes, extending the material axis of Blanchot's thought far beyond literary language:

> The forces within man enter into a relation with forces from the outside, those of silicon which supersedes carbon, or genetic components which supersede the organism, or agrammaticalities which supersede the signifier... What is the overman? It is the formal compound of the forces within man and these new forces. It is the form that results from a new relation between forces.[25]

As such, the outside here emerges as an effect of those inhuman forces and materials which might help us overcome the Western philosophical subject. The outside is a site of novelty and change, and an eschewal of habitudes which might point us towards a 'people to come', no longer strictly human beings but rather inhuman becomings. As Deleuze continues:

> the overman is much less than the disappearance of living men, and much more than a change of concept: it is the advent of a new form that is neither God nor man and which, it is hoped, will not prove worse than its two previous forms.[26]

And indeed, it is this political and inhuman outside, drawn from both Blanchot and Foucault, that Deleuze takes up in the latter stages of his work on cinema.

At the time of writing the cinema books, as Marie-Claire Ropars-Wuilleumier has noted,[27] Deleuze was already involved in preparations for the book on Foucault, and there's little doubt that Blanchot, an occasional reference throughout the Deleuzian corpus, appears here in a thoroughly Foucauldian aspect. Deleuze's originality, however, lies in his eschewal of a linguistic or literary outside, instead setting the concept to work in the context of perception, thought and images. As Gregory Flaxman writes:

> By way of Blanchot, who baptised the concept as "the impower [*impouvoir*] of thought," and Foucault, who resumed it as "the figure of nothingness," Deleuze defines the outside as the point where and when we dispense with presuppositions and define thought itself as a problem. Inasmuch as

Deleuze adds his name to this conceptual lineage, he does so according to his own philosophical taste. In a word, he does so *cinematically*.[28]

The problem of thought constitutes a central preoccupation throughout Deleuze's *oeuvre*, perhaps most explicitly stated in the third chapter of *Difference and Repetition*. And while there are difficulties attendant to reading concepts across Deleuze's works, given the significant mutations they invariably undergo,[29] we will now briefly summarise this chapter, in order to clarify our subsequent postulation of a Deleuzian 'outside' *vis-à-vis* noesis and the cinematic image.

The Dogmatic Image of Thought

Deleuze's critique of a certain 'image' of thought to which Western philosophy has cleaved continues his long-standing project to posit new forms of thinking, such as would be creative, nebulous and changing – irreducible to *any* particular image. Thus, in *Difference and Repetition*, Deleuze does not just disavow a certain conservative mode of thought, but opens up a critical territory within which we might formulate new modes, such as would be capable – in keeping with the central objectives of the book – of thinking *difference in itself*, without recourse to *identity*. As Deleuze explains in the preface to the English edition, published in 1994:

> Finally, in this book it seemed to me that the powers of difference and repetition could be reached only by putting into question the traditional image of thought. By this I mean not only that we think according to a given method, but also that there is a more or less implicit, tacit or presupposed image of thought which determines our goals when we try to think. (*DR*, xvi)

There is no shortage of commentaries on this critique, which identifies a 'dogmatic image of thought' animating the Western philosophical tradition. As such, my own treatment of it here will remain relatively circumscribed, and by no means aims to be definitive. I refer the interested reader to works by James Williams, Daniela Voss and Henry Somers-Hall for thorough and compelling exegeses.[30]

This critique, as I've suggested, is most clearly presented in chapter 3 of *Difference and Repetition*, but as Williams has cautioned, we must be wary of reading it in isolation from the broader metaphysical intervention Deleuze makes throughout the book.[31] Here, as we have said, Deleuze seeks to think difference not via recourse to 'identity' – with differences derived from already constituted individuals – but as an ontogenesis which is the very condition for individual bodies, a *differentiating difference* which adheres 'all the way down'. This form of 'difference in itself', Deleuze claims, is obscured by what he will describe – redeploying a term from Kant – as a 'transcendental illusion' (*DR*, 229), according to which we tend to focus on already differentiated or extended bodies, as opposed to the intensive and differential forces which condition and produce them. In the service of this illusion, Deleuze argues, thought claims as its own combined functions of *recognition* and of *representation*,[32] embracing a structural conservatism which inhibits the thought of novelty and change – the operations of difference and repetition.

In this context, Deleuze argues that philosophy has tended to mistake recognition and representation for thought itself, elevating a 'popular' or 'pre-philosophical' – which is to say *doxic* – 'image of thought' to the level of a set of philosophical principles. But for Deleuze, most of our day-to-day mentation does not, in fact, constitute 'thought', in the properly philosophical sense. Certainly, the dogmatic image Deleuze identifies – a good and common sense, fundamentally modelled on recognition and inextricable from an inherent morality associating 'truth' with 'the good' – is what constitutes the mentation of the human being in its everyday milieu. However, this kind of thought shoulders none of philosophy's burden of breaking with *doxa*, of escaping inherited opinion and habituated response in order to effect new modes of thinking and of life. As Deleuze explains:

> acts of recognition exist and occupy a large part of our daily life: this is a table, this is an apple, this the piece of wax, good morning Theaeteus. But who can believe that the destiny of thought is at stake in these acts, and that when we recognise, we are thinking? (*DR*, 135)

For Deleuze, a more properly *philosophical* thought emerges in response to an initial shock or bewilderment, a failure in cognition which echoes the Kantian sublime:[33] 'Something in the world *forces* us to think. This something is an object not of recognition but of a fundamental *encounter*' (emphasis added) (*DR*, 139). This encounter, with what Deleuze enigmatically designates a *sign*, 'moves the soul, perplexes it – in other words, forces it to pose a problem: as though the object of the encounter, the sign, were the bearer of the problem – as though it were a problem' (*DR*, 140).

The sign is a concept with a long history throughout Deleuze's work, and we must here carefully note that Deleuze will later characterise the two cinema volumes as a 'taxonomy' of cinematic signs. Beginning in 1964 with *Proust and Signs*, Deleuze associates the 'sign' with a noetic event which engenders a process of interpretation, writing that 'everything that teaches us something emits signs; every act of learning is an interpretation of signs or hieroglyphs'.[34] While it is thus associated with a process of interpretation, the sign, particularly in the context of Deleuze's later work on cinema, does not accord to a linguistic model. Indeed Deleuze is careful to avoid any analogy between cinematic 'signs' and language, invoking instead the interpretative semiotics of Charles Sanders Peirce.[35] This is to say that the sign, particularly as it emerges after Deleuze's encounter with Guattari, does not accord to the structural(ist) model of a signifier coordinated against a signified, but constitutes instead a productive or individuating intensity, engendering an encounter, and immanent to a regime or ecology of interrelated signs. In this context, as Anne Sauvagnargues explains, 'signs are no longer devalued as degraded material doubles of a representation or thought, but rather unfold upon maps of affects in an ecological semiotics and an ethology of territory'.[36] We will return to the sign and its affects in the following chapter.

For now, and to vulgarise somewhat, we might say that in *Difference and Repetition*, this encounter with a sign, which emerges as the bearer of a problem, constitutes a tripartite articulation of the *new*. It is an encounter with the radically new, the *unthought*, which constitutes thought, and which is elided by any dogmatic or habitual image of thinking we may have. Confronted with something we have never seen, to which we have no immediate means of response, which – in essence – *we do not recognise*, we begin to think in earnest. Such a thought, confronted with the radically new, is thus simultaneously confronted with its own inability to think, a groundlessness which impels thought into action. Reaching out, as it were, for a thought which has not yet been had, the thinker confronts both the limits of thought and the very moment of rupture which calls for thinking to be renewed. Or, as Deleuze and Guattari explain in *A Thousand Plateaus*, drawing on the passages we have already encountered in Artaud:

> Artaud, in his letters to Jacques Rivière, [explains] that thought operates on the basis of a central breakdown, that it lives solely by its own incapacity to take on form, bringing into relief only traits of expression in a material, developing peripherally, in a pure milieu of exteriority, as a function of singularities impossible to universalise, of circumstances impossible to interiorise.[37]

In the context of such a thought – what Deleuze will follow Artaud in calling a 'thought without image' – thinking reveals itself not as something innate or within easy reach, but as that which must be 'engendered' (*DR*, 147), sometimes painfully, in response to our confrontation with the new or the unthinkable.

In keeping with the central preoccupations of *Difference and Repetition*, the new is here characterised as 'difference'. In the context of Deleuze's work on cinema, the vocabulary will change; however, the essential shape and orientation of this encounter remain the same. Confronted with the new, we are forced beyond all habitudes and into thought as a creative practice, in a model which will as such privilege the creativity of art. As Deleuze explains: 'For the new – in other words, difference – calls forth forces in thought which are not the forces of recognition, today or tomorrow, but the powers of a completely other model, from an unrecognised and unrecognisable *terra incognita*' (*DR*, 136).

In *Difference and Repetition*, Deleuze suggests that this encounter with the new has a dramatic series of liberating functions, impelling thought to become a-centred, dynamic and creative. We have noted a trace of the Kantian sublime, and in Deleuze's discussion of the 'faculties' this connection becomes explicit. But whereas in Kant's account of the sublime, a failure of the imagination invokes the powers of reason – engendering a discordant but 'collaborative' relation – for Deleuze, the 'encounter' with difference engenders a disjunctive exercise of simultaneous provocation and constraint, a 'violence' passed between the faculties, in an intensive refraction of their differential natures (*DR*, 141).

The object of the encounter, moreover, given that it is not yet thought, can thus only be *sensed*, and this 'pure' sensation, untrammelled by the intellectual operations of recognition, liberates sensibility itself from its hitherto purposive and habitual exercises.[38] As Deleuze explains, the object 'really gives rise to sensibility with regard to a given sense ... it is not a sensible being but the being *of the sensible*. It is not the given but that by which the given is given' (*DR*, 140). Freed from the strictures of 'common sense' – tied up with the unphilosophical premise of recognition – which had hitherto restricted it, sensibility 'thereby enters into a discordant play, its organs become metaphysical' (*DR*, 140).

Alongside this being of pure sensation, and perhaps more importantly for our purposes, Deleuze will claim that this encounter likewise ushers thought into the presence of a *pure being of memory*.

In searching – and failing to find – a memory commensurate with the object of the encounter, memory, like sense, comes into contact with the *very being* of memory, a *transcendental memory*, the *a priori* ground for the empirical memory of the subject, hitherto invariably obscured by the conditions of dogmatic recognition. As Deleuze explains:

> Empirical memory is addressed to those things which can and even must be grasped: what is recalled must have been seen, heard, imagined or thought ... transcendental memory, by contrast, grasps that which from the outset can only be recalled, even the first time: not a contingent past, but the being of the past as such and the past of every time. (*DR*, 140)

This dual model of memory refers to chapter 2 of *Difference and Repetition*, in which we encounter three 'syntheses' of time. And Deleuze's philosophy of time also lies at the heart of his work on cinema, which restages a long-standing engagement with Henri Bergson's temporal metaphysics. As such, before we can return to the cinematic outside, we must clarify the idiosyncratic role played by *time* in Deleuze's account of thought – in particular as it emerges in the form of the 'three syntheses' of time in *Difference and Repetition*.

The Three Syntheses of Time

The three syntheses are ostensibly divisible into the familiar temporal categories of past, present and future; however, in keeping with the anti-*doxic* project to which Deleuze is dedicated, these three faces of temporality must be apprehended in an altogether new way. Central once more is Kant, to whom Deleuze imputes the formulation of a profound new notion of time, according to which time becomes a pure and empty form, a lacuna through which change itself might be apprehended.[39] As opposed to classical conceptions of time, such as philosophy had largely inherited from ancient Greek cosmology, and whereby time – the Platonic 'moving image of eternity' – was conceived in terms of the rotation of the planets – that is to say, as both cyclical and kinetic – Kant, Deleuze claims, liberates time from movement, such that it becomes 'unrolled, straightened...' assuming 'the ultimate shape of the labyrinth, the straight line labyrinth which is, as Borges says, "invisible, incessant"' (*DR*, 111).

And this 'pure' form of time, no longer indexed to movement, likewise alters the subject, which becomes, in Kant, fundamentally 'split' by 'the form of time which runs through it' (*DR*, 169). This 'splitting' results from the fact that subjectivity is *situated* in time, such that its habitual foundations are gnawed away by time's passage, which requires the formation of new selves in an interminable 'othering'. As such, the subject is divided between the synthetic functions of thought and the empirical experience of thought as though it were prosecuted by another. In this context, Deleuze turns to Rimbaud's famous formula, 'I is another',[40] or, more precisely, as Deleuze explains, 'it is not the other which is another I, but the I which is an other, a fractured I' (*DR*, 261). This dual 'event' in the philosophy of time, such that temporality becomes a pure and empty form through which we might apprehend change and appearance, and such that the subject becomes internally cleft between an *I* which is subject to the syntheses of time and an *I* which is the subject of its empirical demands and flux, constitutes a temporality which lies at the very heart of Deleuze's account of thought. But before we can turn to this complex endpoint to Deleuze's 'noetics' of time, we must elaborate briefly the content of the three syntheses.

First, and perhaps most intuitively, there is the synthesis of habit, or of the present. Here, temporality emerges in a thoroughly Bergsonian aspect, with the synthesis understood as a 'contraction' such as constitutes a habit. Important to note is that for Deleuze, this synthesis is not the product of subjectivity; rather its functioning is 'passive'. In this sense, we are not speaking at the level of psychology or of phenomenology. A human being constitutes exactly such a 'synthesis' in the form of a collection of biochemical 'habits' which are contracted in the context of a horizon of possible (inter)actions. As Sean Bowden explains, this synthesis

> takes place insofar as otherwise indifferent moments of sensation come to be related to one another through the contraction of a habit, where this latter is defined as the formation of a horizon of anticipations on the basis of the qualitative impressions generated by received sensations.[41]

But, Deleuze observes, this first form of temporality – the synthesis of the present – engenders a paradox, which necessarily ushers in a *second* form of temporality. For if the present constitutes time, yet nevertheless continues to 'pass' and make way for new presents, it appears as if the present passes into one of its own dimensions. As such, Deleuze claims: 'We cannot avoid the necessary conclusion – *that there must be another time in which the first synthesis of time can occur*' (*DR*, 79). Thus, while the first synthesis constitutes the 'foundation' of time, the second, claims Deleuze, constitutes the 'ground' within which this foundation is embedded. This ground – the condition for the fundamental changeability of the present – is a kind of 'memory'. But this is not the memory of an individual subject – the temporal form to which Deleuze refers must once more be understood in the most rigorously metaphysical and suprasubjective, which is to say 'passive', sense.

This form of memory, what Deleuze calls the 'pure past', is the *a priori*, transcendental condition for the contraction of a habit which constitutes the passing present. It is thus a past which was never present, and which does not pass, yet which nevertheless allows the differentiation of *former* and *present* presents. As such, this transcendental form comprises the originary temporality of which presents constitute particular dimensions. We have spoken of Bergson, and we might here recall that for the latter, conscious perception is constituted by a combination of memory and what he describes as the 'sensory-motor' (*MM*, 168) condition of preparedness for future action. In order for memories to penetrate into the present, to be *actualised*, they are thus contracted from a hitherto virtual – though perfectly real, and, as we shall see, for Deleuze, *fully determined* – memory which coexists with the present, which is indeed the very condition of the present; a situation Bergson illustrates via recourse to his famous temporal 'cone'.[42] This distinction between pure memory and memories activated in the service of the subject's sensory-motor exigencies, between *virtual* memory and its *actualisation* in sensory-motor response, lies at the heart of Deleuze's subsequent account of the unique temporality expressed in the cinematic image. This opening onto a pure complexity of time constitutes the central architecture of the *time-image*, in which multiple and interconnected temporal loops, freed from such sensory-motor imperatives as narrative and chronology, are made manifest. We will return to this idea in the following chapter.

For now, we might note that in addition to these two syntheses, which comprise the present and the past-as-condition for the present, Deleuze will argue that there must also be a *third* synthesis, perhaps the most complex of the three: that of *difference* or the *future*. The third synthesis, Deleuze explains, is simultaneously *static*, *formal* and *serial*, inasmuch as it is the synthesis which serves to distribute past, present and future as delineable categories. This distribution, importantly, takes place in the context of an *event* or *act*, constituting what Deleuze describes as a 'caesura', on either side of which are formally distributed a past as condition for the subject, the present as that situation in which the subject is confronted with a problem to which it has no apparent solution, and a future in which the subject will arrive at a solution to this problem – but only inasmuch as it becomes *other than it is*. Thus, Deleuze explains, evoking a concept of time which is no longer subordinate to movement, such as will recur throughout his work on cinema:

> The synthesis is necessarily static, since time is no longer subordinated to movement; time is the most radical form of change, but the form of change does not change. The caesura, along with the before and after which it ordains once and for all, constitutes the fracture in the I (the caesura is exactly the point at which the fracture appears). (*DR*, 89)

This serial distribution of temporality, occasioned by an 'encounter' with the un-thought, thus suggests a subjectivity which is no longer unitary, but cleft by its constitution through time, through which it becomes constantly 'other' to itself. The third synthesis thus ties temporality's dimensions together, with the past as 'ground' or condition, the present as agent or event, and the future as the necessary production of difference and novelty in response to this event.[43]

The 'encounter' of thought, as we have said, engenders this trifold activity of time, in the context of a confrontation with a pure difference which is no longer subsumed within identity (and as such, cannot be recognised). The creativity incumbent upon the agent here, such that it might confront the present, searching the pure past for resources with which to produce the future, constitutes the fundamentally temporal architecture of a thought which is no longer 'dogmatic', but which is instead creative. But thought, as we have said, is rare. This latter synthesis, which transcends habit in a creative production of the new, is open to the subject only when it *embraces* the encounter, *choosing* to eschew habitude in favour of difference in itself.

In this way, Deleuze's metaphysics opens resolutely onto an ethics, which he conceives both in terms of artistic creation and the Nietzschean 'eternal return'. Indeed, it is only in the context of an *affirmation* of the event, such as sees the 'subject' make way for an 'author' or 'actor' of time, that this third synthesis can properly adhere, projecting a future which is no longer simply the repetition of a habit. As Deleuze explains, the third synthesis is rather a 'royal repetition', a *repetition of difference*, which 'constitutes a future which affirms at once both the unconditioned character of the product in relation to the conditions of its production, and the independence of the work in relation to its author or actor' (*DR*, 94).

In other words, we encounter, in the third synthesis, a future which exceeds the initial conditions of its production, likewise overflowing the capacities of a subject to fully comprehend or respond to it. It is only in the context of a Nietzschean *amor fati*,[44] an ethics of openness to difference in all of its catastrophic and unthinkable excess, that the subject is able to 'become equal to [...] the unequal in itself' (*DR*, 90), producing difference through an embrace of the difference which is its own condition.

For our purposes, we might say that it is only in embracing a formless 'thought from outside' – from the future, or from the purest past – that the subject is able to move beyond the limits of the present, producing – and being produced by – a new which is radically undetermined. But philosophy, Deleuze suggests, has been for the most part unable to stage the kind of encounter which might lead us to this creative production of the future – predicated as it is upon the *doxic* model of enchained *recognition* and *representation*. In this context, alongside Guattari, he will ask, 'is there a hope for philosophy, which for a long time has been an official, referential genre?'[45] It is in search of an answer to this question that Deleuze enacts a protracted philosophical encounter with *art*, concluding that 'the search for a new means of philosophical expression must be pursued today in relation to the renewal of certain other arts, such as the theatre or the cinema' (*DR*, xxi).

In his books on Francis Bacon, Kafka and Proust, this pursuit takes the form of an exploration of the 'signs' constituted by painting and literature. But cinema, in its temporal and kinetic dimensions, not to mention its strange affinity with cognition, seems uniquely predisposed to produce such encounters. In this context, as Gregory Flaxman explains:

> Whatever their intricacies and digressions, *The Movement-Image* and *The Time-Image* fundamentally contend that, beyond all other arts, the cinema opens the possibility for deterritorializing the cogito, the rigid "image of thought" that in one form or another has dominated Western philosophy.[46]

The elaborate cinematic philosophy these books enact thus continues the project to engender a thought which, in confronting its own radical ungroundedness, opens itself to difference and novelty – to the intensive and differentiating forces which produce extended or

Where is the Outside?

actualised states. But by the time Deleuze comes to elaborate this philosophy *vis-à-vis* cinema, the notion of a 'thought without image' has been replaced by an 'outside'. Why does Deleuze make this move? Is this simply a change in vocabulary, or something more significant? It is to these questions that we now turn, and to the cinematic image.

Notes

1. As Reza Negarestani has written, in a characteristically heterodox exploration of motifs of 'openness' in philosophy: 'From pre-Islamic Zoroastrian mages to Sade to Nietzsche, Bataille and Deleuze, the investigations into openness have always been accompanied by at least five supplements: life, death, horror, outside and intensity. Openness has been diagrammed as both a tactical line and strategy traversing these five supplements while crushing the dimensions between them.' R. Negarestani, 'Death as a Perversion: Openness and Germinal Death', in J. Johnson (ed.), *Dark Trajectories: Politics of the Outside* (Creative Commons, 2013), p. 55. Deleuze's thinking is perhaps less consistently oriented by ideas of horror and death, but this is certainly an accurate precis of one part of his project *vis-à-vis* life, intensity and the outside.
2. See primarily *Faux Pas* (1943), *The Work of Fire* (1949), *The Space of Literature* (1955) and *The Book to Come* (1959).
3. M. Blanchot, *The Work of Fire*, trans. C. Mandell (Stanford, CA: Stanford University Press, 1995), p. 300.
4. For more on this connection, see L. Hill, *Blanchot: Extreme Contemporary* (London: Routledge, 1997), p. 123.
5. M. Blanchot, *The Space of Literature*, trans. A. Smock (Lincoln, NE: University of Nebraska Press, 1982), p. 23.
6. M. Heidegger, *Off the Beaten Track*, trans. J. Young and K. Haynes (Cambridge: Cambridge University Press, 2002), p. 2.
7. M. Blanchot, *Faux Pas*, trans. C. Mandell (Stanford, CA: Stanford University Press, 2001), p. 137.
8. U. Haas and W. Large, *Maurice Blanchot* (London: Routledge, 2001), p. 28.
9. Blanchot, *Space of Literature*, p. 27.
10. Ibid., p. 26.
11. Ibid., p. 31.
12. Ibid.
13. Ibid., p. 77.
14. Hill, *Blanchot*, p. 108.
15. A. Artaud, 'There's an Anguish', in *Artaud Anthology*, ed. J. Hirschman (San Francisco: City Lights, 1965), p. 32.
16. M. Blanchot, *The Book to Come*, trans. C. Mandell (Stanford, CA: Stanford University Press, 2003), p. 36.

17 Blanchot, *Space of Literature*, p. 27.
18 Blanchot, *Book to Come*, p. 40.
19 In *Difference and Repetition*, Deleuze thus explicates Blanchot in his own terms, centralising the formulation of 'problems' which animates this era of his work: 'Imperatives in the form of questions thus signify our greatest powerlessness, but also that point of which Maurice Blanchot speaks endlessly: that blind, acephalic, aphasic and aleatory original point which designates "the impossibility of thinking that is thought," that point at which "powerlessness" is translated into power, that point which develops the work in the form of a problem' (*DR*, 199).
20 The concept is by no means exclusive to Blanchot, and I don't seek to suggest that Deleuze derives it primarily from his work. Indeed, the 'shock' as it emerges in Deleuze no doubt more fully derives from the work of Jean Wahl, whose classes at the Sorbonne Deleuze attended while he was there in 1944–48, and who remained a profound influence. In Wahl's *Vers le concret*, we find an account of the noetic 'shock' deployed in order to transcend the realist/idealist schism in philosophy. According to Wahl, both realist and idealist schemes begin in response to a 'shock' engendered in their thinking by the 'concrete', a term Wahl uses in order to avoid the partisan ring of the 'real'. See J. Wahl, *Vers le concret: Études d'histoire de la philosophie contemporaine* (Paris: J. Vrin, 1932).
21 M. Foucault, 'Maurice Blanchot: The Thought from Outside', in M. Blanchot and M. Foucault, *Foucault / Blanchot*, trans. B. Massumi and J. Mehlman (New York: Zone Books, 1987), p. 11.
22 Ibid., p. 57.
23 Ibid., p. 55.
24 Ibid., p. 58.
25 G. Deleuze, *Foucault*, trans. S. Hand (Minneapolis, MN: University of Minnesota Press, 1988), p. 131 (translation slightly modified).
26 Ibid., p. 132.
27 M. Ropars-Wuilleumier, 'Image or Time? The Thought of the Outside in *The Time-Image* (Deleuze and Blanchot)', in D. N. Rodowick (ed.), *Afterimages of Gilles Deleuze's Film Philosophy* (Minneapolis, MN: University of Minnesota Press, 2010), p. 20.
28 Flaxman, 'Out of Field', p. 129.
29 Deleuze himself offers a meditation on the 'shifting', consistently dynamic quality of his work in his 'Author's Note for the Italian Edition of Logic of Sense', when he writes: 'It is difficult for an author to reflect on a book written several years ago. One is tempted to act clever, or to feign indifference, or even worse, to become the commentator of oneself. Not that the book has necessarily been surpassed; but even if it remains relevant, it is an "adjacent" relevance... We all move forward

or backward; we are hesitant in the middle of these directions; we construct our topology, celestial map, underground den, measurements of surface planes, and other things as well. While moving in these different directions, one does not speak in the same way, just as the subject matter which one encounters is not the same...' (Deleuze, *Two Regimes*, p. 63). In this sense, we can see that of the utmost significance to Deleuze is a methodological dynamism, an anti-essentialist 'movement' of thought that he derives from both Bergson and Nietzsche.

30 J. Williams, *Gilles Deleuze's Difference and Repetition: A Critical Introduction and Guide* (Edinburgh: Edinburgh University Press, 2013); D. Voss, *Conditions of Thought: Deleuze and Transcendental Ideas* (Edinburgh: Edinburgh University Press, 2013); H. Somers-Hall, *Deleuze's Difference and Repetition* (Edinburgh: Edinburgh University Press, 2013).

31 Williams, *Gilles Deleuze's Difference and Repetition*, p. 118.

32 The 'conservatism' inherent to the model of recognition may already seem self-evident: we can only *re-cognise* that which we have already encountered. Representation, however, is equally the target of Deleuze's critique. Leaving aside an in-depth explication of this critique – which primarily hinges on a rejection of both Aristotelian and Platonic 'hierarchies of being' – it's helpful to think here in terms of art. If a painting, for instance, is conceived in terms of 'representation', its relation to the real is already subsumed in a mediated or analogous (Aristotelian) difference which is essentially *equivocal*. The painting's 'difference' from the reality 'to be represented' is established under the auspices of a predetermined distribution of sense, whereby 'real' object and 'copy' occupy determinate relations of analogy, according to which copies can only ever be a degraded, secondary expression of a reality more properly filled with being. But for Deleuze, the work of art is not of the order of representation. It is *productive*, in terms of the affects and percepts which it concretises, and of the thought which they are able to provoke. As a result, Deleuze's philosophical taste will consistently run to artforms which problematise the figurative, indeed which *put figures in motion*, as does film. For perhaps the most sustained Deleuzian critique of representation, see 'The Simulacrum and Ancient Philosophy', published as an appendix to *The Logic of Sense*. See also the authoritative account in D. Olkowski, *Gilles Deleuze and the Ruin of Representation* (Berkeley, CA: University of California Press, 1999).

33 There is nothing innocent in Deleuze's choice of the sublime as a model for the moment which might instigate a thought freed from the auspices of the dogmatic image – what Deleuze describes as a 'thought without an image'. Indeed the sublime, as the response to an object which is 'devoid of form', which excites a 'negative pleasure' and is 'ill adapted to our faculty of presentation', offers up a simultaneously noetic-aesthetic

experience which is reliant on no representational schema, no model of recognition. The sublime, that which, Kant writes, might 'do violence, as it were, to the imagination, and yet [be] judged all the more sublime on that account', offers Deleuze a model by which we might conceive of thought not as a harmonious exercise which takes place in accordance with a pre-distributed regime of sense, but as that which, in Kant's terms, might 'transcend [...] every standard of the senses'. See I. Kant, *Critique of Judgement*, trans. W. S. Pluhar (Indianapolis, IN: Hackett, 1987), pp. 75–81. Of course, Kant's project – the (re-)elevation of a purified and *a priori* schemata of philosophical reason to the apex of human knowledge – draws from the sublime dramatically different conclusions to those of Deleuze. Their point of departure, as we show in this chapter, is the way the sublime experience causes the faculties to function.

34. G. Deleuze, *Proust and Signs*, trans. R. Howard (Minneapolis, MN: University of Minnesota Press, 2000), p. 4.
35. As Deleuze explains, in this context: 'the cinema seems to us to be a composition of images and of signs, that is, a pre-verbal intelligible content (pure semiotics)' (*CI*, xi).
36. A. Sauvagnargues, *Artmachines – Deleuze, Guattari, Simondon*, trans. S. Verderber and E. W. Holland (Edinburgh: Edinburgh University Press, 2016), p. 46.
37. G. Deleuze and F. Guattari, *A Thousand Plateaus: Capitalism and Schizophrenia*, trans B. Massumi (Minneapolis, MN: University of Minnesota Press, 2009), p. 378.
38. Deleuze deals with the concept of 'sense' in his identification of one of the 'dogmatic image's' key postulates, the so-called 'postulate of the ideal'. According to this postulate, both common sense and good sense are the distribution which guarantees the 'concord' between thought, truth and goodness (*DR*, 167). Deleuze's critique of this postulate, which responds to Descartes' foundational claim that 'good sense is the most evenly distributed thing in the world' (R. Descartes, *A Discourse on the Method of Correctly Conducting One's Reason and Seeking Truth in the Sciences*, trans. I. Maclean [Oxford: Oxford University Press, 2006], p. 5), is also taken up in *The Logic of Sense*, in which Deleuze associates 'good sense' with the concrete functioning of particular forms of social organisation – he is explicit in naming agrarian 'enclosure' and middle-class 'regulation' – and 'common sense' with an 'organ' dedicated to the collapse of diversity into a homogenising function of 'identity'. See G. Deleuze, *The Logic of Sense*, trans. M. Lester and C. Stivale, ed. C. V. Boundas (London: Athlone Press, 1990), pp. 76–8. But sense, for Deleuze, must be grasped in its dimensions prior to any particular structuration, for example as a propositional determinant of the order 'true/false'. The properly philosophical

problem, for Deleuze, is not to determine the truth or falsehood of propositions cleaved from their situation in a complex and chaotic real, but rather to understand the structure and genesis of sense itself, in its multiple and contradictory forms (good sense, nonsense, common sense and so on).

39 For more on this, see D. Voss, 'Deleuze's Third Synthesis of Time', *Deleuze Studies*, 8(1) (2013), p. 195.
40 Rimbaud's formulation, in an 1871 letter to Paul Demeny, takes the form of a meditation on the 'future of poetry'. Here, Rimbaud writes: 'I am present at the birth of my thought: I watch it and listen to it... If old imbeciles had not discovered only the false meaning of the Ego, we would not have to sweep away those millions of skeletons which, for time immemorial! have accumulated the results of their one-eyed intellects by claiming to be the authors!' A. Rimbaud, *Complete Works, Selected Letters*, trans. W. Fowlie (Chicago: University of Chicago Press, 2005), p. 375.
41 S. Bowden, '"Becoming Equal to the Act": The Temporality of Action and Agential Responsibility', in R. Braidotti and S. Bignall (eds), *Posthuman Ecologies: Complexity and Process after Deleuze* (Lanham, MD: Rowman and Littlefield, 2019), p. 124.
42 See *MM*, 152.
43 For a compelling account of this structure, and its ethical and agential implications, see Bowden, 'Becoming Equal', p. 129.
44 As Deleuze explains in his book on Nietzsche – evoking the Nietzschean motif of dice throwing and his conception of the world as a gambling table – this process can be seen as an affirmation of the imbricated nature of chance and necessity immanent to *all* becomings: 'The dice which are thrown once are the affirmation of *chance*, the combination which they form on falling is the affirmation of *necessity*. Necessity is affirmed of chance in exactly the sense that being is affirmed of becoming and unity is affirmed of multiplicity. It will be replied, in vain, that thrown to chance, the dice do not necessarily produce the winning combination, the double six which brings back the dicethrow. This is true, but only insofar as the player did not know how to *affirm* chance from the outset.' Deleuze, *Nietzsche and Philosophy*, p. 26.
45 G. Deleuze and F. Guattari, *Kafka: Toward a Minor Literature*, trans. D. Polan (Minneapolis, MN: University of Minnesota Press, 2003).
46 G. Flaxman, 'Introduction', in G. Flaxman (ed.), *The Brain is the Screen: Deleuze and the Philosophy of Cinema* (Minneapolis, MN: University of Minnesota Press, 2000), p. 2.

2

The Image and the Out-of-Field

Why, having criticised philosophy for embracing a certain 'image' of thought, would Deleuze look to cinema, the art of moving images, for a way out of the *impasse*? The answer to this question lies in the idiosyncratic conception of the image Deleuze takes up from Henri Bergson, which sees the image fundamentally change its form. No longer a 'representation' of matter or memory – the product of an interested and orthodox reduction – the image becomes, in Bergson, the *very identity* of matter and memory, a metaphysical category through which we might overcome dualisms at the heart of philosophy. Bergson's thought more generally, indeed, responds to the problem of dualism, in particular the Cartesian distinction between extended bodies and thought. In this context, Bergson turns to the idea of the 'image', which he feels can help to mediate between realist and idealist philosophical presuppositions. But while Bergson, claims Deleuze, misconstrues the *cinematic* image as emblematic of the spatialising tendencies of the intellect – such as obscure the properly temporal and dynamic character of both bodies and of thinking – for the latter, the unique experiments of the cinematic image are intimately related to the *durations* which comprise both thought and matter.

In this chapter, I map this evolution of the image, tracing Deleuze's account of thought into his work on cinema, where the 'unthought' becomes implicated with the image and its 'out-of-field' (*hors-champ*). I attempt to articulate the trajectory by which this out-of-field changes, in the context of the horrors of the Second World War, from an 'open' to an 'outside', reflecting profound alterations in the structure of Western thought and sensibility. In this context, the image no longer opens onto a 'whole' which might vouchsafe its meaning, but rather a fundamental incomprehensibility immanent to the post-war world. Far, however, from greeting this development with pessimism, Deleuze – in keeping with the affirmative ethics we encountered in the previous chapter – claims that this 'intolerable' outside forces our hitherto habitual cognition into a thought of virtuality and difference, 'a thought from outside' which might be the condition for radically unforeseen becomings.

The Image

But before we can discuss these functions of the cinematic image, we must briefly return to the image as it appears in Bergson, tied as it is to a certain 'crisis of psychology' (*CI*, xviii) emerging at the end of the nineteenth century. This crisis corresponds to the increasing difficulty of a dual metaphysics of mind and matter, problematised on fronts as diverse as physiology – which had gradually come to understand the function of the brain as an electro-chemical organ; psychiatry – which, abiding in the shadow of Freud, now embraced a broadly processual rather than essential concept of the psyche; and physics – which, via thermodynamics, had thoroughly problematised any notion of stable essences in favour of a universe of movement, change and flux. For Bergson, this situation had made redundant the long-standing schism between realism and idealism, which had characterised philosophy arguably since Plato. In this context, he begins *Matter and Memory* by deploying the image as a kind of naive first principle, writing:

> We will assume for the moment that we know nothing of theories of matter and theories of spirit, nothing of the discussions as to the reality or ideality of the external world. Here I am in the presence of images, in the vaguest sense of the word, images perceived when my senses are opened to them, unperceived when they are closed. (*MM*, 17)

Prior, in other words, to adopting any particular philosophical stance *vis-à-vis* reality, we are able to intuit an 'aggregate of images' – a 'whole' which is perceptual before any intellectual partitioning. And of the utmost significance is Bergson's insistence that the centres which enact this perception, the body and the brain, cannot be extricated from or privileged above this whole, or image of all images. To do so would be to enact a paradox, given that, as he explains, 'to make of the brain the condition on which the whole image depends is, in truth, a contradiction in terms, since the brain is by hypothesis a part of this image' (*MM*, 19). The difference between mind, body and their outside, Bergson thus suggests, is only one of function, not of any profound metaphysical difference. Mind and body are simply images among images, albeit with particular qualities to which we will return.

In making this move, as we have said, Bergson hopes to overcome the long-standing struggle in philosophy over the distinction between mind and world. In conceiving of the material universe itself as an 'aggregate of images' (*MM*, 18), with the perceiving brain included as just another image, we appear to have arrived at a model via which we might overcome certain epistemic confusions which have plagued philosophy since Plato. In this context, Bergson writes:

> Every image is within certain images and without others; but of the aggregate of images we cannot say that it is within us or without us, since interiority and exteriority are only relations among images. To ask whether the universe exists only in our thought, or outside of our thought, is to put the problem in terms that are insoluble, even if we suppose them to be intelligible; it is to condemn ourselves to a barren discussion, in which the terms *thought, being, universe*, will always be taken on either hand in entirely different senses. (*MM*, 25)

Inside and outside, or a mind which is radically distinct from matter, are thus only the residue of a wrongheaded intellectual schism, which might be overcome if we return to the intuitive experience of perception. The rejection of these 'false problems' to which philosophy has cleaved does not, however, amount to a claim that consciousness is simply illusory or unimportant. Indeed, it is exactly conscious operations of both memory and perception with which Bergson seeks to model the 'appearance' of images or phenomena in general.

For Bergson, perception is a selective process whereby the perceptive centre, in the paradigm case – though not, as we shall see, necessarily – a nervous system, discards that which does not interest it, perceiving only those stimuli which directly affect its capacity for extending actions. A chair might be the site of all manner of subatomic processes and transformations, but to me it is just a chair, by virtue of the fact that I might sit on it. In this way, images are selectively produced, or 'framed', by the perceptual centres of mind and body in terms of their utility (*MM*, 31).

This is not, however, the route to a kind of Kantian anthropocentrism, of 'things in themselves' which are 'hidden behind' these images. The collapse of transcendence which occurs once we consider both matter and mind as united in the category of the image is such that a complex and multidirectional 'perception' of images constitutes the total fabric of the real. Thus, the leaf of a tree, by neglecting those elements of sunlight which do not 'interest' it – its beauty, for instance – and extracting those that *do* – the protons

The Image and the Out-of-Field

which fuel photosynthesis – creates an *image* of sunlight, in a model we can extend to account for relations or appearances in general. Bodies – which are images – thus differentiate or perceive *other bodies as images*, in keeping with the movements they communicate and the action which these movements might in turn effect.

This seemingly innocent, 'rhetorical' use of the image thus elevates it to a metaphysical status, whereby the aggregate of selectively framed images is synonymous with that which can be said to exist. These images communicate movements to one another, forming the open, qualitatively evolving 'whole' or multiplicity which is the Bergsonian universe. As Anne Sauvagnargues explains:

> Rigorously speaking, images are the only things that exist. Such a realism of the image must be taken literally ... the image is thus not a mental snapshot, a double or a fiction, but a real composition of relations of differential forces, consisting of varying speeds and of fluctuating actions and reactions, and which also experience variations of power of affects.[1]

And Deleuze, in the context of his long-standing hostility towards philosophies of transcendence, will see in this strange use of the image a means both of prosecuting his critique of dogmatic forms of thought, and – what amounts to the same thing – articulating a resolutely immanent metaphysics.

Immanence, Deleuze's often heterodox rearticulation of Spinozist substance, is the cornerstone of his philosophical project, and is consistently levelled at philosophies of transcendence, which emerge, so he claims, as the 'poisoned gift' of Plato (CC, 137). Deleuze follows Spinoza in dedicating himself to a metaphysics which is ethico-political in its rejection of transcendence, and which thus involves the difficult task of articulating a power of distinction or of differentiation which comes from no 'beyond'. Rather, Deleuze seeks to localise processes of differentiation which are immanent to a single infinite plane or substance, which involves the complex thought of an immanence immanent only to itself. In this context, Nathan Widder explains:

> Deleuzian immanence is ... a domain of complex and subtle folds, which are both spatial and temporal in nature, and whose exteriority is unlike that posited by philosophies of transcendence. Indeed, for Deleuze, transcendence is nothing more than an erroneous interpretation of these folds, one that misconstrues them as ruptures or breaks that point to a beyond.[2]

The impossibility of such a beyond, and the dubious ends this fiction has served – be it the reactionary denial of life diagnosed in Nietzsche, the repressive function of desire conceived as lack in psychoanalysis, or hierarchised models of thought which buttress the modern state – determine a Deleuzian metaphysics consistently oriented towards total immanence and the rejection of any transcendent scheme.

Caution, however, when characterising this 'metaphysics of immanence' is essential. Gregory Flaxman has rightly noted the difficulties attendant to any kind of systematised or programmatic reading of Deleuze's philosophy, at least in ways which are not rigorously self-critical.[3] This is because Deleuze subjects his own concepts to a process of internal differentiation, such that they change shape and implication across his various works. The question of a Deleuzian 'ontology' is likewise fraught, given, as François Zourabichvili has written, 'if there is an attitude of Deleuze's philosophy, it is pretty much this: extinguishing the word being, and through this, ontology'.[4] In this context, Deleuze's immanent metaphysics must be grasped not as a purely 'descriptive' project, such as aspires to stabilise any particular ontology, but rather as consistently ethico-aesthetic[5] – a kind of demonstrative performance, which responds to our always already creative situation in a universe of forces which is contingent, multiple and open.[6] This means being attentive to the problems of creativity itself, in particular as they play out in art. And it is precisely in this context that the Bergsonian account of the image appears so fertile to Deleuze, such as he will think it alongside cinema.

In conceiving of the universe as an aggregate of moving images, each selectively 'perceived' by what is ultimately another image, Bergson gives us

> The material universe, the plane of immanence, [as] the *machine-assemblage of movement-images*. Here Bergson is startlingly ahead of his time: it is the universe as cinema itself, a metacinema. This implies a view of the cinema itself which is totally different from that which Bergson proposed in his explicit critique. (*CI*, 67)

This last remark refers to the final section of *Creative Evolution*, a chapter entitled 'The Cinematographical Mechanism of Thought and the Mechanistic Illusion', which sees Bergson return to his long-standing critique of a tendency of the intellect to mistake time for space.[7] This tendency, which subdivides temporal duration into discontinuous, static units (the paradigm case being the homogeneous instants of 'clock time'), serves to *spatialise* time, as such misunderstanding fundamentally temporal phenomena like free will and evolution. These are the product of *durations* – continuous temporal multiplicities which are indivisible without introducing qualitative change, which as such obscures their fundamentally creative or ontogenetic character.[8] This 'spatialising' method is likewise taken up in modern science, where movement is recomposed from series of discrete instants, as in Kepler's astronomy or Newton and Leibniz's calculus (*CI*, 5). While practically useful, such models give us a 'false' image of movement, as divisible and determined, artificially isolated from the whole within which all movements are in fact indivisible, qualitative transformations. And for Bergson, the cinematic moving image, artificially composed as it is of a series of spatially discrete, 'discontinuous' frames or images, is paradigmatic of this false movement of the intellect, which erroneously conceives of both time and movement as quantitatively measurable, divisible and reversible.[9]

Deleuze, however, claims that Bergson has here misapprehended the essence of the cinematic image, which gives us not a series of static images to which movement is 'added', but rather an immediate *movement-image*, which, in keeping with Bergson's account of temporal duration, is a qualitative or continuous multiplicity – irreducible to its component sections (*CI*, 3–4). More than this, cinema gives us certain 'false' movements, achieved through technical means and communicated to thought, yet irreducible to habitual subjective experience. This is the meaning of Bergson's 'startling' contemporality, a contemporality of which Bergson himself is not fully aware. If philosophy, as we saw in the last chapter, must seek out new modes of expression – being particularly attentive to developments in art – then Bergson in a sense achieves a confrontation with the art of cinema without fully or necessarily realising it. This is because his thought and cinema are alike in emerging from the same *techniques* of movement, and a techno-scientific paradigm which generates 'false' movements, a 'false' time, from series of discrete instants.

Contrary to a superficial and all-too-common misreading, this is not a model to which Bergson was somehow fundamentally opposed.[10] Rather, he is insistent that philosophy ought to transform itself in response to this new science, providing it, in Deleuze's words, with 'the metaphysic which corresponds to it, which it lacks as one half lacks the other' (*CI*, 8). Bergson's use of the image in the first part of *Matter and Memory*, like his subsequent turn to biology,[11] constitutes an attempt to enact just this metaphysics, rearticulating the creative movements which mechanistic science obscures. For Deleuze, this is also something cinema achieves, once it transcends an initially 'scientific' function of recording and discovers a capacity for synthesising 'aberrant' movements through editing and montage (*CI*, 3–4). And while Bergson himself is unable or unwilling to forge this connection, for reasons to which we will return, Deleuze intuits that this cinematic *mechanisation* of the image constitutes the condition for philosophy to rearticulate certain problems in an entirely new way.

The Out-of-Field

The image of the cinema books, then, is not the 'dogmatic image' of *Difference and Repetition*, which is still fundamentally implicated with representation and transcendence. It has become dynamic, kinetic and productive, in a way which both Bergson and film help Deleuze to think. This change reflects the fact not only that Deleuze's method deploys a rigorous 'anexactness', according to which concepts are constructed as non-identical, and thus engineered to produce thought, but also the influence of Guattari, who had pushed Deleuze further from linguistic semiotics in search of new forms of the sign through their decade-long collaboration.[12] In this context, the image itself *becomes a sign*, such as might confront thought, in a semiotics radically untethered from questions of representation or meaning.[13]

It is in this context that Deleuze turns to the vocabulary of set and information theories at the beginning of *Cinema I*, in his discussion of the pre-war or 'classical' cinematic movement-image. Here, the framed cinematic image constitutes a 'relatively closed system' or 'set' (*CI*, 15), which contains as its parts a diversity of elements: characters, props, scenery and so on. This set is informational, presenting 'data' which varies in complexity from frame to frame. Fundamental to this presentation, and to its supposedly informational character, is an inherent function of limitation. As in Bergson's account of perception, the frame selects and limits the components of a set, simultaneously determining what is not to be included.

It's important to note that Deleuze has here evoked the concept of information, writing, 'if the frame has an analogue, it is to be found in an information system [*une système informatique*] rather than a linguistic one' (*CI*, 15). This claim, as we have suggested, must be read in the context of Deleuze's hostility to the reductive overlay of a linguistic model of the sign over what are always mixed assemblages of semiotic materials – a critique Deleuze had developed through his collaborations with Guattari. In simple terms, this amounts to a

The Image and the Out-of-Field

rejection of the notion of cinema as simply or strictly a vehicle for narrative, given its deployment of a variety of sonic, visual and otherwise non-linguistic semiotics (*sonsigns, opsigns, chronosigns*), each of which generates singular affects. In order, however, to avoid slipping into what he describes as 'an empty aestheticism' (*CI*, 18), each framing must nevertheless be 'explained' in some way, through its interrelation with other shots, establishing the regularity or normality of a given distribution of parts. This necessity, Deleuze emphasises, adheres even in non-narrative film, and constitutes the essentially communicative function of the cinematic image. The problem, as we shall see, is when this 'informational' tendency is exacerbated, such that the communicative function of the image eclipses its more problematic and productive dimensions, a contention to which we will return in due course.

Thus, albeit in idiosyncratic terms, we may feel as though we are faced with a familiar account of cinematic art. Its images are arranged in such a way as to communicate information to the viewer, which different directors do in a variety of ways. It is in the relation that these framed 'sets' maintain with what they exclude, however, *with their outside*, that the specificities of the Deleuzian approach begin to emerge. Of the utmost significance is Deleuze's claim that what adheres outside of the frame is a state of affairs which is neither immediately perceptible nor comprehensible, yet which is nevertheless *perfectly present*. As he explains:

> There remains the out-of-field [*hors-champ*]. This is not a negation; neither is it sufficient to define it by the non-coincidence between two frames, one visual and the other sound (for example in Bresson, when the sound testifies to what is not seen, and "relays" the visual instead of duplicating it). The out-of-field refers to what is neither seen nor understood, but is nevertheless perfectly present. (*CI*, 19)

Important here is Deleuze's distinction between the out-of-field and those devices by which the 'out-of-shot' is traditionally deployed by film-makers. In the guise of off-camera noise or space suggested by eye-line, the out-of-shot would constitute the proliferation of further 'framings'. What is at stake here is rather a fundamental unknown which nevertheless effects the very possibility of a given image. And the process goes both ways. 'All framing determines an out-of-field', writes Deleuze (*CI*, 19), which means that while a set may tend towards closure, it is fundamentally constituted by an inability ever to fully do so. As he explains, '[framed] content is defined both by the tendency to constitute closed systems and by the fact that this tendency never reaches completion. Every closed system also communicates' (*CI*, 20).

The language of closed systems again refers to Bergson, and his claim that scientific analysis – like matter – is characterised by a tendency to isolate its objects through an artificial act of the intellect.[14] The study of such closed systems, Bergson argues, necessarily precludes a thought of genesis or emergence, which can only be understood in the context of a system's openness to the whole within which it is situated. This whole is *temporal*, inasmuch as it is the condition by which closed systems – modelled in terms of Euclidean geometry, which is to say *spatially* – inevitably communicate, becoming as such non-identical and indeterminate; they change. As Bergson writes:

> The universe *endures*. The more we study the nature of time, the more we shall comprehend that duration means invention, the creation of forms, the continual elaboration of the absolutely new. The systems marked off by science endure only because they are bound up inseparably with the rest of the universe.[15]

This process, Bergson claims, the endless 'elaboration of the absolutely new', is obscured by mechanistic science in the Newtonian mould,[16] which takes the probabilities and reversibility it is able to derive from closed systems as its exclusive object. But the proper object of philosophy is this very whole, or 'open', the condition for transformation and the emergence of the new.

Again, Deleuze identifies a profound resonance between these 'epistemic'[17] interventions and the cinematic image, in particular the *frame*, which, in producing an out-of-field, tends consistently towards a closure that eludes it. In the classical cinema, Deleuze claims, this can take one of two forms. In some cases, the out-of-field works to situate the framed set within a larger set that contains it. In this context, the relation is with an actual or actualisable reality which the extended set expresses (*CI*, 19). In other cases, however, the frame expresses a relation with the *whole*, which is to say the impossibility of any set being fully closed – and this relation, importantly, is *virtual*. We will return in depth to virtuality shortly; suffice it to say that in this latter situation, the cinematic image opens onto both temporality and thought, the virtual multiplicities which Bergsonism aspires to think. But how is this achieved in cinema, concretely?

The Image and the Out-of-Field

We might think, by way of example, of Hitchcock's magisterial exercise in framing(s), *Rear Window* (1954). The film begins as a distinctly 'closed system', imbuing us with the immobility of its protagonist, photojournalist L. B. 'Jeff' Jeffries, who is resting a broken leg. His view onto the courtyard behind his apartment constitutes a rigorous framing, within which we are afforded tertiary frames in the form of the windows of his various neighbours, each of which exists in relation to an outside or absence which conditions the distribution of values in that 'set'. Thus 'Miss Torso' and her string of suitors adhere in the context of an absent lover, set to return from the army at the end of the film. 'Miss Lonelyhearts' potters sadly in her apartment, unaware of the single pianist in the upstairs apartment, later to be her match. The killer, Thorwald, performs a series of acts – cleaning a knife, moving heavy objects, apparently killing a neighbour's dog – all of which are conditioned by the sudden absence of his wife from that set.

Jeffries, able to perceive these absences in God-like fashion, and, importantly, able to *infer from them*, is himself unaware of the distribution of values within his own set, the prescience of girlfriend Lisa and nurse Stella – the true *actors* of the film – whose admonitions ultimately win out over his own sense of self as a restless adventurer. Each frame, including the meta-frame constituted by the view from Jeffries' apartment, extends a set into a larger set which includes it, a situation that their inhabitants are often trying actively to deny. Hitchcock, meanwhile, signs this proliferation of sets with his trademark flourish, appearing briefly as a guest in the pianist's apartment. This gesture, crystallising a consistent tendency in Hitchcock to foreground the *filmic* character of film-worlds, represents the thread by which the closed system of the film is connected to the external world, in which we find ourselves as spectators.

The assemblage of Hitchcock's film thus takes us *beyond* a logic of sets, forcing us into a thought of the whole, as open, temporal multiplicity – the condition through which closed systems always 'communicate' and whereby our best-laid plans are always overcome by circumstance, perhaps Hitchcock's ultimate theme.[18] But more than this, or what amounts perhaps to the same thing, Hitchcock forces us into a thought of thought itself, using the figure of Jeffries and his inferences to produce an 'image of thought', in an altogether new sense of that term. For now, we might recapitulate this schism in Deleuze, between framings that posit further, more comprehensive sets, and those that express the whole which prevents the closure of any set. As Deleuze explains:

> Framing is the art of choosing the parts of all kinds which become part of a set. This set is a closed system, relatively and artificially closed. The closed system determined by the frame can be considered in relation to the data it communicates to the spectators: it is "informatic..." [yet] it determines an out-of-field, sometimes in the form of a larger set which extends it, sometimes in the form of a whole into which it is integrated. (*CI*, 22)

This 'whole', or 'open', is distinct from sets, given that it is the condition by which sets are never able to be absolute or definitive – a situation expressed equally in Russell's Paradox. For Deleuze, following Bergson, this is because the whole is *time*, the 'duration which is immanent to the whole universe, which is no longer a set and which does not belong to the order of the visible' (*CI*, 20) because it is noetic, and ultimately, 'spiritual' (*CI*, 21). The movement-images of classical cinema express this whole, which, as we have seen, is fundamentally open, necessarily oriented towards the 'continual elaboration of the absolutely new', and as such profoundly futural. That cinema begins to express this state of affairs from the beginning of the twentieth century, at the time when Bergson was writing, suggests a parallel evolution in sensibility, tied, as we have seen, to particular temporal technics/techniques. But something happens to this function of the image, and to the Bergsonian whole – such that time is no longer implicated with movement, and the open becomes an outside. It is this change, which is both political and historical, and tied to the demise of the classical movement-image, to which we will now turn.

From the Open to the Outside

Classical cinema – Golden Era Hollywood, but also Soviet montage, French poetic realism and German Expressionism – still *believed* in movement, which is to say in the *power of movements* to change and rearticulate the world (the whole). Perhaps the characteristic image of this cinema is thus the 'action-image' (*CI*, 159), which sees characters, situated within milieux, respond to and interact with these environments, propelling forward narrative arcs predicated on their action. Deleuze associates the action-image with cinematic 'realism', which is not to be confused with a 'realistic' depiction of reality, but instead forms a conceptual topology in which all of a film's material is contiguous, and such stylised or exaggerated motifs as we encounter – dream sequences, hallucinations, the quirks of

The Image and the Out-of-Field

genre – make 'sense' insofar as they do not puncture the milieu/action relation. As he explains:

> What constitutes realism is simply this: milieux and modes of behaviour, milieux which actualise and modes of behaviour which embody. The action-image is the relation between the two and all the varieties of this relation. It is this model which produced the universal triumph of the American cinema, to the point of acting as a passport to foreign directors who contributed to its formation. (*CI*, 159)

And indeed, this remains the dominant form of popular cinema today, from romantic comedies and dramas through to action films, which perhaps perfect the form. We can easily see how John McClane's body accumulates traumas as it moves through the terrorist-infested urban milieux of the *Die Hard* films, re-extending these affects in a carnage of explosions, shattered glass and machine-gunned extras, as such propelling forward narrative. Deleuze, however, claims that the mid-twentieth century presents the action image with a kind of 'crisis' (*CI*, 229), part of a broader crisis of movement-images, from which emerges a new kind of image, a *pure time-image*, the subject of his second cinema volume.

While we may, of course, object that the action-image still appears to be the dominant cinematic model,[19] Deleuze, in keeping with his conviction that we might differentiate the 'essence of cinema' from the vast majority of films (*CI*, xviii), identifies the disconnected, meandering films of the post-war New Wave(s) as fundamentally problematising the form. This is because they express a situation in which action itself *begins to appear impossible*, in keeping with broader alterations in thought and life emerging from the war. As Deleuze explains:

> the crisis which has shaken the action-image has depended on many factors which only had their full effect after the war, some of which were social, economic, political, moral and others more internal to art, to literature and to cinema in particular. We might mention, in no particular order, the war and its consequences, the unsteadiness of the 'American Dream' in all its aspects, the new consciousness of minorities, the rise and inflation of images both in the external world and in people's minds, the influence on the cinema of the new modes of narrative with which literature had experimented, the crisis of Hollywood and its old genres... (*CI*, 229)

What Deleuze is here describing, in other words, are the conditions of 'post-modernity',[20] and the simultaneous collapse of both narrative and of a political *sensus communis* which takes place in the post-war world. In this context, Deleuze claims that while 'people continue to make [action-image] films: the greatest commercial successes always take that route ... the soul of the cinema no longer does' (*CI*, 229). This 'soul' must be understood in terms of cinema's capacity for forcing unique movements in thought, a destiny the action-image eschews in its tracing of familiar cognitive circuitries.

Deleuze, however, is no postmodernist, and his claim is that these entwined political, social and aesthetic conditions, far from creating a situation in which there's 'nothing new to say', cause the openness of the image to reach unprecedented intensity, unfurling radically new noetic powers. In post-war film – Italian neo-realism, the French New Wave, New Hollywood, post-colonial cinemas – the 'open' gives way to an outside; no longer a whole which might be thinkable, but rather a situation which is 'unthinkable', and which as such calls for thought to be reborn. As Deleuze explains:

> the time-image puts thought into contact with an unthought, the unsummonable, the inexplicable, the undecidable, the incommensurable. The outside or the obverse of the images has replaced the whole, at the same time as the interstice or the cut has replaced association. (*CII*, 220)

We will return to the role of temporality here shortly. For now, we might note that the question of thought, and its relation to the unthought, such as we encountered in *Difference and Repetition*, is forcefully returned. But whereas Blanchot and Foucault pursue the 'thought from outside' in literature, Deleuze's conviction is that this problem might be uniquely posed in the context of the cinematic image.

'[T]he essence of cinema', he writes, '– which is not the majority of films – has thought as its higher purpose, nothing but thought and its functioning' (*CII*, 173), and while this claim may seem strident or surprising, it certainly has precedent. From Hugo Münsterberg to Sergei Eisenstein,[21] Nöel Carroll to David Bordwell,[22] theorists have returned ceaselessly to an affinity between cinema's flow of images and the operations of consciousness. Deleuze, following Eisenstein, draws on the most dramatic of these theses: if cinema frames, composes and 'legislates' over images, then it is like a kind of brain – a *kino-brain*, capable of thinking in radically new and inhuman ways. But its motion, like the motion of our own thought, is forced and artificial – automatic – consisting of aberrant movements and heterodox relations to the world of extended 'things'. As such, it is perhaps uniquely predisposed to affect and displace our own, 'human' cognition, something post-war cinema begins to do in earnest.

This is because in the post-war world it is no longer possible to think in terms of a whole which might situate and rationalise the image, a situation that the disjunctive 'cuts' of New Wave *auteurs* like Godard render explicit.[23] In this context, the new cinematic image reflects a new philosophical reality: in the post-war world we are *unable to think the whole*, we have lost a thought of the absolute. But thought's failure, we will recall, is the paradoxical condition for its rebirth, albeit in a radically new form. As Deleuze explains:

> What Blanchot diagnoses everywhere in literature is particularly clear in cinema: on the one hand the presence of an unthinkable in thought, which would be both its source and barrier; on the other hand the presence of another thinker in the thinker, who shatters every monologue of a thinking self. (*CII*, 173)

This simultaneous 'source and barrier', as we have seen, is the 'impossible' moment at which thought is confronted with that which it has *never thought* – a confrontation which impels it into creativity. This 'other thinker' is the author or agent of such a creativity, who does not pre-exist this process, but who must be brought into being through an affirmation of those forces which have so shattered its peace and self-identity.[24] And while this 'shattering' has often been the destiny of those outlying, 'untimely' *personae* who so consistently fascinate Deleuze – Rimbaud, Kafka, Artaud, Schreber – this noetic structure proliferates widely after the Second World War. Faced with the unthinkable realities of that conflict – from the Holocaust to Hiroshima – the habitual exercise of both thought and action appear to shudder and collapse *on an industrial scale*.

In this context, in *Cinema II*, Deleuze once more advances a 'commentary' on Bergson, in particular the latter's theory of action. Bergson had dubbed the set of habitual response mechanisms we employ in the face of external stimuli the 'sensori-motor system' (*MM*, 152), a set of regulatory neural affects conditioned by past experience and disposed to respond 'sensibly' to events. This is the system or schema which legislates over images, 'framing' them in terms of their utility or lack thereof for the purposes of motricity. And while this schema is practically useful, its habituated character predisposes it to certain conservatisms from the perspective of philosophy. This, indeed, is the model upon which the action-images of classical cinema draw in constructing narrative, as Ronald Bogue explains:

> The sensory-motor schema provides the commonsense temporal and spatial coordinates of our everyday world, and the signs of the movement-image, which are the signs of the classic cinema, ultimately conform to the coordinates of that commonsense world.[25]

But it is exactly 'common sense' which has become an impossibility in the post-war world. And cinema, claims Deleuze, begins to express this situation directly, producing 'a cinema of the seer and no longer of the agent [*de voyant, non plus d'actant*]' (*CII*, 3). In this context, 'it is no longer a motor extension which is established, but rather a dreamlike connection through the intermediary of the liberated sense organs' (*CII*, 5).

The paradigm case is Rossellini's *Germany, Year Zero* (1948), in which 12-year-old Edmund Kohler, wandering the streets of a shattered Berlin, consecrates a new kind of image, which is primarily temporal, and only incidentally spatial-kinetic. The plot of the film is as simple as it is unimportant. Trying to survive in the ruins of the city – until so recently the capital of the 'Thousand Year Reich' – Edmund floats from situation to situation: a squabble over the meat of a dead horse, a young girl selling her body for cigarettes, the death of his father and the arrest of his brother – a soldier unregistered with the authorities. What we see, however, is not a chain of linked and purposive events, unfurling in a spatial trajectory of *beginning*, *middle* and *end*. Rather, we are confronted with a series of floating and disconnected images: Edmund's ragged body, the crumbling façades of ruined buildings, vistas of twisted metal, the furrowed brow of Edmund's father. Walking through this wasteland, adrift in a destruction which far outstrips his comprehension, much less his agency, Edmund becomes a *seer*, bearing witness to a situation in which 'action' is no longer possible. In this context:

> the character has become a kind of viewer. He shifts, runs and becomes animated in vain, the situation he is in outstrips his motor capacities on all sides, and makes him see and hear what is no longer subject to the rules of a response or an action. (*CII*, 3)

And it is this disconnection, this 'liberation' of sense from its traditional moorings in the service of habitual mentation and activity – the sensory-motor schema – which places post-war cinema in contact with the outside; the problematic inner limit of thought. The sensory-motor break confronts both character and spectator with a world which is 'unthinkable', likewise confronting thought with its own, internal 'powerlessness' (*CII*, 175). But this 'powerlessness' must be understood in the context of the affirmation Deleuze claims is the key to bringing about the new, in thought and as such in life. This dispossession of both the human being and its world must serve, in the context of a Nietzschean *amor fati*, as the condition for the creative becoming of both a new thinker and, potentially, a new world. But how might this actually occur? What does this cinema of the seer actually *see*?

Actuality, indeed, or rather *actualisation*, is just what's at stake in the time-image, which presents us with a situation in which certain movements are no longer actualisable. This circumstance, Deleuze claims, forces us into a thought of the *virtual* – the condition for all actualisations, which our habitual sensory-motor framings tend to obscure. In this context, the image begins to express both a 'pure' temporality and a 'pure' thought, no longer subordinated to these all-too-human interests. This account is once again framed as a commentary on Bergson, who understands temporality in terms of a mutual interpenetration of virtual past and actual present (*duration*) – a synthesis which is the condition for the production of the qualitatively new (*creative evolution*). And while classical and action-image cinema produced an *indirect* image of this virtual multiplicity (the whole) as subordinated to movement, post-war cinema, Deleuze claims, expresses time directly. In this way, the virtual saturates and penetrates the actual, confronting thought likewise with its radically temporal character. Before, however, we can turn to these developments as they relate to the Deleuzian outside, we must briefly explicate the concept of the virtual as it emerges in Bergson, Deleuze and cinema.

The Virtual in Bergson

The virtual is one of the most frequently misconstrued concepts in Deleuze's *oeuvre*, given that, as Keith Ansell-Pearson rightly notes, it is often treated in vague way, as 'all the other stuff that is not actual, something like the universe in its totality and unfathomable complexity'.[26] At the very least, what this characterisation neglects is the way in which the virtual differs and repeats throughout Deleuze's work – at times appearing in a thoroughly Bergsonian aspect (as duration or *élan vital*), in a refitted Kantianism as the stuff of 'Ideas' in *Difference and Repetition*, or indeed, as closely associated in various works with the concept of the 'event'.[27] In this first sense, we must remember that for Bergson, far from some kind of woolly metaphysical totality, the virtual cannot be understood without recourse to an actual, individuated body, for which it serves as the condition for action, memory and the particular contractions of duration which ultimately form consciousness. Thus, in *Matter and Memory*, Bergson introduces the virtual in the context of his discussion of the nervous system, which he explains as a particular arrangement of matter allowing the body to draw upon the virtual in positing ever more complex and multiple courses of action.[28]

Bergson, as we saw, uses the concept of the image to move beyond Cartesian dualism, articulating a mind which is rigorously immanent to the universe of material movement-images. But this does not mean that the mind, nor the bodies of certain living things, are not also particular in their functions, with unique capacities for selecting and differentiating communicated movements. The image that is our body receives movement in the form of stimuli, but depending upon the nature of these stimuli it does not re-extend or translate this movement automatically. This is because the nervous system creates a 'delay' or 'interval' between stimulus received and action (re-)extended, 'slowing' incoming movements in order to form a lacuna which is ultimately constitutive of our subjectivity (*MM*, 30–2). This interval allows the organism to escape from the mechanism of pure reactivity, drawing on a store of previously accumulated nervous responses which will be more diverse and sophisticated depending on the organism's perceptual and *mnemetic* capabilities. Put differently, this interval allows the organism to *transcend the actual*, allowing it to select from among a plurality of *virtual* actions, which are virtual inasmuch as they have been retained as memories.

It is this virtual world which we encounter in dreams and imagination, albeit now even more liberated from – Bergson would say less 'contracted' by – the exigencies of action in the present. This line of thought, indeed, leads Bergson to the notion of a 'pure memory', a memory yoked to no particular sensory-motor activity, and as such *fully virtual*. To reach this memory, or rather to reach a thought of it, Bergson writes, 'we must have the power to value the useless, we must have the will to dream' (*MM*, 83). Such, indeed, is also the power of art, and Deleuze will link Bergson's account of pure memory to the well-known passages in Proust, where memory is no longer purposive and intentional, but rather involuntary, 'pure' and a-centred. In the explosive so-called 'episode of the madeleine', which sees the unmoored multiplicity of life in Combray emerge, filling

The Image and the Out-of-Field

Proust's narrator with 'an exquisite pleasure' causing 'the vicissitudes of life [to become] indifferent',[29] we encounter pure memory, no longer tethered to the exigencies of action, but linked rather to the persistence of the past, which lies dormant, virtual, and which might be actualised by all manner of haphazard and unexpected events. This is the virtuality actualised by the subject when it escapes simple reactivity, and the scope of our access to it is thus also the scope of our freedom.

As always, however, Bergson is not thinking in terms simply of psychology. A particular nervous system contracts a local zone of this absolute virtuality, but what it contracts is actually the past itself, a *pure past*, which persists as the condition for actualisation or individuation *tout court*, and which is irreducible to any particular subject. This 'pure past' is perfectly present, albeit in a way which our 'spatialised' conception of time tends to obscure, as Deleuze explains in his book on Bergson:

> We have great difficulty in understanding a survival of the past in itself because we believe that the past is no longer, that it has ceased to be. We have thus confused Being with being-present. Nevertheless, the present is not; rather, it is pure becoming, always outside itself. It *is* not, but it acts. Its proper element is not being but the active or the useful. The past, on the other hand, has ceased to act or to be useful. But it has not ceased to be. Useless and inactive, impassive, it IS, in the full sense of the word...[30]

In this sense, it is important to understand that 'pure memory' refers less to the operation of a particular psyche, and rather to a generalised virtuality presupposed by the present of action, whereby individual psyches might 'leap into the past as into a proper element'.[31] This is because the past, far from being somehow reconstituted by a brain which maintains a record of it, is perfectly real and present – albeit virtual – until it is actualised in the form of localised memories or sensory-motor responses. Or in Deleuze's words, 'in the same way that we do not perceive things in ourselves, but at the place where they are, we only grasp the past at the place where it is in itself, and not in ourselves, in our present'.[32]

In this context, Bergson claims that our existence is fundamentally *cleft*, the site of a schism between virtual and actual, which flow into functions of memory and of perception respectively. Our experience is comprised of these two 'jets' or 'flows' of time, one flowing back into virtuality, the other contracting an actualised present – in a model we have already encountered in Deleuze. And for Bergson, *déjà vu* is only the most immediately perceptible instance of this 'splitting', a glimmer of the consistent structure of the present, whereby

> Our actual existence [...] whilst it is unrolled in time, duplicates itself all along with a virtual existence, a mirror-image. Every moment of our life presents two aspects, it is actual and virtual, perception on one side and memory on the other. Each moment of life is split up as and when it is posited. Or rather, it consists in this very splitting...[33]

The virtual aspect of this splitting – memory – as we have said, establishes a kind of reservoir for 'counter actualisations',[34] the condition by which individuals, understood in the broadest possible sense, are able to become other than they are. In this way, the virtual works to keep Bergson's metaphysics fundamentally open, providing an account of the way in which actual states – or closed systems – are in effect conditioned by the reservoir of virtuality they serve ceaselessly to actualise.

The Virtual in Difference and Repetition

In *Difference and Repetition*, Deleuze takes up this model of the virtual, linking it to an idiosyncratic structuralism which supplements Bergson's own, at times obscure, vitalism. In the service of his project to think 'difference-in-itself', Deleuze evokes the virtual, tying it to Gilbert Simondon's philosophy of individuation, in order to posit a processual differentiation which would be the condition of constituted individuals, a differentiating difference 'all the way down'.[35] In the service of this project, Deleuze establishes as distinct virtual differen*t*iation (with a *t*) and actualisation as differen*c*iation (with a *c*), to refer to the two 'parts' or 'moments' of difference (*DR*, 207). Essential here is Deleuze's insistence that objects are 'double', in the sense of their having both virtual and actual reality. By way of Deleuze's example from linguistics,[36] we might say that the virtual aspects of language – differential relationships between and within series of phonemes, morphemes, lexemes, conventions of syntax and grammar – remain ideal (yet perfectly real) until actualised through speech or writing, laryngeal and facial muscles, ink, paper or symbols on a computer screen.

It is in this sense that Deleuze claims that 'the reality of the virtual is structure' (*DR*, 209), a genetic or generative structure, comprised of singularities with no identity beyond that which is determined by their differential relations. Deleuze's focus here, in keeping with the noetic 'critique' advanced throughout *Difference and Repetition*, is on the virtual structure of *Ideas*, which he defines in the once more Bergsonian (and Riemannian) terms of 'qualitative' or 'continuous' multiplicity (*DR*, 182): multiplicities which are indivisible, change only qualitatively, and are intensive (a term to which we will return). Or as Deleuze explains:

> An Idea is an *n*-dimensional, continuous, defined multiplicity ... by dimensions, we mean the variables or co-ordinates upon which a phenomenon depends; by continuity, we mean the set of relations between changes in these variables ... by definition, we mean the elements reciprocally determined by these relations, elements which cannot change unless the multiplicity changes its order and its metric. (*DR*, 182)

As the above passage suggests, 'virtual structure', far from being closed or static, is therefore fundamentally relational and dynamic. Events are constantly redistributing the singularities which comprise a given structure, causing some to become defunct, and producing others which ensure that structure as mobile and evolving. Indeed evolution, in the biological sense, offers a helpful model of just how this process might be conceived, with the virtual structure of DNA composed – and re-composed – through constant contact with actualised environmental and physical factors which cause some gene sequences to become obsolete, new ones gradually to emerge.

Important therefore to note is that while the object is 'double' in the sense of having both a virtual and an actual reality, these two aspects of the object are not identical, nor indeed do they resemble one another (*DR*, 209). Fundamental to this 'asymmetry' between virtual and actual faces of the object is the role played by *intensity*, to which we have already briefly referred. Deleuze's concept of intensity is perhaps best understood via recourse, once more, to the Bergsonian distinction between quantitative and qualitative multiplicities. Quantitative multiplicities, we may recall, depend upon an enumeration of parts which are spatially distinct from one another, and thus divisible.[37] Qualitative multiplicities, meanwhile – like durations – are divisible only inasmuch as an alteration to any constitutive part effects a change to the whole. As Daniel Smith and John Protevi explain, 'extensive differences, such as length, area or volume, are intrinsically divisible ... intensive differences, by contrast, refer to properties such as temperature or pressure that cannot be so divided'.[38]

Indeed, Deleuze's evocation of intensity in the fifth chapter of *Difference and Repetition* draws heavily on a thermodynamic conception of intensive quantity, which, contra classical thermodynamics, posits differences of potentiality or energy in intensive forces as the productive condition of extended states or systems.[39] Put briefly, what interests Deleuze in the thermodynamic conception of intensive quantity is the fact that it is differentially productive, as illustrated by the example of steam-powered engines – which produce motion through the juxtaposition of different temperatures that, in accordance with the second law of thermodynamics, work to re-establish equilibrium. Leaving aside, here, the specificities of Deleuze's engagement with thermodynamics – in which he ultimately seeks to reject the thesis of an entropic 'heat-death' of the universe – we might say that the differentially productive mode of intensities conceived in an initially thermodynamic mould appears to Deleuze a particularly fertile means of conceiving of differentiation and individuation in a more thoroughly metaphysical sense. 'Everything which happens and everything which appears is correlated with orders of differences...' he writes, 'differences of level, temperature, pressure, tension, potential, *difference of intensity*' (DR, 222).

It is for this reason that Deleuze attributes to intensities a generative or genetic role, such that intensive differences work ceaselessly to resolve themselves and their tensions through differenciation in actual bodies, constituting a concrete mechanics to the qualitatively productive operations Bergson will attribute to temporality. In keeping with Deleuze's account of the 'transcendental illusion', however – whereby we invariably dedicate ourselves to the empirical study of actual individuals – it is important to note that this 'cancellation' of intensive difference in the context of actualisation is only ever an empirical effect. Intensity abides, 'uncancelled', both in its own order and in the extensities it produces (as the condition for potential future 'counter-actualisations').

This 'dualism' – which is anything but a dualism, once we properly understand the two moments of difference as continually implicated in multilateral and reciprocal operations, 'threshold' moments, metastability and phase-shifts – must likewise be understood in the context of Deleuze's noetic project to establish modes of thought hospitable to the movements of difference and of differenciation *without* recourse to concrete identity. We have already seen how, for Bergson, temporality-as-duration is characterised by a constant, creative evolution which makes suspect our intellectual habitudes – our tendency to think in calcified and abstract modes, neglecting certain noetic motions proper to philosophy.

The Image and the Out-of-Field

In positing intensive differen*t*iation as the condition for the extensive and localised resolutions of differen*c*iation, Deleuze has expanded this project into a complex metaphysics, in the service of his critique of a thought of difference predicated on the notion of 'identity' – such as precludes certain processual and problematising dimensions of reality. As such, he will claim of these two 'moments' of difference, that the first constitutes *problems* – the genetic and differen*t*ial relations of singularities in the virtual – while the second constitutes *solutions*, in the localised and actual expression of individuals, bodies, organs and so on. For Deleuze, our conceptualisation of real difference (difference-in-itself) is hampered by a focus on extensive magnitudes – or solutions – as opposed to the intensive qualities – or problems – which generate them, guaranteeing their processual character. This error of thought – the 'transcendental illusion' (*DR*, 266) – sees us assign to both intensities and virtual singularities the same characteristics as the extensive and actual states they engender.

It is not only the task of a 'thought without image', as it is sketched in relation to philosophy in chapter 3 of *Difference and Repetition*, but also a potential of art, which might overcome this illusion – this obliteration of virtual difference in favour of an actualised (differen*c*iated) 'difference' that we grasp via recourse to identity. 'The search for new means of philosophical expression [...] must be pursued today in relation to the renewal of certain other arts', Deleuze writes, 'such as the theatre or the cinema' (*DR*, xxi). And cinema, as we have briefly suggested, ushers in a new relationship between actuality and the virtual, creating circuitries and crystallisations between the virtual and the actual which offer themselves up to perception, causing the 'two sides' of the object to merge in a catalytic cross-pollination.

Cinema and the Virtual: La Jetée

These crystallisations adhere as a result of the profound indeterminacies of the cinematic image, structured as it is of inter-bleeding images of reality, falsehood, dream, memory and hallucination – collaged together as a uniform perceptual 'fact' by the automatic visuality of the camera and the editing table. And this process reaches a particular intensity in the context of the post-war cinema, where:

> perception and recollection, the real and the imaginary, the physical and the mental, or rather their images, continually follow [...] each other,

running behind each other and referring back to each other around a point of indiscernibility. But this point of indiscernibility is precisely constituted by the smallest circle, that is, the coalescence of the actual image and the virtual image, the image with two sides, actual and virtual at the same time. (*CII*, 72)

If the object has two sides – virtual and actual – then so indeed does the cinematic image, with one side facing a relatively closed set and the other opening onto a virtual whole or outside. But in this latter situation, and with the collapse of the sensory-motor schema, these two sides of the image begin to interpenetrate and become indiscernible, forming a kind of *crystal*, which confronts our thought with the virtuality its dogmatic exercise obscures.

In the background here again is Simondon, for whom crystallisation is a paradigm for processes of individuation *tout court*. Just as a crystal gradually 'organises' a supersaturated liquid through a successive polarisation of its molecules, as such rendering it solid, individuation generally can be conceived in terms of the systematisation of energetic tensions immanent to pre-individual milieux.[40] While Deleuze only refers to Simondon obliquely here, we might say that the crystalline cinematic image expresses this situation directly – taking in both actualised 'individuals' and the virtual potentials which *in-form* them to give us an image of individuation in both its processual and pre-individual dimensions. The films Deleuze treats as emblematic of the crystal-image – Welles' *Citizen Kane* (1941) and *The Lady from Shanghai* (1947), Zanussi's *The Structure of Crystals* (1969) and Carné's *Daybreak* (1939) – work in just this way, with individuals simultaneously constituted and torn apart by virtual states of recollection, dream and hallucination, the complex folds of which constitute these films' narrative 'present'.

This tendency perhaps finds its apogee in *La Jetée* (1962), Chris Marker's 28-minute 'photo novel', in which the protagonist, a condemned prisoner, simultaneously inhabits a present, past and future which coalesce into a u-chronic world of interwoven dream and post-apocalyptic reality. While Deleuze himself doesn't discuss the film, it offers up a rich expression of the forces he will attribute to 'crystalline' forms of the time-image, and as such we will turn to a brief analysis of it here. *La Jetée*, indeed, constitutes an incredibly pure time-image, composed as it is of a montage of still shots which are themselves evacuated of all movement, in the context of an apocalypse where the only possible action takes the form of an exploration of time. Humanity, we are told – in the austere narration which constitutes the only dialogue – has almost been eradicated in a Third World War. In a network of subterranean galleries beneath the Chaillot in Paris, the 'victors' struggle to find a means of saving humanity, following the destruction of all life on the surface of the planet. Space, we are told, is 'off limits', and as such, 'the only hope for survival lay in time'.[41] A group of experimenters are thus looking for a 'loophole in time', through which it might be possible to retrieve food, medicine and energy sources capable of restarting large-scale industry.

We may already grasp the Bergsonian implications of the film's narrative – such that a virtual temporality is actualised in the service of action in the present; however, it is important to recall Deleuze's methodological conviction that films don't simply 'illustrate' a pre-established philosophical system. Rather, film offers philosophy a new means of expression, and in this context *La Jetée* itself produces a new image of time, a temporal-cinematic 'sign', or 'crystallisation', such as philosophy might experience as provocation. *La Jetée* achieves this through its sly deployment of still images, which – in a style reminiscent of Eisenstein's montage – coagulate gradually to produce a complex and evolving virtuality, explosively actualised in the film's single motion shot.

The film's protagonist, a prisoner who is earmarked as a guinea pig for this experimental time-travel, is chosen by his jailers because of the visceral presence of an image from his childhood: a woman he had seen on the viewing platform (*la jetée*) at Orly Airport, in pre-apocalypse Paris. On the basis of this fragment of the past, his jailers hope to throw him (in French, *jeter* –he will become 'the thrown', *la jetée*) into the past itself, the pure, virtual past, actualising this virtuality in the service of the present. This one, fragmentary image – the face of a young woman – is graven in his memory; however, it is disconnected from all sensory-motor context. Around it trembles a world of indistinct, virtual images, of which he is only vaguely aware. On their obscure evidence alone, 'he knew he had seen a man die'. The prisoner's eyes are covered, and he is restrained and drugged, such that his only possible motion is into the labyrinths of memory. Here, after suffering horribly, he encounters a constellation of images from before the war: a peacetime morning – with grass, sun and sheep – a peacetime bedroom, real children, real birds, real cats (Marker's signature, present in every film), and on the sixteenth day, the 'jetty' at Orly Airport. Here he meets the woman from his vision, and on repeated visits to the past they begin a relationship, gradually falling in love.

Here, the film's temporality is once more complicated. In the pure past, which the prisoner begins to move through with confidence and ease, the two lovers gradually forge an alternate temporality built out of the 'event' which is their love. In the context of this love, the narrator explains, 'they are without memories, without plans. Time builds itself painlessly around them.' The affair reaches its crescendo in the stunning moment of the film's single motion shot, which sees the woman's eyes slowly open as she lies opposite the prisoner in bed, accompanied by a symphony of singing birds. Tarkovsky famously refers to the 'pressure' of time in a given shot,[42] and this solitary movement-image, emerging from the timeless temporality of love, seems likewise to emerge from the overwhelming pressure of the static images which surround it, causing it to spread out in an eternity redolent with potentials, such as lovers will well know.

It is here – in this solitary image – that the film's unique temporal sign is consecrated, implicating the rigorously particular temporality of love. Deleuze had already dedicated important passages to the coalescence of time, love and the sign in *Proust and Signs*, where he writes, in terms not un-Bergsonian, that 'signs are the object of a temporal apprenticeship, not of an abstract knowledge'.[43] This apprenticeship, which takes the form of a gradual discernment and interpretation of signs, reaches particular intensity in the case of love, whereby 'the beloved appears as a sign, a "soul"; the beloved expresses a possible world unknown to us, implying, enveloping, imprisoning a world that must be deciphered...'[44] But the experience of love, or of the sign of love, is not just the experience of a new world. This confrontation with a 'new world' necessarily implies a *plurality* of worlds, such that

> the pluralism of love does not concern only the multiplicity of loved beings, but the multiplicity of souls or worlds in each of them. To love is to try to *explicate*, to *develop* these unknown worlds that remain enveloped within the beloved.[45]

Indeed, to return to the explicit terms of *Difference and Repetition*, we might say that love, even in its most domesticated and atomised forms – as experienced by two individuals, as under patriarchal or capitalist norms – produces an imbalanced, differential axis of potentiality, which sees the individual's world 'opened up' through contact with that which it is not. But more important still, lest we slip back

The Image and the Out-of-Field

into dualism, is the fact that this contact with another world – with an outside, exceeding the logics of our own – engenders the necessary thought of a plurality of worlds, a multiplicity of multiplicities, each implying their own complex of virtual–actual relations.

In using these few seconds of motion-picture footage (here, Marker used a 35mm Arriflex camera as opposed to the Pentax Spotomatic used for the stills – the story goes that he could only afford to hire the former for an afternoon), Marker makes explicit the *qualitative change* that takes place in the context of an intensive event such as love. In this 'opening' of the hitherto static world of the film onto the possibility of movement, an 'aberrant movement' – even as small as an opening of eyes – Marker fabricates a cinematic sign which expresses the explosive potentials that lie dormant, virtual, within any given image or image system.

The reprieve, however, is brief, and after returning to the present and discovering that he is slated for liquidation, the prisoner makes a final, last-ditch attempt to escape into the past with his beloved. Running towards her on the platform at Orly he spots an agent from the present, and realises, as the agent fires, that the memory which had projected itself so insistently throughout his life was that of his own death. The film's denouement, however, accompanied by the Heraclitean realisation that 'there [is] no way to escape time', must be understood not simply in terms of science fiction or glib speculations about time travel. Essential is the way in which a series of temporal structures are literally actualised, differenciated through the montage flow of images. A timeless temporality of love; a present evacuated of movement by catastrophe and violence; a future to which that present might open itself and orient its experiments – these various temporal regimes are thus combined in a complex assemblage which is real in the fullest sense.

This composition of images, which no longer privileges sensory-motor action, confronts thought with these actual situations as they are individuated through and by virtuality, giving us an image of individuation itself. If the sensory-motor schema is predisposed to 'see' conservatively, focusing on actualised individuals and habituated response, then this composition is also concretely political, as Marker's work aspires consistently to be. Indeed, as Matthew Croombs has noted, a critical focus on the film's play with stasis, movement and temporality has often obscured its 'radically political content',[46] a central and 'undertheorised' depiction of torture which, he argues, is influenced by Henri Alleg's book *La Question*, and its detailed descriptions of the brutal methods deployed by French paratroopers during the Algerian War of Independence.[47] The tension between the scenes in which the prisoner is restrained, blindfolded and injected with drugs and the idyllic images from a pre-war Paris must be read as emerging from this decidedly actual sociopolitical juncture. As Croombs explains:

> Marker ultimately uses a series of subversive formal strategies [...] superimposition in particular, to create an abject frontier between these consumer and colonial contexts, unravelling the binary opposition that sustained 'modern' French subjectivity.[48]

As such, the images which constitute *La Jetée*, far from simply being those of science fiction, respond to the visceral and contemporary problems not only of nuclear war, but of colonial power and state repression. In the face of these 'intolerable' situations, Marker, and we must hope the spectator, is forced into a kind of thought which reaches outside the habitual experience of affluent, Western subjectivity, and into a problematic virtuality upon which it might draw in order to expand and alter its perception.

'Art is real', writes Anne Sauvagnargues, 'it produces real effects on the plane of forces...',[49] and everything that occurs in the film, once we understand the virtual as perfectly real – 'completely determined' (*DR*, 209) as a genetic structure capable of expressing an axis of intensity[50] – must likewise be understood as 'real' in the sense of communicating concrete affects and movements to our thought. Time and time again – to use an appropriate cliché – the images of *La Jetée* race towards a virtuality which is actualised in disparate forms discussed by Bergson and Deleuze alike: dream, hallucination, involuntary memory, *déjà vu*. But what is essential to its crystalline descriptions is the notion that these 'leaps' into the virtual constitute not just illusory effects of consciousness, but genuine explorations of time's differential forms and contours, rigorously uncoupled from the successive, purposive and actualised functioning of sensory-motor perception. In this context, the film, like its protagonist, emerges from the virtual bearing all manner of 'seeds',[51] such as might counter-actualise or crystallise new realities.

In this way, Deleuze writes, 'something takes shape inside the crystal which will succeed in leaving through the crack and spreading freely' (*CII*, 89). The crystal-image, in its rendering indiscernible the virtual–actual schism, is thus the site of a 'new distinction [...] a new reality which was not pre-existent' (*CII*, 91). This reality is not

The Image and the Out-of-Field

guaranteed, and it is always possible that 'everything that has happened falls back into the crystal and stays there' (*CII*, 91), provided we are not equal to the unequal in the image, which is to say, if we capitulate to the notion that 'it's only a film', and that images only instantiate a secondary kind of reality. Again, what's at stake here is an ethics of noesis, and a willingness to affirm the differential forces expressed in the image, believing in thought and art as ways to change the world. In this context, Deleuze continues:

> Time in the crystal is differentiated into two movements, but one of them takes charge of the future and freedom, provided that it leaves the crystal. Then the real will be created ... what we see in the crystal is always the bursting forth of life, of time, in its dividing in two or differentiation... (*CII*, 91–4)

Intensity, *life* and *time* – these constitute multiple faces of the outside, that event which displaces thought, forcing it to confront itself and its present as problematic. The problems of *La Jetée* are manifold and pertinent: how might we live, love and act in a world evacuated of all movement, through an apocalypse of our own making but apparently beyond our control? How might we seek not only lessons from the past, but from a utopian future, such as might save us from a present which presents itself as inevitable? How might we concretise new temporalities which escape from the pressures of a hegemonic, 'official' time, imposed as if from above? How is Western subjectivity generated through the systematic exploitation of colonial and racialised 'peripheries'? These questions, in *La Jetée*, are posed in the context of a nuclear apocalypse, but they seem no less pertinent as we face up to the prospect of the Sixth Mass Extinction Event. But perhaps we have remained too obscure, treating 'thought' as an abstract and academic enterprise. A thought from outside, as I have suggested, precipitates unforeseeable becomings in the most immanent and concrete sense. Indeed, it is to the most concrete problem we must now turn, if we are to outline the stakes and implications of Deleuze's engagement with the image and its outside: the problem of the political itself.

Notes

1 Sauvagnargues, *Artmachines*, p. 87.
2 N. Widder, *Political Theory After Deleuze* (London: Continuum, 2012), p. 19.

3   See G. Flaxman, *Gilles Deleuze and the Fabulation of Philosophy: Vol. I – The Powers of the False* (Minneapolis, MN: University of Minnesota Press, 2012), p. 270.
4   Quoted in ibid., p. 305.
5   Deleuze's 1961 essay on Lucretius in many ways articulates the entwined ethical and metaphysical orientations which would inform all of his subsequent work. In the context of Lucretius' (Epicurean) project to use the 'atom' to articulate a radical naturalism, Deleuze writes, 'never has one pushed so far the enterprise of "demystification." Myth is always the expression of false infinity and the disturbance of the soul. One of the most profound constants of naturalism is to denounce everything that is sad, everything that is the cause of sadness, everything that requires sadness in order to exercise its power. From Lucretius to Nietzsche, the same goal is pursued and attained. Naturalism makes thought and sensibility into an affirmation.' G. Deleuze, 'Lucretius and Naturalism', trans. J. C. Bly, in A. Greenstine and R. Johnson (eds), *Contemporary Encounters with Ancient Metaphysics* (Edinburgh: Edinburgh University Press, 2017), p. 252.
6   As Claire Colebrook writes, 'immanence begins with a commitment to the given. There is just one flow of life... This plane ought not to be thought of as some thing or being – some object towards which we bear a relation – but as an open and dynamic flow of becoming.' C. Colebrook, *Understanding Deleuze* (London: Allen and Unwin, 2002), p. 57.
7   See primarily *Time and Free Will* (1889), *Matter and Memory* (1896) and *Creative Evolution* (1907).
8   Duration, for Bergson, begins as the contiguous and indivisible coexistence of *all times* experienced by consciousness, and is developed throughout his works from an initially psychological structure into an ontogenetic account of the universe itself. As he explains in *Time and Free Will*: 'Pure duration is the form which the succession of our conscious states assumes when our ego lets itself *live*, when it refrains from separating its present states from its former states. For this purpose it need not entirely be absorbed in the passing sensation or idea; for then, on the contrary, it would no longer *endure*. Nor need it forget its former states: it is enough that, in recalling these states, it does not set them alongside its actual state as one point alongside another, but forms both the past and the present states into an organic whole, as happens when we recall the notes of a tune, melting, so to speak, into one another.' H. Bergson, *Time and Free Will: An Essay on the Immediate Data of Consciousness*, trans. F. I. Pogson (Mineola, NY: Dover, 2001), p. 113. Implicit in this passage is the idea that we cannot stress, substitute or remove a note without introducing a *qualitative* change to the entire melody. It is just this impossibility

of extricating the different temporal categories of past, present and future – of a *quantitative* distribution of temporality – which causes Bergson to assert that mathematised and 'spatial' approaches to time are unable to give us a full account of life.

9   As Bergson writes: 'such is the contrivance of the cinematograph. And such is also that of our knowledge. Instead of attaching ourselves to the inner becoming of things, we place ourselves outside them in order to recompose their becoming artificially. We take snapshots, as it were, of the passing reality, and, as these are characteristic of the reality, we have only to string them on a becoming, abstract, uniform and invisible, situated at the back of the apparatus of knowledge, in order to imitate what there is that is characteristic in this becoming itself.' H. Bergson, *Creative Evolution*, trans. A. Mitchell (Mineola, NY: Dover, 1998), p. 306.

10 Commentators have often sought to characterise Bergson as somehow 'anti-scientific' or hostile to what he calls the intellect. This position finds little textual support, given his consistent emphasis on the need for philosophy to complement science, and for his 'intuitive' method to be combined with the operations of the intellect. Bergson characterises this reciprocal relationship thus: 'As soon as we have intuitively apprehended the truth, our intelligence corrects itself, and gives intellectual form to its error. Having received a hint, it provides in its turn control. As the divers will touch in the depths of the ocean the shipwreck that the aviator has spotted from high in the air, so our intelligence – immersed as it is in a conceptual environment – will analytically verify, point by point, what had been apprehended in a synthetic, supra-intellectual manner.' H. Bergson, *The Creative Mind: An Introduction to Metaphysics*, trans. M. L. Andison (Mineola, NY: Dover, 2007), p. 66.

11 For the underexamined influence of Weismannian biology on Bergson's thought, and subsequently that of Deleuze, see K. Ansell Pearson, *Germinal Life: The Difference and Repetition of Deleuze* (London: Routledge, 1999), pp. 1–10, 43–5.

12 As Anne Sauvagnargues explains: 'The image shifts, according to the logic of the sign in which it is taken up, away from an interpretation deemed mental in 1964 toward the machinic experimentation defined by Guattari, which infused their collaborative writing with a new tension. In *The Logic of Sense* and in the second edition of *Proust and Signs*, Deleuze remained invested in an interpretation of the image founded on signification. Beginning with the collaboration with Guattari, this regime of interpretation definitively gives way to a pluralism of regimes of signs, semiotic clusters that they define as "rhizomes" that do not privilege the mental or linguistic sphere.' Sauvagnargues, *Artmachines*, p. 46.

13 In this context, Deleuze is trying to break definitively with a then-dominant trend in film theory, dedicated to treating cinema in terms of structural linguistics. Paradigmatic of this approach is the work of Christian Metz; see C. Metz, *Film Language: A Semiotics of the Cinema*, trans. M. Taylor (Chicago: University of Chicago Press, 1991).
14 Again, Bergson is not categorically hostile to this tendency, which reflects certain practical realities, as he concedes: 'certainly, the operation by which science isolates and closes a system is not altogether artificial. If it had no objective foundation, we could not explain why it is clearly indicated in some cases and impossible in others. We shall see that matter has a tendency to constitute isolable systems ... but it is only a tendency. Matter does not go to the end, and the isolation is never complete.' Bergson, *Creative Evolution*, p. 10.
15 Ibid., p. 11.
16 It should be made clear that the 'mechanistic' model in Bergson's sights is far from universally adopted within science itself, particularly in its developments since his death. A great deal of chaos and complex systems theory, as well as work in quantum physics, bears a striking resemblance to some of Bergson's positions *vis-à-vis* what might now be called 'emergence'. See, for instance, the work of Ilya Prigogine and Isabelle Stengers, who link Bergson's thought to a plurality of physical systems which function in indeterminate and unpredictable ways, producing increased complexity and order out of apparent entropic chaos. Here, the question of the 'openness' of a given system is of fundamental importance. See I. Prigogine and I. Stengers, *Order out of Chaos: Man's New Dialogue with Nature* (Toronto: Bantam Books, 1984).
17 Although, as Deleuze argues, these interventions are not 'epistemological' in the traditional sense of 'reflecting' upon scientific knowledge and its conditions; instead, 'on the contrary in the sense of an invention of autonomous concepts capable of corresponding with the new symbols of science' (*CI*, 68). I have here used the term for the sake of brevity and convenience, while conceding scare quotes to Deleuze.
18 We might think, for instance, of *Rope* (1948), in which the two students' 'perfect crime' unravels gradually under the glare of Rupert Cadell's gaze and the film's single, inquisitorial shot. Or of the infamous scene in *Torn Curtain* (1966), in which, as Hitchcock once explained to François Truffaut, he wanted to show how difficult it was to kill a man. See H. Maxford, *The A-Z of Hitchcock* (London: Batsford, 2002), p. 266. Throughout Hitchcock's *oeuvre*, in a mechanism subsequently perfected by the Coen Brothers in *Fargo* (1996) and *No Country for Old Men* (2007), there is a fascination with the ways in which the best-laid plans inevitably go wrong.
19 Indeed, the rise of small screens has seen cinema turn increasingly to a hyperbolic action-image of vast special effects and spectacular scenes of

destruction, in order to capitalise on the immersive environment of the big screen, and turn the tide of a consistently diminishing market share.
20 See F. Jameson: *Postmodernism, or The Cultural Logic of Late Capitalism* (London: Verso, 1991), and J. F. Lyotard: *The Postmodern Condition: A Report on Knowledge*, trans. G. Bennington and B. Massumi (Minneapolis, MN: University of Minnesota Press, 1984). Both thinkers approach the epistemic consequences of this same set of conditions, albeit in what are at times completely contradictory ways.
21 See H. Münsterberg, *The Photoplay – A Psychological Study* (New York: D. Appleton and Co., 1916); R. Arnheim, *Film as Art* (Berkeley, CA: University of California Press, 1957); S. Eisenstein, *Film Form: Essays in Film Theory*, trans. J. Leyda (New York: Harvest and Harcourt Brace Jovanovich, 1977).
22 In the late 1980s and 1990s, Carroll and Bordwell, working in the tradition of analytic aesthetics, popularised the use of 'cognitivist' and 'neuroscientific' theories in film analysis. Broadly, their work focuses on the ways in which cinematic spectatorship might be used to model theories of cognition more generally. See, in particular, Bordwell's 'mission statement', 'A Case for Cognitivism', *Iris: A Journal of Theory on Image and Sound*, 9 (1989), pp. 11–33.
23 Godard's famous riposte to Georges Franju's question as to whether a film ought to have a beginning, middle and an end – 'Yes, but not necessarily in that order' – captures perfectly the temporal destabilisations which begin to occur in the post-war cinema. Quoted in D. Sterritt, *The Films of Jean-Luc Godard: Seeing the Invisible* (Cambridge: Cambridge University Press, 1999), p. 20.
24 In *Cinema II*, Deleuze thus resumes his discussion of Artaud, positing this 'creativity' as implicated with a form of 'automatic writing', analogous to the operations of cinema, and calling into being a new form of thinker, no longer conscious or unconscious, but rather wedding the aleatory and undetermined with a wilful process of creation. See *CII*, 171.
25 Bogue, *Deleuze on Cinema*, p. 5.
26 K. Ansell-Pearson, 'The Reality of the Virtual: Bergson and Deleuze', *Modern Language Notes*, 120(5) (2005), p. 1112.
27 For a concise treatment, see C. V. Boundas, 'Virtual/Virtuality', in A. Parr (ed.), *The Deleuze Dictionary – Revised Edition* (Edinburgh: Edinburgh University Press, 2010), p. 301.
28 See chapters 1 and 2 of *Matter and Memory*, pp. 17–133, throughout which this theory is gradually elaborated.
29 M. Proust, *In Search of Lost Time: Volume 1 – Swann's Way*, trans C. K. Scott Moncrieff and T. Kilmartin (New York: The Modern Library, 1992), p. 60.

30. G. Deleuze, *Bergsonism*, trans. H. Tomlinson and B. Habberjam (New York: Zone Books, 1991), p. 55.
31. Ibid., p. 56.
32. Ibid.
33. H. Bergson, *Mind – Energy: Lectures and Essays*, trans. H. W. Carr (Westport, CT: Greenwood Press, 1975), p. 165.
34. The term is Deleuze's, and emerges in *The Logic of Sense*, in the context of the virtual/actual 'doubling' of every event. As Deleuze explains: 'On the one side, there is the part of the event which is realized and accomplished; on the other, there is that "part of the event which cannot realize its accomplishment." There are thus two accomplishments, which are like actualisation and counter-actualisation.' Deleuze, *Logic of Sense*, p. 151.
35. For an accomplished study of the 'renovation' undergone by the virtual in *Difference and Repetition*, in particular its re-emergence under the influence of Simondon's philosophy of individuation, see S. Bowden, *The Priority of Events: Deleuze's Logic of Sense* (Edinburgh: Edinburgh University Press, 2011), ch. 3, pp. 95–151.
36. This example features in *Difference and Repetition*, but is also comprehensively stated in the essay 'How do we Recognise Structuralism?' collected in D. Lapoujade (ed.), *Desert Islands and Other Texts: 1953–1974*, trans. M. Taormina (Los Angeles: Semiotext(e), 2004), p. 176.
37. See, in particular, Bergson's elaboration of this distinction in the early chapters of *Time and Free Will*.
38. D. Smith and J. Protevi, 'Gilles Deleuze', in *The Stanford Encyclopedia of Philosophy* (spring 2018 edition), ed. E. N. Zalta, https://plato.stanford.edu/archives/spr2018/entries/deleuze/.
39. For a detailed treatment of Deleuze's use of the concept of 'intensity' in the context of thermodynamics, see D. Clisby, 'Intensity in Context: Thermodynamics and Transcendental Philosophy', *Deleuze and Guattari Studies*, 11(2) (2017), pp. 240–58.
40. See G. Simondon, *Individuation in Light of Notions of Form and Information*, trans. T. Adkins (Minneapolis, MN: University of Minnesota Press, 2020), pp. 13–14.
41. *La Jetée*, dir. C. Marker, Argos Films, 1962.
42. A. Tarkovsky, *Sculpting in Time: Reflections on the Cinema*, trans. K. Hunter-Blair (Austin, TX: University of Texas Press, 1989), p. 117.
43. Deleuze, *Proust and Signs*, p. 4.
44. Ibid., p. 7.
45. Ibid.
46. M. Croombs, '*La Jetée* in Historical Time: Torture, Visuality, Displacement', *Cinema Journal*, 56(2) (2017), p. 25.
47. As Croombs explains (ibid., pp. 25–8), the journalist and activist Alleg was responsible for the widespread proliferation of news regarding the

French military's use of torture during the Algerian War, following the smuggled-out account of his own torture in the El-Biar and Lodi prisons. The book sold 60,000 copies in the first two weeks after publication and was hugely influential not only in activist but in artistic circles in metropole France.

48 Ibid., p. 26.
49 A. Sauvagnargues, *Deleuze and Art*, trans. S. Bankston (London: Bloomsbury, 2018), p. 19.
50 The terms here owe a debt to Anne Sauvagnargues' explication of the two 'moments' of difference. As she explains: 'These two regimes of difference express the energy axis of an intensity, which is individuated by resolving its difference in potential: a differen*t*iated (with a *t*) body on the virtual plane differen*c*iates (with a *c*) itself by individuating itself ... the two moments of difference take up the axis of virtual forces (differen*t*iation with a *t*) and actual forms (differen*c*iation with a *c*)' (ibid., p. 59).
51 Indeed, Deleuze identifies three modes by which 'exchange' and 'indiscernibility' might be understood to take place in such crystal-images, enumerating alongside the actual–virtual couplet, the limpid and opaque sides of crystallisation, and, again drawing on Simondon's account of individuation as crystallisation, a relationship between 'seed and the environment'. Unifying these three movements, explains Deleuze, is the notion of 'expression'. As Deleuze writes: 'The crystal is expression ... the seed is on the one hand the virtual image which will crystallize an environment which is at present [*actuellement*] amorphous; but on the other hand the latter must have a structure which is virtually crystallisable, in relation to which the seed now plays the role of actual image' (*CII*, 77).

3

A Politics of the Out-of-Field

It's clear, as we saw in the previous chapter, that the transition from the *whole* to the *outside* of the image has social and political dimensions, taking place as it does under the auspices of the profound changes in Western thought attendant to the Second World War. But the cinema of the time-image is political in another, more active sense, according to Deleuze's idiosyncratic account of the political implications of art. For the 'seer' of the post-war cinema doesn't simply enact a mute and apolitical vision of the status quo. What she encounters is a fundamental 'impossibility' which is the condition for Deleuze's politics *tout court*.

In this chapter, I engage and explicate this politics, of which the cinema volumes constitute two of the most complex and protracted expressions. In so doing, I reject claims advanced by the likes of Slavoj Žižek and Alain Badiou, that no meaningful politics can be derived from Deleuze's thought, alongside an often implicit assumption within Deleuze scholarship itself, that the latter's politics is fundamentally articulated in the two volumes of *Capitalism and Schizophrenia*, co-authored with Félix Guattari. Against these positions, I elaborate the difficult and entwined political claims Deleuze makes on behalf of cinema: that it is capable of reflecting capital's 'time–money conspiracy'; that it might engender a tentative 'belief in the world', such as is the necessary correlate of political action; that it captures the contemporary political fact that 'the people are missing', as a unified or coherent political agent; and finally that it might reveal those 'impossible' or 'intolerable' situations which would provoke such a people into being. These operations are immanent to new forms of cinematic image – the meandering time-images of the various New Waves, the 'minor' works of post-colonial cinema – which emerge from and respond to the political realities of the post-war world. This world, claims Deleuze, in which habitual forms of acting and of thinking seem impossible, must become the condition for a new kind of politics rooted in this very impossibility – a situation these 'unthinkable' cinematic images render perceptible.

A Politics of the Out-of-Field

This model, moreover, which is contiguous with what I call Deleuze's broader 'political ontology of thought', offers up a unique set of tools for thinking about politics and the digital image as they intersect in the twenty-first century. If, as we saw in the introduction, the future of cinema – our present – is the site of a profound and political struggle with control through informatics, then Deleuze's account of the politics of the cinematic image is potentially of great value in helping us to think through this difficult confluence. In treating this politics, I claim, we identify entwined noetic and aesthetic powers which might 'resist' control as it is manifest in contemporary digital media – our objective in the coming chapters.

The Political Deleuze

Before, however, we can turn to these latter claims, it's important to acknowledge the difficulties attendant to any reading of Deleuze which is 'political' in the generally accepted sense. Indeed the political efficacy of Deleuze's thought, in particular of his 'schizoanalytic' work alongside Guattari, has been the subject of ample debate, not least because of certain deflationary remarks made by Deleuze and Guattari themselves. 'Schizoanalysis *as such* has strictly no political program to propose', they write: 'if it did have one, it would be grotesque and disquieting at the same time'.[1] This is because the molecular and multivalent operations of their critique are fundamentally opposed to the kind of 'molar' organisation required in order for a programmatic or 'party' politics to adhere – a claim we might apply to Deleuze's philosophy more broadly. Yet as numerous commentators have noted,[2] political concerns are nevertheless so marbled throughout the Deleuzian corpus, and so consistently dedicated to a clutch of recurrent themes – capitalism, organisation, minority, resistance, control – that we must read such remarks with the sceptical attention they deserve. Indeed, in the same breath (or at least in the following volume), Deleuze and Guattari will also write, in an apparently paradoxical and somewhat grandiose moment, that 'schizoanalysis, as the analysis of desire, is immediately practical and political ... for politics precedes being'.[3]

Many commentators have laid the blame for this apparent incoherence, as well as the sweepingly 'unphilosophical' attitude encapsulated in this latter remark, at the feet of Guattari – who has often been characterised as that 'bad influence' drawing Deleuze away from his lucid metaphysical and properly meta-philosophical treatises. Deleuze, so the story goes, having hitherto dedicated himself to studiously apolitical readings of the history of philosophy – Hume, Nietzsche, Kant, Spinoza – is led astray by the unfortunate confluence of Guattari's institutional analysis and the long shadow of May '68. Paradigmatic of this 'anti-Guattari' reading is Slavoj Žižek, who, with characteristic expeditiousness, claims that *'not a single one* of Deleuze's own texts is in any way directly political; Deleuze "in himself" is a highly elitist author, indifferent towards politics'.[4] Indeed Žižek here adopts a position lamentably taken up by many so-called 'Deleuzians' themselves, which serves not only to misrecognise certain ethico-political themes at work in Deleuze's philosophy *long before* his encounter with Guattari, but also those solo-authored works *after* their initial collaboration, which continue to advance protracted political lucubrations. Here, we can most certainly locate Deleuze's two volumes dedicated to cinema, which use the artform to re-pose the question of politics in an entirely new way.

Of course, the idea of a 'political cinema' is far from unique to Deleuze, with thinkers from Eisenstein to Bazin, Benjamin to Baudry dedicated to thinking the unique ideological potentialities of the motion picture. Deleuze's originality, indeed, lies in an eschewal of these authors' more obviously 'political' concerns – ideology, the 'culture industry', pedagogy and so on – in favour of a political ontology which centralises the specific forms of luminous, affective and noetic 'individuals' which the cinema is able to produce. '[T]he essence of cinema', as we have already seen Deleuze suggest, '– which is not the majority of films – has thought as its higher purpose, nothing but thought and its functioning' (*CII*, 173), and in this sense the cinema books plug into the broader ontology of thought we have encountered in works like *Difference and Repetition*.

While we have noted the importance of caution when reading concepts and critiques as interchangeable across Deleuze's *oeuvre*, given the demonstrative differenciation to which they are invariably subjected, we might, in broad strokes, recapitulate this noetic project thus: thought is a particular form of intensive individuation, a noetic event which takes place in response to an encounter with that which is 'unthought', or unthinkable. As such, thought does not take the form of a habitual recognition (as in Descartes), nor of a unitary representation (*à la* Kant); rather, thinking is always something unexpected, undetermined and uncontrollable, the creative response to an event which cannot yet be thought, and as such, can only be sensed.

A Politics of the Out-of-Field

The political consequences of this model are several. First, thought is rigorously material, composed of, and responding to, sensible states of affairs and the actualised events of life. At the same time, thought is set up in opposition to *doxa* – to habits, lassitude and conservatisms – with which its intensive, creative functioning is fundamentally incompatible. Finally, thought involves a movement into territories which *are not yet actualised* – which are *virtual* – in order to draw on the differential genetic structures which enable actualised states to become other than they are. In terms of this participation in virtual structure – in yet-to-be-actualised dimensions of the real – thought therefore has a fundamental solidarity with, and orientation towards, the future, and the creation of new worlds. This is the noetic model present at least as early as *Difference and Repetition*, and while we may quibble as to its *efficacy* as politics, it is certainly oriented by political concerns, as Deleuze himself acknowledges.[5]

On meeting and collaborating with Guattari, of course, who had already long been engaged in an activism far more 'actualised' than that of Deleuze,[6] the latter eschews his meta-philosophical approach to themes of *doxa*, conservatism and reactionary modes of life in favour of an explicit vocabulary of micro-politics, molecular revolution and revolutionary desiring production, themes we will leave to one side for now. Suffice it to say that Deleuze and Guattari's project to identify the processes of axiomatised individuation which constitute capitalism is the most explicitly political moment in Deleuze's career. It is far, however, from the last, and in turning his attention, after the laborious completion of *A Thousand Plateaus*, to a study of 'aesthetics' across painting and cinema, Deleuze carries over ethico-political concerns already present, yet thoroughly enriched by Guattari's provocations.

Thus, in *Francis Bacon: The Logic of Sensation*, the latter's canvases constitute the site of a diagrammatic 'battle' against cliché, as against figuration and representation in their 'Royal' modalities.[7] In the cinema books, meanwhile, Deleuze's noetic philosophy is forcefully returned, drawing upon a long critical tradition – from the Soviet School to contemporary French criticism in the *Cahiers du Cinéma* – dedicated to the proposition that the fluid and dynamic interaction of images on the cinema screen might enter into catalytic relations with a spectator whose mentation is constructed in a complementary fashion.

But Deleuze's intervention is at once more idiosyncratic and far more contemporary than this. For the 'pre-war' model of a political cinema, such as might 'shock' the spectator into action, evokes a stable or coherent 'people' which might serve as the subjects for such ideological demystifications. By the 1980s, however, a multiplicity of factors – the break-up of traditional labour movements in the developed West, the consolidation of totalitarianism in the Soviet sphere, a generalised 'incredulity towards metanarratives', to use the Lyotardian parlance – problematise this traditionally political model. It is to this clutch of issues that Deleuze turns, advancing, across the latter stages of *Cinema II*, a protracted discussion of how such a 'people' might be thought in the post-war world.

But how might cinema participate in this lofty project, given the well-known thesis that it is ideology or distraction, an apparatus for the production of subjects who 'enjoy their own dehumanisation' – to use an appropriate phrase of Adorno's?[8] That the capital of cinema is Hollywood, and that its global triumph in the twentieth century is the triumph of American-style consumerism, cannot be simply brushed aside. Thus, before we can turn to the political claims Deleuze makes on cinema's behalf, we must look to its intimate relationship with capital, and the complex question of Deleuze's relationship to Marx.

Time is Money

Of course, cinema is always already contaminated by its relationship with capital, being an industrial, popular form, fundamentally indexed to the rise of a globalised consumer culture. As such, it might seem unusual to associate it with powers of 'resistance', even in its most rarefied and avant-garde guises. Deleuze is well aware of this tension, pointing to the 'rubbish' which dominates cinematic production. The vast majority of films, however, do not obscure the powers cinema possesses 'once it stops being bad' (*CII*, 172) and embraces its 'essence' as that which communicates shocks and false movements to thought. As he explains, in the preface to *Cinema I*:

> One cannot object by pointing to the vast proportion of rubbish in cinematographic production – it is no worse than anywhere else, although it does have unparalleled economic and industrial consequences. The great cinema directors are hence merely more vulnerable – it is infinitely easier to prevent them from doing their work. (*CI*, xix)

What this amounts to is a claim that cinema, for Deleuze, is engaged in a kind of continual, internal struggle with the conditions of its production, a situation which affords it a unique perspective on these very conditions.

In this respect, his work is indeed contiguous with a great deal of Marxian thought on film, from Eisenstein to Adorno, which emphasises the internal contradictions of bourgeois culture – an approach rendered most explicit in Deleuze's discussion of the relationship between film and money in *Cinema II*. Money, he here suggests, is cinema's 'most internal presupposition', rejecting Benjamin's famous thesis in order to claim that 'what defines industrial art is not mechanical reproduction but the internalised relation with money' (*CII*, 80). This internalised relation reflects the fact that the materials which comprise the cinematic image – labour, film stock, equipment – but also, importantly, *space* and *time*, become commodities under the capitalist mode of production, a situation cinema is uniquely predisposed to express. As Deleuze continues, quoting the film-maker Marcel L'Herbier, 'space and time becoming more expensive in the modern world, art had to make itself international, industrial art, that is, cinema, in order to *buy* space and time as "imaginary warrants of human capital"' (*CII*, 81).[9]

While film thus literally enacts the cliché that 'time is money', being an artform in which 'a minute of image [...] costs a day of collective work' (*CII*, 80), it is simultaneously capable of foregrounding and problematising this very state of affairs, something the self-reflexive cinema of the time-image begins to do in earnest. Indeed post-war cinema, in the 1960s and 1970s in particular, sees a gradual proliferation of films foregrounding the problematic facts of film production, in particular the central role of *money*. The causes of this development are once more multiple and complex. In America, the rise of television and the collapse of the old studio system saw an unprecedented period of experimentation and risk-taking, with young directors given free rein to entertain an ever-more aesthetically literate public. In Europe, the Western powers attempted to differentiate their 'liberal' culture industries from those in the East through similarly adventurous and subversive production techniques. In this context, Deleuze writes, '*cinema confronts its most internal presupposition, money, and the movement-image makes way for the time-image in one and the same operation*' (*CII*, 81). Paradigmatic of this new style of film-making, which is also linked to the collapse of sensory-motor narrative, is the 'film within a film', a device we encounter in the likes of Fellini, Truffaut, Godard and Kazan.

We might think, for instance, of *8½* (1963), in which the 'director's block' of Fellini's thinly veiled self-portrayal, Guido Anselmi (Marcello Mastroianni), constitutes a self-reflexive commentary on the impossibility of making a film in the context of financial pressures. The more Anselmi is hounded by producers and journalists, the less decisive he is able to be regarding his production, which begins to fall apart (at the same time as the narrative of *8½* falls apart, opening onto a vista of incomprehensible yet strangely beautiful images). Likewise, in Godard's *Contempt* (1963), the confrontation staged between brash Hollywood producer Jeremy Prokosch (Jack Palance) and Fritz Lang's delightful self-portrayal as a relic from an artistically incorruptible old world, speaks to the creative tensions in Godard's own practice. Lang's determination to finish his adaptation of Homer's *Odyssey*, even after its producer has died and the script has been given up as a disaster, constitutes a profound statement on artistic will, played out likewise across Godard's subsequent half-century of obscure and deeply personal films.

In these ways, the film within a film draws to the surface contradictions immanent to the 'time–money conspiracy', as such perhaps pointing us beyond it. While cinema is invariably implicated in this conspiracy as the condition of its production, it is simultaneously, at its best, capable of exploiting this confluence in aesthetically and pedagogically valuable ways. Taking up the Marxian thesis of money as an instrument towards the 'general equivalency' of value, Deleuze gestures to the ways in which the time-image, in superseding the movement-image (in which we encounter a set of movements as exchanges of equivalence), thus injects temporal questions of inflation, disparity and dissymmetry into the image, rendering problematic any transcendent logic of 'equivalence'. As Deleuze explains:

> What the film within the film expresses is this infernal circuit between the image and money, this inflation which time puts into the exchange, this "overwhelming rise." The film is movement, but the film within the film is money, is time ... endlessly relaunching exchange which is dissymmetrical, unequal and without equivalence, giving image for money, giving time for images, converting time, the transparent side, and money, the opaque side, like a spinning top on its end. (*CII*, 81)

Deleuze's examples here are from his preferred canon of high-brow art films – Wenders' *The State of Things* (1982), in which a beleaguered film crew are marooned in Portugal after the production runs out of money; Godard's *Passion* (1982), in which the extravagant film restaging works of classical painting eventually stalls and falls apart – but there are other, less rarefied examples of this production of asymmetrical and abortive time–money exchanges.

We might think of Michael Bay's blockbusters, which seem to come apart at the seams through an overinflation and overinvestment of capital, poured into ever smaller temporal instants. *Armageddon* (1998), for instance – famous for its catastrophic digital editing, which proliferates unintentional disjunctive cuts and irrational connections – gradually reveals the overdeterminations of capital which constitute contemporary Hollywood images.[10] The film, which critic Roger Ebert described as 'an assault on the eyes, the ears, the brain, common sense and the human desire to be entertained',[11] reportedly has an average shot length of 1.5 seconds, the condensation of over a million feet of Kodak film (a feat for which, apparently, the company gifts film-makers with six bottles of Korbel champagne).[12] And this condensation of unbelievable amounts of labour, money, technology and time into ever smaller and more abrupt cinematic instants creates a disorienting, chaotic experience, rendering patently clear the impossibility of any equitable or equivalent 'exchange' of abstract money for concrete temporality. The time–money 'exchange' here simply does not work, and it is difficult to watch Bay's film without constantly encountering, in Deleuze's sense of that term, the impossibility of such an exchange – the very nature of labour under capitalism.

The fact that film possesses these powers, intentional or not, for revealing its own monetary materiality – for inflating, overdetermining and opening up the closed circuits of film–money causality – will be of the utmost importance when we turn to our discussion of contemporary digital media. For now, we might note that this aspect of Deleuze's thinking on cinema conforms with an approach to capitalism that he and Guattari develop throughout their collaboration, according to which, again following Marx, the forces capable of overcoming capitalism must be understood as immanent to capitalism itself.[13] Indeed, Guattari neatly summarises this disposition when he writes, in *The Machinic Unconscious*, 'liberation from capitalistic constraints happens, not through a politics of return to archaic territorialities, but through the crossing of an additional degree of deterritorialization'.[14] For Deleuze and Guattari, in other words, resistance to capital – a task they unabashedly and continually affirm – cannot but take the forms we are afforded by the vast deterritorialisations of capitalism itself.[15] It is in this context, following their postulation of capitalism as 'axiomatic' in its ability to transform heterogeneous flows of matter or desire into uniform flows of capital, that they will write, in *A Thousand Plateaus*:

> Some people invoke the high technology of the world system of enslavement; but even, and especially, this machinic enslavement abounds in undecidable propositions and movements that, far from being a domain of knowledge reserved for sworn specialists, provides so many weapons for the becoming of everybody/everything, becoming radio, becoming electronic, becoming molecular... Every struggle is a function of all of these undecidable propositions and constructs *revolutionary connections* in opposition to the *conjugation of the axiomatic*.[16]

In this context, Deleuze and Guattari famously gesture to 'schizophrenic' tendencies immanent to capitalism, which see its immense productivity produce all manner of disjunctive and undecidable connections – such, indeed, as the 'irrational cuts' of the New Wave – which may well afford potentialities for revolutionary connections in turn.

Revolution, for Deleuze and Guattari, can of course not be understood in any teleological sense – as a coherent party-political programme or the product of a self-achieving *Geist*. However, *forces* – which here remain couched in an explicitly libidinal vocabulary of 'desire' – can either form conjugated, 'captured' and quantitatively productive flows, commensurate with capitalistic forms of encoding, or enter into new and 'undecidable' connections which throw out unpredictable, differential and intensive sparks. The distinction between these forms of connectivity – which of course cannot be posed as a simple duality, but rather as a series of crossed thresholds and indeterminacies – might well be expressed as being between those connections which are *axiomatic* and those which are *problematic*. Or as Eugene Holland explains:

> in most cases, such subversion gets absorbed – axiomatized and reterritorialized – by the existing system, which simply adds one more axiom to its structure of domination-appropriation (e.g. trade-unionism, Fordism, or the French Communist Party as ways of absorbing various workers' movements).[17]

However, alongside these 'apparatuses of capture' there are the constant, empirical conflagrations and complexifications which take place as an inevitable by-product of production, or more properly, as the true nature of desiring-production, once it escapes from molar and abstract overcodings. Thus, as Holland continues, evoking the

A Politics of the Out-of-Field

distinction between 'subjugated' and 'subject' groups which Guattari will lift from Sartre:

> Happily, as ubiquitous as they are, subjugated groups under capitalism only ever have one leg to stand on: decoding and deterritorialization are constantly pulling the rug out from under any permanent formation (including those of capital itself.) And this is where the chances for revolution lie... Schizo-revolutionary strategy thus seeks to reinforce and magnify the subversive thrust of capitalist decoding and deterritorialization; to provoke the transmutation or schism of subjugated groups into subject groups ... so as to attain critical mass and overthrow power...[18]

Technologies play just as prominent a role in these moments of conflagration and chaos as do works of art, profoundly open as they are to all manner of material and inhuman forces. And cinema occupies a particularly important role here, given its coalescence of modern, industrial technology, noesis and aesthetic experimentation. But classical Marxist accounts of cinema, both pessimistic and laudatory, tend to differ from Deleuze's in their sense that subject groups ('the people') are a stable or self-evident proposition. It is in Deleuze's strange account of both *belief in the world* and of a *people to come* that the specificities of his approach most fully emerge, rendering his thought particularly valuable in thinking a politics apt to the post-Marxian world.

Belief in the World

'Restoring our belief in the world', writes Deleuze, '– this is the power of modern cinema (when it stops being bad). Whether we are Christians or atheists, in our universal schizophrenia, *we need reasons to believe in this world*' (CII, 177). This is certainly one of Deleuze's most unexpected claims, and its context and implications require careful excavation. Importantly, this is not a belief in any preordained or pre-distributed world, such as would replicate the 'belief' of religious orthodoxy. Rather, drawing on the unique confluence of Nietzsche, Marx and Spinoza which informs his politics, this is a revolutionary belief in the world's immanent and infinite capacity to become *other than it is* – a fact with which cinema is intimately connected, as we shall see.

The idea that we no longer 'believe' in the world is perhaps a familiar one. A universe of contemporary conditions – from mood-deadening pharmacological interventions to stubborn, obstructive inaction in response to climate change – seems to attest to a generalised scepticism about the 'world' as an object with which we might meaningfully interact. This is what Mark Fisher has called 'capitalist realism', an episteme encapsulated in that apparently irrevocable sentiment, attributed to both Fredric Jameson and Slavoj Žižek, 'that it is easier to imagine the end of the world than it is to imagine the end of capitalism'.[19] And it is most certainly towards this same confluence that Deleuze addresses himself, writing, 'the modern fact is that we no longer believe in this world. We do not even believe in the events which happen to us, love, death, as though they only half concerned us' (*CII*, 177). In place of a 'world' in which we might participate, he explains, 'it is the world which looks to us like a bad film' (*CII*, 177).

Deleuze once more approaches this problem on the noetic register. This lack of belief follows from the demise of what we saw Bergson call the 'sensory-motor schema', a milieu-responsive network of nervous affects which ensures that incoming sense data and outgoing motor action are meaningfully coordinated. This schema, while practically useful, is also fundamentally conservative – constituting a predetermined space of possible actions, in a model which sees both action and movement 'obey laws which are based on the distribution of *centres of forces* in space' (*CII*, 133). The sensory-motor schema, in other words, far from a 'natural' orientation of the nervous system, replicates habitual and culturally determined ways of seeing and of acting – a fact which renders its workings eminently political.

For Deleuze, as we saw in the last chapter, this schema is reproduced in and by the 'classical' or 'action-images' of most commercial cinema, which sees characters propel forward narrative arcs through sensible interactions with milieux. This model sees all events in diegetic space rendered 'meaningful' by the trajectories of narrative, which subordinates all manner of alternate and aberrant movements to its own hegemonic and central structure. But it is just this schema which has become impossible in the post-war world. The catastrophes of the twentieth century, Deleuze claims, have thoroughly confounded it at both the individual and collective levels, causing it to shatter and to collapse – a fact he finds reflected in the listless wanderings and vague trajectories of Italian neo-realism and the films of the various post-war New Waves. As Deleuze explains:

> The fact is that, in Europe, the post-war period has greatly increased the situations that we no longer know how to react to, in spaces which we no

longer know how to describe. These are "any-spaces-whatever" [*espaces quelconques*], deserted but inhabited, disused warehouses, waste ground, cities in the course of demolition or reconstruction. And in these any-spaces-whatever a new race of characters was stirring, kind of mutant: they saw rather than acted, they were seers. (*CII*, x)

The themes here are again familiar – echoing the interventions of Lyotard and Adorno. There is simply no action commensurate with a horror as vast as Auschwitz, or indeed a banality as irrevocable as the unfurling of post-war suburbia. The contemporary world is simply too big, too autonomous, its political subjects – importantly – too diffuse and atomised, for any meaningful motricity, much less political action to adhere. In Deleuze's words, 'the link between man and the world is broken. Henceforth, this link must become an object of belief' (*CII*, 177).

Deleuze's claim, here, is not that political action ceases in the twentieth century. Rather, as we shall see, his argument is at once more difficult and precise: sensory-motor action has come to appear impossible in the post-war world – it is 'unthinkable' – and it is this very impossibility which must serve as the condition for new styles of thinking and of acting to emerge. Indeed, the political becomings which increasingly interest Deleuze after his encounter with Guattari, and which we might describe in their terms as 'minor' – the struggles of decolonisation, of women, students, prisoners, the 'mad' – are those which crystallise at just this juncture, as dominant modes of collective political action fragment into a multiplicity of disparate and disjunctively related resistances.

For Deleuze, this new political reality is expressed in the time-images of the post-war cinema. In the sumptuous and difficult films of neo-realism and the New Waves – from Resnais to Varda, Antonioni to Tarkovsky – the ordering movement of sensory-motor narrative subsides, allowing a multiple and multivalent temporality to saturate the screen. Thus, in Antonioni's *L'Avventura* (1960), an initial 'mystery' – the disappearance of a young woman during a pleasure cruise on the Mediterranean – is strangely and abruptly forgotten by both characters and director, submerged in an ocean of confused and apparently disconnected images. In Scorsese's *Taxi Driver* (1976), meanwhile, protagonists float through scenes of urban decay, unable to act 'meaningfully' because adrift on the plural rhythms of a vast and indifferent city.

These are films which express situations so complex, powers so profound, that the sensory-motor schema can no longer bring its powers of recognition to bear. And in keeping with Deleuze's broader political ontology of thought, this incapacity, this 'unthinkable' state of affairs, is that which causes thought to be reborn. But this new thought – the condition likewise for new styles of acting – is indifferent to the *certainties* engendered by the sensory-motor schema. Rather than images about which we can be 'sure', the post-war cinema produces images which serve as the object of a tentative and nascent perceptual *belief*.

The fundamental role of belief in the functioning of thought is a theme that we can trace as far back as Deleuze's first monograph, his 1953 study of Hume. Hume, Deleuze explains, 'laicised belief',[20] removing, through his artful elaboration and ultimate transcendence of scepticism, the epistemological fetish for a means by which subjectivity might 'hook on' to the given, in favour of a pragmatics according to which the subject is composed of a series of habitually practised 'beliefs' about its world – that there are objects, that they are subject to causation, that there is an experiencing 'I' and so on. By *Difference and Repetition*, belief is associated with the third synthesis of time, and the Nietzschean eternal return, which Deleuze describes as 'a belief of the future, a belief in the future' (*DR*, 90), a creative belief in the world's capacity for change.

In *Cinema II*, Deleuze returns to this theme, arguing that the constitutive role played by belief in the context of thought is brought to particular intensity in the case of cinema, which, in terms of its inherently 'illusory' reality, constitutes an artform uniquely implicated with belief. While in theatre, for instance, the fact of our embodied presence before the events means that we can be perceptually 'sure' of what we see, the cinematographic illusion – in its consistent deployment of experientially impossible space-times, its constant commingling of dream, flashback and hallucination – offers up no such certainty, drawing out a particularly intense form of perceptual belief. 'It is clear from the outset that cinema had a special relationship with belief', Deleuze explains; 'there is a Catholic quality to cinema' (*CII*, 176).

At face value, this latter claim may seem strange indeed; however, it is not without precedent. Erwin Panofsky, writing in 1934, claimed that film, 'called into being by a co-operative effort in which all contributions have the same degree of permanence, is the nearest modern equivalent of a medieval cathedral'.[21] In *Fonction du Cinéma*, meanwhile, the art historian, medical doctor and critic Élie Faure wrote that cinema is, 'today, the most "Catholic," means of expression that the evolution of ideas and techniques has put at the disposal of man, if we want to return to this word its original, human sense'.[22] And indeed, the basis for these claims is persuasive. Cinema, like Catholicism, deploys a set of universalist tropes which have demonstrated an impressive capacity for translation into different semiotic situations globally. Catholicism itself is distinctly cinematic, deploying a grand *mise en scène* of Apostles, villains and heroes, spread across audacious and exotic sets – while cinema, with its great art deco temples occupying pride of place on street corners and in the weekly routine (a Saturday night mass to replace that of Sunday morning), constitutes in turn, in Deleuze's words, which echo those of Faure, 'a cult which takes over the circuit of the cathedrals' (*CII*, 176).

But there is more than collaborative effort, universalising semiotics and the question of a certain perceptual 'faith' in common between church and cinema. Essential, for Deleuze, is the fact that cinema constitutes an art of the masses – in the dual sense of the word – such as imbues it with a simultaneously spiritual and political power. As Deleuze explains:

> from the outset, Christianity and revolution, the Christian faith and the revolutionary faith, were the two poles which attracted the art of the masses ... hence it developed either in the direction of a transformation of the world by man, or in the discovery of an internal and higher world than man himself... (*CII*, 176)

Cinema, indeed, constitutes an art at the apex of this latter pole, its confluence with revolutionary faith finding ultimate expression in the figure of Eisenstein, for whom, in the early years of the Bolshevik experiment, a largely illiterate Russian public might be awakened to their revolutionary consciousness by the dialectical collisions of the celluloid image. Alongside his fervent belief in the revolutionary promise of the cinematic form, Eisenstein also described cinema as 'one of the most characteristic reflections of man's spiritual activity',[23] and indeed a strangely secular spirituality crystallises across twentieth-century cinema, commensurate with its luminous distance from the everyday world.

Tarkovsky's sprawling films, for instance, constitute a self-professed attempt to generate a 'new spirituality',[24] uniquely conditioned by the material circumstances of presenting religious content in the context of strict Soviet censorship. *Andrei Rublev*'s (1961) vistas of medieval Russia, in which we move from molecular treatments of cracked or spattered paint, drops of water or flittering ashes, up to vast tableaux of extras engaged in battle or industry – often in the same shot – constitute a cinematic cosmology which oscillates between patterns observable in both the vast and the minute. *Stalker*'s (1979) saturated *mise en scène*, in which religious iconography, syringes, weapons, coins and clocks form a montage of interlocking symbols submerged beneath a 'film' of tepid water, gives us a worn-out collection of worldly matters, later sublimated by the messianic emergence in full-colour of the telepathic little girl, riding atop the Stalker's shoulders. Such films constitute a high-water mark in the production of a cinematic spirituality, one in which our 'link' with the world, in all of its tenuousness and complexity, is made manifest.

There can be little doubt that the specific vocabulary of a spiritual/ revolutionary tendency towards 'belief in the world' in Deleuze's work on cinema emerges from the influence of both Eisenstein and Élie Faure. But a third and more thoroughly philosophical axis, formed by Deleuze's Nietzschean and Spinozist commitments, determines the unique specificities of this belief. For in order for it to have a *revolutionary* function, this cannot be belief in the 'link' with a given world, in which all values are already distributed – such as in the orthodoxies of organised religion. Indeed, it is via recourse to Deleuze's profound – and often perverse – Spinozism that we might grasp exactly how the notion of belief might be purified of its *doxic* residues, opening the way for a style of thought synonymous with the revolutionary production of the new.

A Cinematic Spinozism

When, in the *Ethics*, Spinoza provides his famous definition VI, writing 'by reality and perfection I understand the same thing' (IId6), we may rightly question the efficacy of his philosophy from any political (much less revolutionary) point of view. If reality and perfection are absolutely equivalent, then according to what orientation would we strive to change anything, *to act at all*? However, as Antonio Negri has noted, the history of philosophy has in effect afforded us 'two Spinozas', one who is broadly rationalist and materialist, who 'expresses the highest and most extensive development of the cultural history of its time', and the other, who 'accomplishes a dislocation and projection of the ideas of crisis and revolution'.[25] This tension, Negri claims, is such that 'the first is the author of the capitalist order, the second is perhaps the author of a future constitution'.²⁶ Spinoza, in other words, presents us with an anomaly which resists subsumption within our (already ideological) history of ideas, an 'absolute exception',²⁷ irreducible to any systemisation with which we might approach it.

We might well argue, indeed, that this 'anomalous' status is the common thread linking Spinoza to Deleuze, particularly given that criticisms of the former's political utility often closely resemble those levelled at the latter. Paradigmatic are those of Alain Badiou, who accuses Deleuze of an unconscious *status quo* monism, writing, for instance, that

> [Deleuze] came to tolerate the fact that most of his concepts were sucked up ... by the *doxa* of the body, desire, affect, networks, the multitude, nomadism and enjoyment into which a whole contemporary "politics" sinks, as if into a poor man's Spinozism.²⁸

Leaving aside the complexities of the Badiou–Deleuze schism, it is important to note that Badiou has here misread Deleuze in the terms of this 'first Spinoza', rather than the second, for whom we might well say that reality is perfection inasmuch as reality is *difference* and *change*. Reality, thus conceived, requires of us a style of thought which is fundamentally open to novelty and emergence, in a model according to which thinking itself might become revolutionary praxis. To explicate this complex axis of Deleuze's political philosophy, however, we must briefly explicate Spinoza.

Spinoza famously argues throughout the *Ethics* that there is a single immanent substance, which is God or nature (Ip14). As such, everything exists and acts in such a way as is necessary in accordance with God's nature, and does so without an external end or purpose. This rejection of any transcendent conception of divinity thus problematises the very possibility of normative 'natural law' as it had hitherto been imposed by both state and church. As Spinoza writes, in the *Tractatus Theologico-Politicus*:

> We conclude therefore that God is described as a legislator or a prince, and as just, merciful etc., only because of the limited understanding of the common people and their lack of knowledge, and that in reality God acts and governs all things from the necessity of his own nature and perfection alone, and his decrees and volitions are eternal truths and always involve necessity.²⁹

The implications of this philosophical manoeuvre are vast. Not only does it call into question the very premise of state and religious power – that legislative proscriptions over and above human behaviours can be derived from scripture – it opens up the space for a radical self-determination of individuals, given that their natures and actions must invariably be seen as modular expressions of divine will.

Far, therefore, from creating a kind of imbricated homogeneity from which we can no longer derive difference or multiplicity, Deleuze reads this 'univocal' premise (alongside that of Duns Scotus) as a condition for thinking *genuine* difference or singularity. As he explains, in *Difference and Repetition*:

> the essential in univocity is not that Being is said in a single and same sense, but that it is said, in a single and same sense, *of* all its individuating differences or intrinsic modalities. Being is the same for all these modalities, but these modalities are not the same ... the essence of univocal being is to include individuating differences, while these differences do not have the same essence and do not change the essence of being... (*DR*, 36)

And while Deleuze will claim that Spinoza, in positing the modes as dependent on substance (and not vice versa), does not ultimately succeed in thinking difference without identity,[30] the former's commitment to radical immanence sees substance and its plural modes understood as fundamentally inextricable.

Importantly, this univocal metaphysics is therefore – for Deleuze as for Spinoza – simultaneously the condition for an ethics. The architecture of this Spinozist-Deleuzian ethics is complex, and involves a highly specific lexicon, which constraints of space do not allow me to treat fully here.[31] Suffice it to say that from these metaphysical terms, Spinoza advances a definition of *freedom* according to which singular 'bodies' (understood in the broadest possible sense) are free inasmuch as they express divine substance to the full extent and in the full exercise of their unique (modal) powers. The essence of singular beings must be properly understood to accord with their own capacities to self-determine and individuate – to affect and be affected – expressing their singularity in ways which extend capacities for action and resist external limitations. This is therefore an ethics dedicated to the multilateral increase of potentialities, and such as *must* become a politics, given that such singularities exist together. Or as Negri explains:

> The singularity is free. Freedom is the form of the singular being. There is an identity between the singular being and its practical nature. Necessity is not contradictory with freedom but only a sign of the ontological absoluteness of freedom.[32]

In other words, Spinoza's metaphysical premise – that reality, as God, is perfection – becomes an ethical premise – that difference and multiplicity are to be affirmed as the necessary expression of this perfection, in a move consonant with Spinoza's advocacy for religious tolerance and individual liberty. This ethics thus also implies a politics, given that the ideal state is one which would afford the conditions for the broadest possible diversity and difference of individuation(s).

Deleuze adopts this model in various places across his *oeuvre*, given its fertility for thinking a politics adequate to his metaphysical commitments to both multiplicity and immanence. For our purposes, what is important is that it is therefore belief in a rigorously particular world which Deleuze advocates, indeed an open plurality of *worlds*, ushered in when we take seriously a Spinozist natural philosophy of necessity. Belief in the world must be understood as belief in the world's capacity to be multiple, to elaborate itself by becoming other than it is, a belief which is therefore thoroughly compatible with a revolutionary politics. From an ethico-political perspective, this approach may still seem vague or abstract, especially once removed from the political circumstances of Spinoza's own milieu.[33] However, Kathrin Thiele rightly notes the radical pragmatism inherent to Deleuze's deployment of Spinozism, when she writes:

> First we have to adequately understand the rigorous philosophical demand for an immanence immanent only to itself that is so fundamental to Deleuze's thought. His strong commitment to immanence and nothing but immanence already turns every ontological endeavour into a practical one, and that is into an endeavour driven by an ethico-political impetus.[34]

In this sense, a Deleuzian injunction towards belief must be understood in pragmatic terms, such that in the very act of believing in a certain kind of world, we commence the task of bringing it into being (or, more properly, becoming).

Thus the 'link' between humanity and the world, properly understood, constitutes a belief in the world's capacity to change, to become an open plurality of worlds and not to calcify in any preordained manner, according to any transcendent principle. And it is this link, argues Deleuze, which has become untenable in the modern world. Evacuated of the potentiality for political action, traditionally understood as a function of the sensory-motor schema, the pure 'optical' and 'sound' situations of the time-image – which is to say, situations which are no longer 'sensory-motor', but rather *unthought* and as such, can only be sensed – precipitate a kind of thinking which must take the reconstruction of such a belief as its essential mission. As Deleuze explains:

> The link between man and the world is broken. Henceforth, this link must become an object of belief: it is the impossible which can only be restored within a faith... Only belief in the world can reconnect man to what he sees and hears. The cinema must film, not the world, but belief in this world, our only link ... restoring our belief in the world – this is the power of modern cinema ... whether we are Christians or atheists, in our universal schizophrenia, *we need reasons to believe in this world*. (CII, 177)

The prescience of this contention, in the context of capitalist realism and anthropogenic climate change – which present themselves as entwined inevitabilities – is profound. It has become all but an impossibility to imagine the emergence of a world, or of worlds, that exceed the logics of the present, a fact that Deleuze not unconvincingly traces to the crisis of modernity in the jaws of the Second World War. But in *believing* that there exists a link between humans and the world they are destroying, and furthermore that this world is radically undetermined and redolent with potentials, we might commence the task of changing it for the better.

Minority Cinema

But who are these believers, given that this shattering and disillusionment is so profound? How might we identify the agents who would enact such a belief, given that the concept of 'humanity' itself is so thoroughly problematised by the catastrophes of the twentieth century, and the impending disasters of the twenty-first? Deleuze's answer to these questions draws on the theme of 'minoritarian' enunciation, developed in his work with Guattari in both *A Thousand Plateaus* and *Kafka: Towards a Minor Literature*. And central once again is the 'unthinkable', the outside, which this time takes the form of an absence, articulated in an incessant refrain across his work alone and with Guattari: *'the people are missing'* (CII, 223). Indeed, as 'minor' literatures and cinema attest, the people also must be thought anew.

Classical Soviet and American cinema, explains Deleuze, deployed a concrete or stable notion of 'the people' as *socius* or body politic. The status or ideal organisation of this 'people' could be the source of bloody contest, but their appearance as *a priori* principle for political thought and aesthetic representation was unquestioned. We might think here of some paradigmatic examples: the crowds in Eisenstein, which surge and seethe as though a single organism, dividing into particulate units before reconverging into a whole. In Hollywood, the musicals of Berkeley, which see showgirls swirl and organise into elaborate geometric shapes, perfectly coalescing the ideal tenets of the American *socius* – democratic interchangeability and Fordist mass-production. And later, this tendency evolves, in Hollywood, into that of the Western, and that *other* Ford, to distribute a 'people' constituted by ragged, self-sufficient individuals, through films which 'testify' to the hardships of their existence (*CII*, 223).

The same conditions, however, which led to the collapse of the sensory-motor schema, have problematised this hitherto stable – if contestable – premise, causing 'the people', as they had hitherto existed, to disappear. As Deleuze explains:

> In American and Soviet cinema, the people are already there, real before being actual, ideal without being abstract. Hence the idea that cinema, as art of the masses, could be the supreme revolutionary or democratic art, which makes the masses a true subject. But a great many factors were to compromise this belief: the rise of Hitler, which gave cinema as its object not the masses become subject but the masses subjected; Stalinism, which replaced the unanimism of peoples with the tyrannical unity of a party; the break up of the American people, who could no longer believe themselves to be either the melting-pot of peoples past or the seed of a people to come (it was the neo-Western that first demonstrated this break-up). In short, if there were a modern political cinema, it would be on this basis: the people no longer exist, or not yet ... *the people are missing*. (*CII*, 223)

Of course, this absence, so keenly and so suddenly felt in the late twentieth-century West, has been the condition of 'third world' and 'minority' cinema since its inception. Here, the people are already missing, insofar as minority identities (paradigmatically post-colonial subjects) have never been permitted to properly appear within hegemonic orders of visibility. That both individual subjectivity and collective identity are thoroughly problematised by the violence of colonisation is a fact that Deleuze will trace through the productions of a number of film-makers working in non-Western contexts, including Lino Brocka, Pierre Perrault, Glauber Rocha, Yilmaz Güney, Youssef Chahine and Ousmane Sembène.[35]

Indeed, it is to such 'minoritarian' enunciations that Deleuze will turn in pursuing a politics of the outside. Reflecting on the impasse encountered by Kafka, who found himself facing the entwined impossibilities of choosing not to write or of writing in the coloniser's language (*CII*, 224), Deleuze identifies a third way, open to 'minority' *auteurs*:

> Kafka pointed to another path, a narrow path between the two dangers: precisely because "great talents" or superior individualities are rare in minor literatures, the author is not in a condition to produce individual utterances which would be like invented stories; but also, because the people are missing, the author is in a situation of producing utterances which are already collective, which are like the seeds of the people to come, and whose political impact is immediate and inescapable. (*CII*, 228)

In this context, Deleuze appoints cinema the grand task of preparing the way for a 'people to come', claiming that 'art, and especially cinematographic art, must take part in this task: not that of addressing a people, which is presupposed already there, but of contributing to the invention of a people' (*CII*, 224).

The notion of a 'people to come' such as are immediately obscure – and obscured – by current power relations and regimes of visibility, but who might emerge in a revolutionary becoming whereby the 'subjected' become 'subjects', offers up a compelling model of how a revolutionary consciousness might be understood in terms beyond the inevitabilities of dialectical materialism. In taking up majoritarian forms like cinema, and using them to produce images which articulate the situation of minority existences, art therefore emerges as a powerful machinery for producing collective subjects and expressive movements from 'outside'. Such subjects, movements and consciousnesses do not pre-exist this process – before which they are, indeed, 'unthinkable' – rather, they are called into becoming through this very action.

Again, this model is far from utopian or hopelessly abstract. The Afrofuturistic experiments in the 'defacement' of public property by early wildstyle graffiti artists like Rammellzee have changed the face of every major metropolis on Earth. Simultaneous investigations into synthesised music and sampling in New York's b-boy underground replicated early African American experiments with electrified instruments to ensure that the world continues to dance to minoritarian music. From the Mississippi Delta to the Harlem Renaissance, isolated and localised expressions of black identity have worked to call forth a people from the catastrophic 'social death' attendant to the Middle Passage. That these minor literatures have been incorporated so completely into majoritarian discourse – and markets – is evidence both of the profundity of capitalist 'apparatuses of capture' and of these praxes' profound dynamism and power in the formation of subject groups. But how might minoritarian becomings elude this 'capture'? What forces and functions could instigate this initially opaque undertaking? It is with Deleuze's account of an encounter with the 'intolerable' that we conclude, washing up once more on the shores of the outside.

The Intolerable

Deleuze's discussion of the 'intolerable' situations which might provoke a people into becoming returns to one of his most profound theoretical axes, the noetic philosophy developed with reference to Antonin Artaud. As far back as *Difference and Repetition*, Artaud's meditation on the gruesome impossibility of thought, of *any* thought, propelled Deleuze towards a critique of habitual, anthropocentric and dogmatic ways of thinking. Deleuze resumes this theme, with a new, political colouring, in the latter part of *Cinema II*, writing:

> Artaud never understood powerlessness to think as a simple inferiority which would strike us in relation to thought. It is a part of thought, so that we should make our way of thinking from it, without claiming to be restoring an all-powerful thought. We should rather make use of this powerlessness to believe in life, and to discover the identity of thought and life... (*CII*, 175)

This 'identity' of thought and life indicates what is at stake in Deleuze's noetic philosophy. Thought, conceived as radically immanent to the planes on which it is situated – be they material, human, inhuman or otherwise – is no mere reflection on an already distributed real. Properly understood, as a 'thought from outside', thinking *creates the new*, bringing forth previously unimaginable forms of life.

This conception, which drives Deleuze to the 'thought without an image' sketched in *Difference and Repetition*, becomes, in *Cinema II*, the remit of a politics sculpted by the apparent hopelessness of the twentieth century. If it is no longer possible to imagine a 'world', or indeed a 'people', which elude capture by the axioms of capital, then this very impossibility must become the condition for our belief, and as such for our becomings. Or as Deleuze explains, 'it is as if modern political cinema were no longer constituted on the basis of a possibility of evolution or revolution, like the classical cinema, but on impossibilities, in the style of Kafka: the intolerable' (*CII*, 226).

Deleuze once more evokes the neo-realists in approaching this cinema of the intolerable – De Sica's *Umberto D* (1952) and its scenes of quotidian squalor, Rossellini's *Germany Year Zero* and its vistas of rubble – in short, as we have seen, we have arrived at a cinema which confronts a power so profound, a situation of such despair, that the sensory-motor schema can no longer bring its powers of recognition to bear. Deleuze illustrates this 'overwhelmed' cinematic perception with an example from *Umberto D*, which, in muted tones and with a cast of non-actors, tells the story of the titular character, an old man desperately trying to maintain his rented room. In one scene, we see

> the young maid going into the kitchen in the morning, making a series of mechanical, weary gestures, cleaning a bit, driving the ants away from a water fountain, picking up the coffee grinder, stretching out her foot to close the door with her toe. And her eyes meet the pregnant woman's belly, and it is as though all the misery in the world were going to be born. This is how, in an ordinary or everyday situation, in the course of a series of gestures, which are insignificant but all the more obedient to simple sensory-motor schemata, what has suddenly been brought about is a pure optical situation to which the little maid has no response or reaction. The eyes, the belly, that is what an encounter is... Of course, encounters can take very different forms ... but they follow the same formula. (*CII*, 2)

Robbed, by concrete sociopolitical circumstances, of the possibility of coherent sensory-motor response, both characters in, and viewers of, neo-realist cinema thus come to grasp new and hitherto obscured aspects of the real. Faced with the raw optical and sonic data afforded by the screen-image, we experience a pure 'encounter' – a perceptual event prior to any predetermined social inscription.

Such encounters, indeed, are capable of engendering visual revelations and dispositions of thought which shatter sociopolitically determined conventions of perception derived from the sensory-motor schema. In one example to which Deleuze frequently returns – from Rossellini's *Europe '51* (1952) – Irene (Ingrid Bergman), the wife of a wealthy industrialist, is driven by the suicide of her son to a new regime of 'pure' perception, in which hitherto subterranean relations structuring the real are suddenly made manifest. Roaming the slums of post-war Rome, entering the factories upon which her affluence is built, Irene sees the factory workers, and in an apparent 'hallucination' believes she is seeing convicts. As Deleuze explains:

if our sensory-motor schemata jam or break, then a different type of image can appear: a pure optical-sound image, the whole image without metaphor, brings out the thing in itself, literally, in its excess of horror or beauty, in its radical or unjustifiable character, because it no longer has to be "justified" for better or for worse... The factory creature gets up, and we can no longer say "Well, people have to work..." I thought I was seeing convicts: the factory is a prison, school is a prison, literally, not metaphorically... (CII, 21)

In this way, the shattering of the sensory-motor schema produces a concrete political affectivity, revealing the 'intolerable' conditions of the capitalist, fascist and otherwise repressive social arrangements within which it has hitherto functioned.

And it is this 'intolerability' which, in keeping with the noetic philosophy we have already discussed, forces us into the activity of forging new, creative and anti-fascistic lines of flight, be they in philosophy, art, or indeed political praxis. As David Lapoujade explains:

Everything begins, each time, with a '"vision" of something intolerable, unjust, or shocking. Such events affect not only individuals; sometimes an entire social field "sees" something intolerable and rises up. *We do not live in a world where all political action is impossible, we live in a world where the impossible is the condition of every action, of every new creation of possibilities.*[36]

In other words, this is not a mere 'revelation' of a political reality which was hitherto obscured. The production of affects in such an image must be understood in the immanent, metaphysical terms of Bergson – not as mimetic double or derived representation, but as an individuation of forces with its own affective powers. Once situated at the level of the intensive variation and becoming of matter, or – to transpose things into terms more hospitable to politics – an individual or social 'body', the 'intolerable' and 'impossible' affects extended by a given cinematic image call forth responses in the 'images' to which they relate (minds, societies, group subjects and so on). Or, as Lapoujade continues:

The perceptual or affective shock is inseparable from the powers it awakens in each of us ... perceptions communicate directly with the plane of intensive matters of which we are composed. A redistribution of powers is effected that makes perception an *event*. At that point, but only at that point, we stop thinking in terms of the future and rather in terms of becoming. A becoming is first of all this: powers that rise up and pull us toward something non-personal and, in this way, "political."[37]

If this vocabulary of 'political becomings' sounds hopelessly abstracted from the bloody struggles of the real, we might turn, in closing, to a concrete example.

Joshua Oppenheimer's *The Act of Killing* (2012) – co-directed with Christine Cynn and an anonymous Indonesian film-maker – provides a compelling example of the capacity of film to extend multilateral affects – in both its subjects and its spectators – which might produce qualitative changes in individual and collective bodies. Focusing on the aftermath of the 1965–66 massacre of between 500,000 and 2–3 million Indonesian 'communists' (though this designation became a shorthand for anyone the perpetrators sought to remove from their communities, including ethnic Chinese Indonesians and Christians) by government-backed militias, the film sees actual perpetrators of the massacres recruited into the project of producing a narrative film about their own exploits.

This film within a film is as chilling as it is absurd, with the group of ageing self-professed paramilitary 'gangsters' producing elaborate costumes and dance routines, stylising their past violence in accordance with their acknowledged obsession with Hollywood genre films: musicals and Westerns. The locus of the film is perpetrator Anwar Congo, who, initially a thug frequenting the local movie houses, eventually found himself leading a death squad in North Sumatra and purportedly killing 1,000 people personally – primarily by garrotting. Early in the film, Congo takes Oppenheimer and his crew to the rooftop of a building where he murdered these 'communists', proudly dancing the cha-cha-cha for which he was infamous at the time.

Through a string of outlandish and gratuitously violent self-staged scenes, however, the unrepentant Congo appears to become gradually aware of the gravity of his crimes. At one point, he is hooded and 'tortured' by his fellow perpetrators, ultimately stopping the shoot as he suffers a nervous breakdown. Through the inhuman presence of the camera, and the impersonal theatricality of performance, Congo's sensory-motor justification for his actions appears to fall away in the context of an 'encounter' with their sheer intolerability. Later, he returns to the rooftop, retching repeatedly in a pure bodily response to his own violence, consecrating one of the most arresting scenes in contemporary cinema.[38]

This transformative production of affects at the individual level is replicated across the social body, with underground showings of the film in Indonesia sparking widespread critical discussion of the killings in the context of a state which still sanctions and protects their perpetrators.[39] The relatively simple machinery of the film – far from a sumptuous blockbuster or complex narrative – judiciously inserted and set to work in Indonesian society – not to mention in a West blithely unaware of its own implication in the killings – demonstrates the powerful political affectivity open to cinema 'when it stops being bad'. At the individual level of Congo's body, and at the molar level of the social body, this is an instance of change. In a world which appears so irrevocably unchangeable, we must make a careful note of it.

In this chapter, we have seen that Deleuze's two-volume study of cinema constitutes a work of political philosophy, albeit in a highly idiosyncratic sense of that term. In reflecting the 'time–money conspiracy', cinema injects questions of inflation and disparity into the image, expressing the problematic tensions of its production. Through its production of images which are 'unthinkable' in terms of our habitual sensory-motor orientations, the time-images of post-war cinema furthermore force thought into a revolutionary production of new beliefs, affects, peoples and modes of life – such as might exceed the logics of a present which presents itself as inescapable. We must carefully note before proceeding, however, that there can be no guarantee that the political affects produced by cinema, nor indeed the 'people' that it might call into being, are to be desired, a fact of which Deleuze is well aware. Deleuze, indeed, closes *Cinema II* with a discussion of Leni Riefenstahl, and the Nazi obsession with cinema, writing:

> it is true that up to the end Nazism thinks of itself in competition with Hollywood. The revolutionary courtship of the movement-image and an art of the masses become subject was broken off, giving way to the masses subjected as psychological automaton, and to their leader as the great spiritual automaton. (*CII*, 271)

Hitler, in other words, consecrates or completes a certain tendency of the movement-image, such as emerges initially in the exhortations to class-consciousness of Eisenstein and the production of a Fordist social machinery in Berkeley. In situating its spectacular movements within a 'whole' which contextualises them, making them seem – in the hands of certain accomplished *auteurs* – inevitable, the movement-image is thus inherently vulnerable to the prosecution of dangerous and repressive ends. Indeed, the endless proliferation of films about Nazism and the Second World War seems to bear witness to the fact that Hitler's staging of a quasi-mythic 'rise' and spectacularly destructive 'fall' are uniquely cinematic in their contours (a fact of which his propagandist Goebbels was well aware).[40]

But the cinema of the post-war *time-image*, we will recall, produces images and affects of a quite different order, engendering not a blind or immediate sensory-motor activity, such as might be hospitable to the imperatives of fascism, but rather a *problematisation*, an 'ungrounding' which causes action itself to seem impossible. Its images emerge not from a pre-established – and as such potentially authoritarian – 'possible' but from an identity-less and as-yet-un-actualised 'impossible', which calls for thought to be reborn. These are the powers of a pure temporality, no longer limited by the movements of action/reaction, but by the virtual production of the impossible event in time, an event which might erupt into a constellation of new becomings.

It is in these same passages, however, that Deleuze warns us of another 'automata' which might replace these 'psychomechanics' of fascism, 'automata of computation and thought, automata with controls and feedback' (*CII*, 272). And whereas Nazism constituted a danger immanent to the movement-image, these 'computational' automata comprise a threat immanent to the time-image, or rather to its electronic successors. It is to this development, and to the ecology of digital images, that we must now turn.

Notes

1. G. Deleuze and F. Guattari, *Anti-Oedipus*, trans. R. Hurley, M. Seem and H. Lane (Minneapolis, MN: University of Minnesota Press, 2000), p. 380.
2. See N. Tampio, *Deleuze's Political Vision* (Lanham, MD: Rowman and Littlefield, 2015); G. Sibertin-Blanc, *State and Politics: Deleuze and Guattari on Marx*, trans. A. Hodges (South Pasadena, CA: Semiotext(e), 2016).
3. Deleuze and Guattari, *A Thousand Plateaus*, p. 203.
4. S. Žižek, *Organs Without Bodies: On Deleuze and Consequences* (Abingdon: Routledge, 2012), p. 18.
5. See *DR*, xx, 137.
6. For a detailed cartography of Guattari's history as a young Trotskyite, including his editorship of *La Voie Communiste* and involvement in the 'events' of May '68, see F. Dosse, *Gilles Deleuze and Félix Guattari: Intersecting Lives*, trans. D. Glassman (New York: Columbia University Press, 2010).

7 See G. Deleuze, *Francis Bacon: The Logic of Sensation*, trans. D. Smith (London: Continuum, 2003), pp. 86–98.
8 T. W. Adorno, *Minima Moralia: Reflections on a Damaged Life*, trans. E. F. N. Jephcott (London: Verso, 2005), p. 206.
9 This claim must be read in the context of the idea that capitalism, as Marx and Weber alike demonstrate, had developed a generalised commodification of both time and space throughout the nineteenth and twentieth centuries. In this context traditional, familial and feudal holdings of space disappear in favour of a general equivalence whereby space becomes property, subject to the homogenising evaluation of markets. Time, likewise, which had hitherto been comprised of seasonal, festival, lunar and other assorted agricultural cycles, gradually becomes a homogeneous and 'abstract' time attendant to 24-hour mechanised labour. In this sense, space and time not only become in a certain sense profoundly *abstract*, but also *costly*. Art, meanwhile, no longer the preserve of 'privileged' space-times – as when produced through religious patronage, or in accordance with agricultural and festival cycles – likewise begins to require ever greater outlays of capital in order to purchase blocks of this homogenised space-time. See K. Marx, *The Poverty of Philosophy: Answer to the Philosophy of Poverty by M. Proudhon*, trans. French Institute of Marxism-Leninism (Paris: Progress, 1955), pp. 20–4, and M. Weber, *The Protestant Ethic and the Spirit of Capitalism*, trans. T. Parsons (London: Routledge, 2001).
10 The script, worked on by nine writers, tells the story of an asteroid hurtling towards the Earth, which, we are told, can only be stopped by a rag-tag group of oil drilling experts who are sent into space to bury a nuclear warhead beneath its surface. At every level of its production, the film is oversaturated with capital, from unprecedented access to NASA's real rocket propulsion facilities to the $20,000 worth of dental work apparently used to make actor Ben Affleck's teeth more big-screen appropriate.
11 R. Ebert, 'Armageddon', *RogerEbert.com*, 1 July 1998, https://www.rogerebert.com/reviews/armageddon-1998.
12 *Armageddon*, dir. M. Bay, Touchstone Pictures, 1998 (DVD Director's Commentary).
13 Deleuze himself claims, in an interview published in the collection *Negotiations*, that: 'I think Félix Guattari and I have remained Marxists, in our two different ways, perhaps, but both of us. You see, we think any political philosophy must turn on the analysis of capitalism and the ways it has developed. What we find most interesting in Marx is his analysis of capitalism as an immanent system that's constantly overcoming its own limitations, and then coming up against them once more in a broader form, because its fundamental limit is Capital itself' (*N*, 171). However, a clean link here is not assured. Not least among

the problems of deriving a Deleuzo-Guattarian Marxism is their persistent rejection of the negative as inherited from the Marxist-Hegelian dialectic. We abide in absence of the phantom limb in Deleuze's corpus, his last book, which was to have been called *The Grandeur of Marx*.

14 F. Guattari, *The Machinic Unconscious: Essays in Schizoanalysis*, trans. T. Adkins (Los Angeles: Semiotext(e), 2011), p. 227.

15 Marx, we will recall, in an important passage, writes: 'Along with the constantly diminishing number of the magnates of capital, who usurp and monopolise all advantages of this process of transformation, grows the mass of misery, oppression, slavery, degradation, exploitation; but with this too grows the revolt of the working-class, a class always increasing in numbers, and trained, united, organised by the very mechanism of the process of capitalist production itself. The monopoly of capital becomes a fetter upon the mode of production, which has sprung up and flourished along with, and under it. Centralisation of the means of production and socialisation of labour at last reach a point where they become incompatible with their capitalist integument ... the knell of capitalist private property sounds.' K. Marx, *Capital: A Critique of Political Economy – Volume One*, trans. B. Fowkes (London: Penguin, 1982), p. 929.

16 Deleuze and Guattari, *A Thousand Plateaus*, p. 473.

17 E. W. Holland, *Deleuze and Guattari's Anti-Oedipus: Introduction to Schizoanalysis* (London: Routledge, 2001), p. 104.

18 Ibid., p. 105.

19 M. Fisher, *Capitalist Realism: Is There No Alternative?* (Alresford: Zero Books, 2009), p. 2.

20 G. Deleuze, *Empiricism and Subjectivity: An Essay on Hume's Theory of Human Nature*, trans. C. V. Boundas (New York: Columbia University Press, 1991), p. ix.

21 E. Panofsky, 'Style and Medium in Motion Pictures', in *Three Essays on Style*, ed. I. Lavin (Cambridge, MA: MIT Press, 1995), p. 30.

22 É. Faure, 'Vocation du Cinéma', in *Fonction du Cinema, De la cinéplastique à son destin social (1921–1937)* (Paris: Éditions d'Histoire et de d'Art, Librairie Plon, 1954), p. 4 (my translation).

23 Eisenstein, *Film Form*, p. 193.

24 N. Skakov, *The Cinema of Tarkovsky: Labyrinths of Space and Time* (London: I.B. Tauris, 2012), p. 213.

25 A. Negri, *The Savage Anomaly: The Power of Spinoza's Metaphysics and Politics*, trans. M. Hardt (Minneapolis, MN: University of Minnesota Press, 1991), pp. 4–5.

26 Ibid., p. 4.

27 Ibid., p. 5.

28 A. Badiou, *Logics of Worlds: Being and Event, 2*, trans. A. Toscano (London: Continuum, 2009), p. 35.

29 B. Spinoza, *Theological-Political Treatise*, ed. J. Israel, trans. M. Silverthorne and J. Israel (Cambridge: Cambridge University Press, 2007), p. 64.
30 In order to arrive at a thought of difference-in-itself, Deleuze claims it is necessary to move beyond Spinoza's ultimately monist modality, according to which, he suggests: 'Spinoza's substance appears independent of the modes, while the modes are dependent on substance, but as though on something other than themselves ... such a condition can be satisfied only at the price of a more general categorical reversal according to which being is said of becoming, identity of that which is different, the one of the multiple, etc.' (*DR*, 40).
31 It is most fully elaborated in Deleuze's two books on Spinoza, *Expressionism in Philosophy: Spinoza* (1968) and *Spinoza: Practical Philosophy* (1970).
32 Negri, *The Savage Anomaly*, p. 83.
33 Spinoza's own project, of course – a rejection of theocratic law and a demonstration of the 'perfection' of individual (modular) being – cannot be extricated from his own status as subject to the writ of *herem* or excommunication from Amsterdam's Sephardic community.
34 K. Thiele, '"To Believe in this World, As It Is": Immanence and the Quest for Political Activism', *Deleuze Studies*, 4 (2010), issue supplement – 'Deleuze and Political Activism', p. 31.
35 Of course, we cannot proceed in this direction without acknowledging critiques of Deleuze from the perspective of postcolonial studies, perhaps most notably that mounted by Spivak in 'Can the Subaltern Speak?', in which the latter charges Deleuze with exemplifying the tendency of Western intellectuals to reinscribe hegemonic conceptions of the subject through their very attempts to a-centre or criticise it. See G. C. Spivak, '"Can the Subaltern Speak" revised edition', in R. Morris (ed.), *Can the Subaltern Speak? Reflections on the History of an Idea* (New York: Columbia University Press, 2010), p. 28. There is undoubtedly a tendency in Deleuze to use examples and concepts taken from postcolonial contexts indelicately. See, for instance, Caren Kaplan's critique of Deleuze and Guattari's concept of 'nomadic' thought in C. Kaplan, *Questions of Travel: Postmodern Discourses of Displacement* (Durham, NC: Duke University Press, 1996). Certainly, these are intractable problems which will continue to emerge as Western intellectual history confronts the colonial genocides with which it is implicated. However, the central Deleuzian preoccupations with difference, novelty, the unknown, the unsubsumable and the violent reflexivity of the encounter would seem well disposed towards opening Western metaphysics and philosophy on to non-Western and counter-hegemonic perspectives. For more on this, see the contributions in S. Bignall and P. Patton (eds), *Deleuze and the Postcolonial* (Edinburgh: Edinburgh University Press, 2010).

36 D. Lapoujade, *Aberrant Movements: The Philosophy of Gilles Deleuze*, trans. J. D. Jordan (Pasadena, CA: Semiotext(e), 2014), p. 275.
37 Ibid.
38 For a compelling reading of this film, and its powerful affective and ethical dimensions (as well as some important caveats around the 'reliability' of its history and the ethics of its production), see R. Sinnerbrink, *Cinematic Ethics: Exploring Ethical Experience Through Film* (Abingdon: Routledge, 2016), ch. 7, pp. 165–84.
39 See B. Simpson, 'It's Our Act of Killing, Too', *The Nation*, 28 February 2014, https://www.thenation.com/article/archive/its-our-act-killing-too.
40 For more on National Socialism's consistent fascination with and use of cinema, see E. Rentschler, *The Ministry of Illusion: Nazi Cinema and Its Afterlife* (Cambridge, MA: Harvard University Press, 2002).

4

The Digital Image

> We are witnessing either a death or a birth, no one can tell for sure yet which. Something crucial is happening in the world of screen and sound... Second birth or death? This is the question facing cinema.¹

Alexandre Arnoux's words, written in 1928, could just as easily have been written today, about the digitisation of the cinematic image. As it is, the source of the French screenwriter and novelist's anxiety was the advent of sound in motion pictures – the birth of the 'talkie' – which seemed to many of his contemporaries to be bringing to a close the 'golden age' of film.² The theme of the exhaustion, end or death of the cinematic image, then, is far from new, being almost as old as the artform itself. Indeed, as André Gaudreault and Philippe Marion observe, 'cinema's entire history has been punctuated by moments when its media identity has been radically called into question'.³ The advent of the talkie, of colour, of the widescreen format, of television, have all been characterised as existential threats to the medium. Each of these developments has, in turn, proved to be a creative stimulant.

Despite, however, this eternal return of the theme of cinema's demise, it is undeniable that a certain conception of cinema – as the experience of viewing a long-form film print projected in a designated public space – no longer occupies pride of place at the very heart of screen culture, as it did for much of the twentieth century. This position has been usurped first by television, and then by online streaming, gaming, social media, user-generated video content and a wealth of other small screen practices. Central to these latter developments is digital encoding, which, in the immense efficiencies it affords in terms of the distribution, storage and production of images, has gradually replaced older, 'analogue' techniques.

At its inception, film was just such a technology – analogue in the sense of its describing a continuous movement or signal through a photo-chemical process for receiving impressions made by waves of light. The moving image of film-stock cinema is constituted through chains of these impressions, with discrete images produced though the exposure to light of a strip of gelatin emulsion and silver halide crystals. Even if, in the case of the individual frames, this exposure takes place at a speed negligible to human perception, the light source and the film must thus coexist throughout a parallel (or analogous) duration or continuity, in order for this impression to be achieved.

Such is the 'indexical' relation famously outlined by French critic André Bazin – whereby the cinematic image and the filmed object are ontologically 'indexed' one against the other, sharing a direct causal relationship which, for Bazin as for Walter Benjamin,[4] has concrete political implications. 'The photographic image is the object itself', Bazin writes, '[...] freed from the conditions of time and space that govern it.'[5] And in this new, mechanised 'objectivity', these thinkers felt that film might avoid the ideological schemata animating earlier pictorial representation, a situation exemplified for Bazin in the unequivocal 'fact images' of Italian neo-realism.[6]

Throughout the 1980s, 1990s and 2000s, however, this analogue technology was gradually superseded by digital encoding, which sees the cinematic image constituted by an electronic sensor which breaks incoming light into millions of pixels – discrete units which are measured for brightness and colour and stored as chains of numbers. In (re)producing the image for the human eye, these numbers are then decoded, and the image is 'reassembled' for projection. And while this change might strike the average moviegoer as technical and esoteric – of limited interest beyond the realm of film production – we must bear in mind that 'digitisation' refers to far more than this simple change of materials.

Indeed, even insofar as it applies just to cinema, 'digitisation' constitutes something of a catch-all term, referring interchangeably to digitally produced special effects, the digital recording and presentation of otherwise ostensibly 'live action' films, and technical practices such as the projection, editing and storage of film materials using digital technologies. The term 'digital cinema' embraces practices on all of these registers, given that developments on any one of them affect the whole of cinematic production. As Gaudreault and Marion explain in their book *The End of Cinema? A Medium in Crisis in the Digital Age*:

> It would be naïve to think that digitalisation could limit its effects to the encoding of data alone. Encoding cannot merely be restricted to an isolated technological operation; it necessarily affects language, for which encoding is, precisely, the primary principle. And when this primary

principle becomes universal, it affects every media language and then all the media that transmit – meaning co-construct – these languages. Put more simply, digital encoding is the process of digitalising our media from top to bottom...[7]

Leaving aside what, as we have seen, is a perhaps problematic application of the linguistic model to cinema, what Gaudreault and Marion rightly identify here is a situation in which digitisation, far from being a circumscribed technical change, has fundamentally altered the way in which cinematic images are produced, perceived, disseminated and thought.

Indeed, this imbrication of technicity and content is illustrated via recourse to a brief resume of the 'big moments' in the digitisation of cinema, which has gradually embraced a new style of film-making commensurate with the possibilities of digital production. Following limited use of digital effects in his 1977 film *Star Wars*, George Lucas established a research division in his production company, Lucasfilm, dedicated entirely to research into digital techniques.[8] In 1982 *Star Trek II: The Wrath of Khan* and *Tron* showcased significant digitally composed content to large audiences for the first time.[9] By the late 1980s 'digital nonlinear editing systems' had begun to replace their mechanical counterparts as the industry standard.[10] In 1993 Steven Spielberg's *Jurassic Park* was one of the first films to generate 'believable' digital images, in terms of their apparent continuity with background images captured photographically.[11] In 1995 *Toy Story* became the first film entirely synthesised using digital technology, while by the early 2000s film negatives were being digitised for work in post-production.[12] By the second decade of the twenty-first century, the experience of seeing a film in a cinema was, generally, that of watching a digitally recorded film, often with extensive digitally fabricated special effects, distributed to cinemas digitally, and projected in the same way.

As we might anticipate from the types of film here enumerated, and as D. N. Rodowick has noted,[13] these developments are marked as much by the economic efficiencies afforded by digital production as by the existential threat posed to cinema by other video, televisual and digital screen forms. In seeking to differentiate itself from ascendant forms of small-screen entertainment, and to resist the trend of gradually diminishing ticket sales, cinema has turned progressively towards the 'spectacular', using digital technologies – particularly elaborate special effects – to capitalise on the awe-inspiring visual and sonic environment of the movie theatre. This evolution is thus symbiotic with the explosion of what Lev Manovich called 'new-media',[14] from video games and social media to computer-based video streaming platforms, which use digital image technics to follow television in proliferating screen culture to almost every corner of our lives.

This situation has been the source of some consternation in the world of film theory, which has struggled to maintain a sense of its identity and purpose in the context of these changes.[15] Rodowick crystallises these anxieties neatly when he writes:

> The celluloid strip with its reassuring physical passage of visible images, the noisy and cumbersome cranking of the mechanical film projector or the Steenbeck editing table, the imposing bulk of the film canister are all disappearing one by one into a virtual space, along with the images they so beautifully recorded and presented.
>
> What is left, then, of cinema as it is replaced, part by part, by digitisation? Is this the end of film, and therefore the end of cinema studies? Does cinema studies have a future in the twenty-first century?[16]

And while we might feel as though we are spectators to a circumscribed debate about the aesthetics of film – coloured, in no small measure, by a certain nostalgia – the implications of this transition, as I have suggested, stretch further than cinema, or the existential crisis of a particular academic discipline.

The digitisation of cinema is, after all, part of a much broader 'revolution' in the latter part of the twentieth century, which has seen information, computing and telecommunications technologies transform human life at a global scale. I do not propose to treat this vast and complex event in its multiple dimensions here;[17] however, my conviction, following both Rodowick and Manovich, is that a long tradition of philosophical thought on film is potentially of great value at this juncture. In offering up a set of well-developed critical tools for thinking about the image as a medium, and given the centrality of the image as a key interface for the techniques of the so-called 'digital revolution', film theory is perhaps uniquely placed to help us navigate and problematise the ecology of digital images which increasingly constitute our habitat. In thinking through the changes undergone by the *cinematic* image, indeed, we might better understand the operations of digital images generally.

There is a temptation, duly noted by the likes of Flaxman and Markos Hadjioannou,[18] to conceive of these new images and their implications in terms of Bazin's 'indexicality' thesis, arguing that the translation of the film image into discrete packets of encoded data breaks the hitherto 'causal' or continuous relation between object and image, interposing a new, and potentially ideological, interlocutor. But as both of these thinkers note, the index was always a fraught line of defence in debates around the so-called 'specificity' of cinema. By what ontological category, after all, might we claim a more properly causal relationship for strips of exposed film stock over colour and movement encoded as numbers? Following Flaxman, indeed, I'd like to suggest that a more fundamental problem – such as we have already briefly encountered – is that digital images risk eschewing the 'out-of-field', or *outside*, which Deleuze takes to be the essence of cinematic art.

Deleuze, as we have seen, seems to tacitly endorse this position, writing that 'the new [numerical] images no longer have any outside (out-of-field)' (*CII*, 272), and while he here uses the term *extériorité* rather than *dehors*, I'd like to follow Flaxman in suggesting that the outside is a vital concept with which we might engage these new techniques of the image. But whereas for the latter, digital media's eschewal of the outside as a *visual*, and as such *noetic*, limit serves as the basis for a defence of the resolute specificity and value of cinema, I intend to take a different tack. Indeed, I'd like to suggest that we need to move beyond cinema, in order to think a uniquely *digital outside* – our task in the coming chapters. But before we can turn to these latter claims, we must introduce Flaxman's critique, which, in many ways, extends and rearticulates Deleuze's own engagement with the image conceived as 'information'. 'The life or the afterlife of cinema depends on its internal struggle with informatics', writes Deleuze (*CII*, 277), and in this sense, his work shows considerable foresight, anticipating the digitisation of cinema from top to bottom at the end of the twentieth century. At what stage, then, do we find the cinematic image today, given the resounding victory of informatics? Are we speaking of life or an afterlife? Have we witnessed the death of cinema?

Digitisation and the Out-of-Field

There has been no shortage of commentary on these very questions, and I do not propose to wade into the 'analogue vs digital' debate in general. For broader, more bird's-eye critical accounts of this transition, including some of its philosophical implications, I refer the interested reader to aforementioned texts by Rodowick, Gaudreault and Marion, Manovich, and, for a more general history of the digitisation of media, Balbi and Magaudda.[19] Rather, I want to take up the argument made by Gregory Flaxman in his short piece, 'Out of Field: The Future of Film Studies', not only because it constitutes one of the most persuasive contemporary extensions of Deleuze's own thinking about new, informatic images, but also because it offers a convincing diagnosis of certain tendencies these images themselves express.

This piece is far from Flaxman's most significant intervention into the film philosophy paradigm, or indeed that of Deleuze scholarship.[20] As such, I do not seek to characterise his work as a whole here, especially given that the question of the 'out of frame' appears to remain, for him, a live one. Instead I hope to use this piece as a tentatively isolated artefact, a theoretical instant from which we might develop the threads of a complementary – though divergent – critical trajectory. I do so because it coalesces the tangle of themes I want to explore in the latter part of this book. Digitisation, as it takes place in cinema, crystallises a series of profound technical, aesthetic and political changes adhering in the late twentieth century, the implications of which extend far beyond film itself. And indeed, the unique interest of Flaxman's piece is to trace these developments in terms of their relation to the cinematic 'outside'.

Flaxman begins by forcefully posing the question of the entwined futures of film and film studies, both thoroughly destabilised by the event of digitisation. As he writes:

> At this critical juncture, we find ourselves at a point of profound and even existential reckoning: if it hasn't happened already, the outgrowth of digital culture seems to dissolve the borders, stakes, and claims that had heretofore delineated film studies. Does the medium have a future, much less a field?[21]

To wrangle with this question, Flaxman revives a debate surrounding the 'specificity thesis', which saw early film theorists (Münsterberg, Bálazs, Eisenstein, Bazin et al.) seek to identify the essential characteristics which distinguish cinema as art from any other form.

Flaxman rightly notes that perhaps the most frequent means of establishing this specificity has been by pointing to the causal or indexical relationship between film and the objects it records. This is the position we have already encountered in Bazin, who imputes to it a simultaneously ontological and political significance. And indeed, the indexical thesis has been the standard defence of film's

The Digital Image

specificity in the face of digitisation, which, like animation, is able to synthesise images without any external or indexical relation to the outside world of 'things'.[22] This idea of cinema's specificity, however, is one which Flaxman eschews, in favour of an approach taken up quite directly from Deleuze. As he writes:

> Is the index really the last line of defence between medium specificity and media studies? This is a crude simplification of course, but it helps to frame the problem that confronts us today and perhaps even to formulate a different manner of response, one that lies "out of frame."[23]

In Flaxman's estimation, indeed, what specifies cinema is its relation to the *outside* – a position which will prove significant in the context of the digitisation of the image. As he continues, returning to Deleuze's account of the out-of-field:

> The perverse nature of this solution consists in eschewing the "thereness" and "thisness" of the image in order to affirm the cinema on the basis of that which lies beyond the limits of the visible. While the out of frame is not specific to cinema – we can trace it back at least as far as rectilinear perspective – the cinema undertakes experiments with the off-screen that divagate from the history of the prior visual arts and, more importantly, mark its historical and philosophical difference from digital media.[24]

And indeed, the reason for my focus on this short piece is a sense of profound solidarity with this thesis.

Flaxman thus effects a twofold motion, on the one hand offering a tentative – and Deleuzian – definition of the cinematic, while simultaneously distancing cinema from the contemporary media which have come, in the twenty-first century, to supplant it. The nexus of this dual movement is the outside, which digital media begins unwittingly to eradicate, as such abandoning its powers for the deterritorialisation of both thought and image. This occurs, for Flaxman, in several key and interconnected ways.

First, in a critique that we have already seen Deleuze suggest, the digital image seems to proliferate frames within the frame, as such eschewing a concept and method of framing as the rigorous determination of exteriorities. As Flaxman explains:

> for some time, the cinema has been in conversation with computer technology, appropriating its displays and interfaces. In these new configurations, the cinema increasingly exchanges off-screen space for something like "a number of coexisting windows." It is as if the out of field had

been folded back into the image, either in the form of so many panels multiplied across the surface of the screen or in the form of so many panels stacked within the display.[25]

This 'conversation' takes place both intrinsically and extrinsically to the cinematic image itself. On the one hand, digital distribution continues an evolution begun by television which sees movies spill out onto laptops and smartphones – no longer a luminous rectangle suspended in the darkness of the movie theatre, but rather a quotidian occurrence which is increasingly interactive. On the other hand, as we have seen, films themselves change, embracing hyper-informatic techniques as part of their style and narrativity – a contention to which we will shortly return.[26]

In this context, Flaxman suggests that the digital is perhaps implicitly oriented by its own 'myth of total cinema',[27] aspiring towards a total, immersive image-space which resists the impression of externality. Flaxman takes the idea of a 'total cinema' from Bazin, who had rejected George Sadoul's gradualist account of cinema's evolution in favour of a psychological history, according to which, even before cinematographic technologies emerged, the arts had presupposed a form that might imitate the movement, colour and shapes of life comprehensively.[28] Such a myth, claims Flaxman, now animates digital technologies' attempts to extend the frame to include all possible dimensions of the image. As he explains:

> the digital domain has already begun to displace the screen with virtual environments, and it does not seem implausible to imagine, at some point in the future, that the frame itself will give way to an animated ambience in which spectators or even users are projected... In the inexorable rush to full-fledged virtual reality, the off-screen is presented not as an aesthetic limit or philosophical problem but as a technological obstacle that we are sure to overcome.[29]

And indeed this development – which we can likewise trace into 'open world' video games like *World of Warcraft* (2004) or *Red Dead Redemption 2* (2018), as into the fractally nested 'Windows' of computer operating systems and URL environments – appears literally to ameliorate externality, in favour of a self-contained and self-perpetuating image-space which is ripe for escapism and addiction.

The second, albeit connected, way in which Flaxman suggests that digital technologies threaten the cinematic outside is commercial, and linked to the exigencies which cause a particular kind of image to be produced. Digital techniques for the synthesis of images allow for a

The Digital Image

level of control and (pre)determination hitherto inaccessible to photographic technics, but this control is placed squarely in the hands of a culture industry furiously monetising its products.[30] 'When images are subject to endless algorithms and equally endless expenditures of capital', Flaxman explains, 'the on-screen is not only overdetermined but overinvested...'[31] The pressures of capital, in other words, combine with the immense efficiencies of digital technology to engender a kind of image production in which non-intentional perceptual 'events' are suppressed, in keeping with the exigencies of market forces.

Flaxman traces these entwined developments as they emerge in the 'overdetermined' digital aesthetic of James Cameron's blockbuster *Avatar* – at the time of writing still the highest-grossing and one of the most expensive films ever made – which, he claims, in using techniques of 360-degree motion-capture and digital rendering, obliterates the cinematic 'shot' in favour of a multi-angle information space. As he writes:

> The vast majority of the "performance'" takes place within what the director and his crew dubbed "the volume," a huge motion capture stage containing as many as eighty or ninety digital cameras that surround the actors. The motion performance technology no longer exists for a given camera: rather, performances are captured from any perspective within the 360 degree spectrum. What this means is that, once the initial images are recorded, Cameron could go back and reshoot the virtual scene from any perspective or angle. At this point, the director is not shooting the film, nor going back and doing retakes, but manipulating the data. There is no shot to speak of, just the information necessary to render the image...[32]

And this change – from framed 'shot' to digitally synthesised, three-dimensional image – is inextricably linked to the 'endless expenditures of capital' with which contemporary Hollywood seeks to differentiate its images from other, small-screen media. Thus, Flaxman continues:

> the spectacle of digital cinema, especially as we find it in *Avatar*, unfolds in an endless series of "money shots." Indeed pornography is not the worst way to think about the on-screen, since the digital cinema of the spectacle follows the very same inclination to "show it all," to disclose every last shred of rapturous action, and to leave nothing unseen (think, for instance, of Michael Bay). Of course, I'm referring here to an enormously big-budgeted cinematic orgasm to describe this inclination, but I think the exorbitant excesses of Cameron's film disclose an imperative, at once aesthetic and economic, that determines the new idea of cinema: *it must be represented*.[33]

And while of course we might object that not all digital films display this tendency, Flaxman's intervention offers a convincing diagnosis of a major trend orienting contemporary screen cultures, one which Deleuze himself had seemed to presage with his observations at the close of *Cinema II*. This new attitude towards the off-screen perhaps betrays what Deleuze would claim is cinema's richest philosophical affect – its refusal or incapacity to articulate a total or 'closed' world, as such provoking us into a thought of openness, virtuality and difference. The endless algorithmic manipulations of major studio productions, combined with an implicit hostility towards the 'unseen', combine in such a way as to foreclose or forget cinema's capacity for engineering the invisible, *the outside* – the unthought within thought.

And in this sense, indeed, Flaxman's diagnosis has broader implications than those just for the cinematic image, subtly articulating a mechanism via which informatics, in the service of capital, works to close down possibilities for thought understood as creation and resistance. In this context, Flaxman returns to Deleuze, writing:

> Today, more than ever, we ought to lay claim to the concept of the outside as the most rigorous description of the cinema and the most unrelenting critique of the digital means and media that claim to have superseded it.[34]

And again, the present work advances in a spirit of solidarity with this claim. It is also, however, animated by what is perhaps a different ethic *vis-à-vis* the digital, and as such a distinct philosophical objective. Deleuze's philosophy, after all, is famously one of *affirmation*, and while Flaxman stages a rich and persuasive affirmation of cinema's specificity, I'd like to suggest that our task, today, is perhaps of an alternate order. I'm interested in the ways in which we might affirm the digital image itself as philosophically valuable – albeit in ways which must remain clear-eyed in the face of its multivalence. While Flaxman's piece constitutes a compelling account of the dangers that the digital image poses to cinema – and, as such, to a particular Deleuzian 'image', or account of thought – in what follows I'd like to explore the ways in which these same dangers might be understood as complex and contradictory, opening up new ways to think with and through the image.

Central to this approach is the concept of *information*, which Flaxman follows Deleuze in suggesting has a particular and potentially deleterious relation to the outside. In treating its images as 'data' to be manipulated, the new, digital cinema simultaneously eschews the frame as a device of exteriorisation and opens the image up to the problematic exigencies of capital, as such avoiding the production of 'unthinkable' materials paradoxically conducive to thought. My contention, however, as I suggested in the introduction, is that we might think information *differently*, as a productive and undetermined 'event' conducive to a new kind of outside. But before we can turn to this claim, we must first understand Deleuze's own concept of information, tied as it is to control, closure and the ambiguous 'afterlife' of film.

Deleuze and Information

One of the fundamental problems Flaxman identifies in the 'new idea of cinema' is its treatment of the image as *information* or *data*. In advancing this position, Flaxman draws implicitly on a protracted critique present throughout Deleuze's later work, associating information with what he calls 'control'. As such, we need to briefly outline this position, exploring Deleuze's disparate remarks about information in texts including his 'Postscript on the Societies of Control', the lecture 'What is the Creative Act?' and in the closing chapters of *Cinema II*. Here, breaking with a more polyvocal and ambiguous deployment of the term across earlier works with Guattari, as well as with Gilbert Simondon's ontological account of information, with which he was obviously familiar,[35] Deleuze associates information primarily with a new form of social organisation which uses information technologies to produce particular forms of subjectivity and subjugation. In this context, information is characterised as a regulatory mechanism in the service of dubious political ends, and as such antithetical to art, which is inherently creative, experimental and liberatory. 'A work of art does not contain the least bit of information', Deleuze claims; 'in contrast, there is a fundamental affinity between a work of art and an act of resistance.'[36]

Information is an idea which has seen no shortage of philosophical commentary since the widespread uptake of informatic technologies throughout the 1980s and 1990s. Indeed Ashley Woodward, in the context of his sophisticated reading of Lyotard's aesthetics, rightly notes that philosophy may well be in the process of making yet another 'turn', in response to the gravity of these developments. As he explains:

> The contemporary theoretical context witnesses many claims to some kind of significant "turn" – ethical, theological, speculative, neuroscientific,

nonhuman, and so on – which would perhaps be comparable to the "linguistic turn" in philosophy which dominated much of the twentieth century. Each declaration of a "turn" stakes a claim as to what is at issue in thought today. One of the most plausible claims is to that of an *informational* turn, plausible both because of the way it traces its development to the linguistic turn itself, and because it undeniably has much broader cultural resonance: we are living today in an "information age," as few would dispute, resulting from what some term the "fourth revolution," that of computation.[37]

Here, Woodward evokes a theme of Luciano Floridi's: that this 'informational turn' may well rival the three other great decentring moments in the history of Western thought – the Copernican, the Darwinian and the Freudian revolutions[38] – fundamentally altering our sense of the world and our place in it. It's in this context that he reads information theory against the backdrop of Lyotard's philosophy, in a project which is indicative of a concerted movement throughout contemporary so-called 'continental' thought.

Indeed, as Woodward notes, this tradition has historically been loath to engage with information as a concept, as with the 'information theory' crystallising out of the Anglo-American war effort in the mid-twentieth century, a situation which his own work, alongside that of others like Floridi, is working to ameliorate. We will return to information theory in the following chapter. For now, it suffices to say that while there are some exceptions – including the likes of Simondon and Raymond Ruyer[39] – the prevailing attitude in European philosophy towards the concept of information has tended to be one of hostility and pessimism, such as we find in interventions like those of Lyotard, Virilio, Baudrillard[40] and indeed Deleuze. While these thinkers approach the question of information in what are at times radically different ways, what they broadly share is a hostility to what they take to be its reductive and instrumentalising tendencies, a position perhaps exemplified in the criticisms made by Martin Heidegger.

For the latter, the instrumentality of a 'technical language' like that of information serves to liquidate a *richesse* of meanings and ambiguities proper to language, and as such to subjectivity. As he writes, in a 1962 lecture later published as 'Traditional Language and Technological Language':

> With the unconditional reign of modern technology there is an increase in power – the demand as well as the performance – of the technological

The Digital Image

language that was devised for the widest possible spread of information. Because this [power] is scattered in systems of formalised reports and signals, the technological language is the severest and most menacing attack on what is peculiar to language: saying as showing and as the letting-appear of what is present and what is absent, of reality in the widest sense.[41]

Heidegger's claim here, in other words, is that 'information' constitutes a technical artifice which might menace language's less instrumental, more philosophically expressive characteristics, a critique which is in some ways echoed by Deleuze.

Deleuze's critique of information, as we have said, is fragmentary and plural, sketched across a series of later works. In the short lecture 'What is the Creative Act?', for instance, delivered at the FEMIS film and television school in Paris, Deleuze returns to his claim that ideas are rare, situated and creative, suggesting:

> I consider that having an idea, in any case, is not on the order of communication. This is the point I was aiming for. Everything we are talking about is irreducible to any communication [...] What does it mean? Primarily, communication is the transmission and propagation of information. What is information? It is not very complicated, everyone knows what it is. Information is a set of imperatives, slogans, directions – order words. When you are informed, you are told what you are supposed to believe.[42]

The 'order-word' is a concept Deleuze had developed in his work with Guattari, indicating functions of language which impel a certain action or obedience in subjects, 'communicating' in the sense that one might communicate a force or an imperative. As such, they are essential components in the political machinery that orders social life. As Verena Conley explains, with an archetypical example of an order-word, 'it is the judge's sentence that transforms the accused into a convict',[43] in a concrete use of words to transform bodies.

It's important to note, however – in keeping with Deleuze and Guattari's immanent and mongrel approach to semiotics – that order-words don't necessarily function in terms of their explicit linguistic content, instead operating by virtue of a certain 'redundancy' of linguistic elements. Their semantic meaning is not necessarily indexed to the effects the order-word is intended to produce, which instead take place at the level of pre-individual and unconscious forces or predispositions. We might think, by way of a quotidian example, of an example evoked several times by Deleuze in tracing the linkage between order-words and information: the newspaper. Ostensibly a source of 'facts', any attentive or sceptical reader of mainstream print media is well aware that buried beneath the explicit content of the written word is a set of presuppositions, imperatives and injunctions – presuppositions about migrants and crime for instance, or injunctions as to how one ought to vote.

Indeed, it's in this context that Deleuze claims, towards the end of *Cinema II*:

> what makes information all-powerful (the newspapers, and then the radio, and then the television) is its very nullity, its radical ineffectiveness. Information plays on its ineffectiveness in order to establish its power, its very power to be ineffective, and thereby all the more dangerous. (CII, 276)

Information, in other words, operates by virtue of an apparent 'neutrality' or 'factuality', a nullity which ultimately masks certain interested and subterranean operations of power – a situation which renders it a particularly nefarious fabric of order-words. In this context, to return to a distinction I established in the introduction, it appears as if Deleuze is using the term 'information' in a *semantic* sense, using it to indicate something like 'facts' – albeit facts thoroughly problematised by the conditions of their genesis. However, Deleuze's use of the term, not only in 'What is the Creative Act?' but also in important passages in *Cinema II* and *What is Philosophy?*, is also explicit in linking this idea of information to *information technologies*, in particular as they are yoked in the service of what he calls 'societies of control'.

Societies of Control

Deleuze turns to this linkage in a short piece from 1990 entitled 'Postscript on the Societies of Control', which, despite its brevity, has proved to be one of his most influential texts.[44] Here, he claims that the so-called 'disciplinary societies' identified by Foucault are in the process of being supplanted by societies in which information technologies are used to engender new forms of modular, self-regulating control – far more sophisticated than the clumsy 'discipline' of state-directed violence and confinement. These new societies, which are also the site of widespread pharmaceutical interventions, hyper-individualistic competition, debt and generalised precarity, thus establish forms of internalised obedience and docility which are

The Digital Image

buttressed by increasingly sophisticated techniques for the surveillance and 'datafication' of populations.

We will recall that, for Foucault, the seventeenth and eighteenth centuries saw the emergence of a new social form in which discipline and punishment were no longer exceptional or circumscribed events, but proliferated into a general social organisation which took a normalising surveillance of the body as its principle.[45] Of the paradigmatic Foucauldian disciplinary spaces, however – schools, prisons and hospitals – Deleuze writes that by the twentieth century:

> The administrations in charge never cease announcing supposedly necessary reforms: to reform schools, to reform industries, hospitals, the armed forces, prisons. But everyone knows that these institutions are finished, whatever the length of their expiration periods. It's only a matter of administering their last rites and of keeping people employed until the installation of the new forces knocking at the door. These are the *societies of control*, which are in the process of replacing the disciplinary societies. (PS, 4; emphasis added)

Opposed to these enclosed and discrete disciplinary spaces, in other words, Deleuze, borrowing the terminology of 'control' from William S. Burroughs – though in the background here is also cybernetics and Norbert Wiener[46] – will posit modular, a-centred and metamorphosing processes which now work to shape subjects; paradigmatically those of debt, drugs and inter-individual competition.

These are control mechanisms which no longer depend upon a logic of closure, capture and surveillance, but rather upon a logic all the more inescapable because it is modular and mobile, adjusting itself to the flux of a subject's unique social and bodily coordinates. As Deleuze explains, in the so-called 'disciplinary society':

> The different internments or spaces of enclosure through which the individual passes are independent variables: each time one is supposed to start from zero, and although a common language for all these places exists, it is *analogical*. On the other hand, the different control mechanisms are inseparable variations, forming a system of variable geometry the language of which is *numerical* (which doesn't mean binary). Enclosures are *molds*, distinct castings, but controls are a *modulation*, like a self-deforming cast that will continuously change from one moment to the other, or like a sieve whose mesh will transmute from point to point. (PS, 4)

In control societies, in other words, processes of subjectivation become mobile and differential, 'flexible', in keeping with the imperatives of an increasingly complex and globalised market.

For Deleuze, this transition is well illustrated in the change from the *factory* to the *corporation* as the paradigmatic institution of production, a development which expresses concrete demographic changes as much as it does the collapse of organised labour. Whereas the factory constituted a relative metastability which was able, at times, to be made to benefit its workers – for instance through collective bargaining – the modular logic of the neoliberal corporation – which pits workers against one another in the service of sales targets and bonuses – threatens the possibility of any such gains. One might, indeed, still work in a factory, if one is lucky, but in the context of a control society this institution will invariably take on a 'corporate' structure or organisation, which sees each worker competing against her colleagues. Or as Deleuze explains:

> the factory was a body that contained internal forces at a level of equilibrium, the highest possible in terms of production ... but in a society of control, the corporation has replaced the factory, and the corporation is a spirit, a gas ... the factory constituted individuals as a single body to the double advantage of the boss who surveyed each element within the mass and the unions who mobilised a mass resistance; but the corporation constantly presents the brashest rivalry as a healthy form of emulation, an excellent motivational force that opposes individuals against one another and runs through each, dividing each within. (PS, 5)

Deleuze's formulation here is noteworthy – control societies, far from delivering the 'individualism' which is either the great boon or bane of capital, *obliterate the individual*, rendering it an interchangeable function or node in their machinery. This destabilisation of the hitherto bipolar movement between the individual and the mass thus sees every worker become his or her own 'boss', taking personal responsibility for the imperatives of their particular zone of productivity.

For Deleuze, this change is likewise illustrated by the use of informatic tools such as the database. Whereas the individual–mass dyad was previously expressed through singularisations of identity like the signature or number – an individual's 'unique' mark in the context of a collective – the society of control, Deleuze suggests, establishes a new kind of *dividuality*, treating its subjects as interchangeable data. Thus:

> In societies of control ... what is important is no longer either a signature or a number, but a code: the code is a *password*... The numerical language of control is made of codes that mark access to information,

or reject it. We no longer find ourselves dealing with the mass/individual pair. Individuals have become "*dividuals*," and masses, samples, data, markets, or "*banks*." (*PS*, 5)

Again, the implications of this claim are noteworthy – while political philosophers have tended to take either the individual or the masses as the locus of political agency, Deleuze's suggestion is that informatic techniques are liquidating this very distinction. The *dividual* constitutes a new kind of political subject, which might be grasped both in terms of an internal or psychological 'splitting', according to which, as Paul Patton writes, 'partial subjects [are] defined by certain functional aspects identified in relation to particular ends',[47] and also in the context of the perpetual self-modulation required by precarious forms of labour: the interminable re-education and 'upskilling' needed to participate in the twenty-first-century workforce.[48]

We might think about these developments as they are expressed in the transition from the taxi to the Uber, which sees a mode of transport explicitly rendered with the name of a corporation. In the ostensibly 'disciplinary' space of the taxi, the worker must surrender her time and efforts, but is afforded at least the consolation of potential rudeness in the face of a long day. In the Uber, however, not only is the worker's behaviour self-monitored in response to the constant collection of information – in the form of user ratings and reviews – but this model is replicated in the experience of the customer, who is reciprocally rated in turn. As such, an ambience of behaviour, or space of possible actions, is self-imposed through the mediating presence of information technology, in a model which proliferates in various forms across the breadth of integrated world capitalism.[49]

We can already intuit the significance of this short text for any attempt to place Deleuze in dialogue with contemporary digital media. While Deleuze doesn't explicitly theorise the Internet – which wasn't made publicly available until 1991, a year after the text was written – the 'Postscript' is nevertheless more than a little prescient, with Deleuze claiming, at one point, that 'the disciplinary man was a discontinuous producer of energy, but the man of control is undulatory, in orbit, in a continuous network. Everywhere *surfing* has already replaced the older *sports*' (*PS*, 5). And strangely, this appears to be the first occurrence of the 'surfing' analogy in the context of telephonically networked information.

Clearly then, computing technologies and telecommunications networks like the Minitel system, rolled out by the French state in 1982, are at the heart of Deleuze's analysis of control societies.[50] This is because for Deleuze, new forms of social organisation are always linked to new machines which facilitate them, a position informed by an idiosyncratic concept of the machine which he had developed with Guattari.[51] As Deleuze explains:

> Types of machines are easily matched with each type of society – not that machines are determining, but because they express those social forms capable of generating them and using them. The old societies of sovereignty made use of simple machines – levers, pulleys, clocks; but the recent disciplinary societies equipped themselves with machines involving energy, with the passive danger of entropy and the active danger of sabotage; the societies of control operate with machines of a third type, computers, whose passive danger is jamming and whose active one is piracy and the introduction of viruses. (PS, 6)

Deleuze, as we have said, is no technophobe or pessimist, and here we get a sense of the complexity he intuits in these developments. While machines like computers, and the networks they support, are thoroughly implicated with the new forms of control, the relation is not one of simple causation. Nor are these machines exclusively or necessarily deployed in the service of any particular social end, such that Deleuze will introduce the machines commensurate with each regime of domination in terms of their potentials for disruption and sabotage.

We will leave these dangers, 'active' and 'passive', to one side, and return to them in a later chapter. For now, we might note that Deleuze, in speaking not only of information as it appears in newspapers or on television, but also as it flows through databases, networks and algorithms, uses the term in both semantic *and* technical senses – designating not only a collection of explicit imperatives and order-words but also an implicit techno-social engineering commensurate with the exigencies of capital. Unsurprisingly, given its contribution to an analysis of this latter phenomenon, the 'Postscript' has thus been the focus of a great deal of secondary scholarship, particularly in the fields of new technology and new media studies. Such approaches should, however, be made cautiously, given some of the pitfalls of Deleuze's own analysis. As Mark Poster has observed, for instance:

> Elements of "control" existed in Europe in the early modern period as the state hired spies to keep track of suspected miscreants. Equally, forms of "discipline" proliferate in the twenty-first century as the United States, for

example, erects more and more prisons under the so called "get-tough" policies of recent administrations. The shift from discipline to control is also Eurocentric, overlooking the very different disposition of these state strategies in the southern hemisphere.[52]

Indeed, both Poster and David Savat have convincingly argued that the 'database' functions of the society of control can, in many ways, be seen as intensifying the hierarchical and normalising forms of visibility that Foucault attributes to disciplinary society.[53]

These objections aside, Deleuze's commentary in this text has a great deal to offer scholars of new and digital media, and indeed contemporary politics, particularly given the ways in which informatic technologies have taken an increasingly prominent role in the prosecution of state interests in the years since he was writing. As Saul Newman writes:

> There can be little doubt that we are living today in a control society. The signs are all around us: ubiquitous CCTV cameras filming public spaces; the introduction of biometric scanning and facial recognition technology in major airports; the planned implementation of ID cards in the United Kingdom and elsewhere – cards which would contain biometric information; widespread DNA testing for even minor offences, and the setting up of national DNA databases; the use of electronic monitoring bracelets for offenders or terrorist suspects placed under home detention; the use of "smart cards" on public transport systems and for accessing health services, and so on. We are seeing the development – bit by bit – of an all-encompassing system of surveillance and regulation, the weaving of an intricate web of overlapping circuits of control, information gathering and identification.[54]

And indeed, the dynamism and intensity of these developments menaces the capacity of theorists to critically engage with them, given that, as Frida Beckman has noted, 'even as you write down the most recent examples in a book manuscript, they will most likely already seem out of date once the book is published'.[55] Leaving aside these critical difficulties, we might observe that all of these mechanisms of surveillance and control depend upon techniques of both the image and the screen, which potentially renders a discussion of cinema particularly fertile in this space. But how does Deleuze himself understand this relationship between information, control and cinema, and what are its implications for the cinematic outside?

Control and Information in The Time-Image

In Chapter 2, we saw Deleuze claim that 'if the frame has an analogue, it is to be found in an information system [*une système informatique*] rather than a linguistic one' (*CI*, 15), given its collection of parts or objects which together form a set. In order to avoid an 'empty aestheticism' (*CI*, 18), cinema, and, we may well extrapolate, art in general, must 'communicate' in at least a marginal sense, deploying certain 'intelligible' (*CI*, xi) materials in order to address the viewer. The expressive and resistant mode which is ultimately that of art, however, emerges from the artwork's relations with material and intensive forces *in excess* of this intelligibility, which communicate to thought a simultaneous experience of violence and constraint. This is the nature of Deleuze's idiosyncratic modernism, according to which art – in the particular sense which he gives that term – is never simply distraction or entertainment, but rather a disruptive and futural event in sensibility and thought, in a model we can trace back to the Kantian sublime. In this context, the informatic system of the cinematic image, as we have seen, is related to a virtual/temporal 'whole' (in classical cinema) and later (in post-war cinema) to an unthinkable 'outside'.

But at the end of *Cinema II*, Deleuze seems to suggest that the informatic or communicative tendencies of the image might menace these more ambiguous potentials, plugging in to the operations of control and obscuring cinema's radical noetic implications. The problem, as we briefly saw in the introduction, is that new forms of 'electronic' and 'numerical' images seem to eschew visuality *tout court*, neglecting aesthetic experimentation in favour of a play with clichés, order-words and predetermined semiotics. In this context, Deleuze's remarks about the new forms of the image relate to his occasional criticism of television – that it constitutes a form of 'social engineering' which is dependent upon a careful domestication of perception. This critique is most fully developed in the short 'Letter to Serge Daney', written as a preface to the latter's *Ciné-Journal* in 1986. Here, Deleuze claims that while there is nothing *in principle* to prevent television from attaining the creative and resistant functions he ascribes to cinematic art, its ultimately 'social' dimensions 'stifle its potential aesthetic function' (*N*, 74). This occurs, claims Deleuze, through television's production of a kind of 'professional' spectatorship – a set of predetermined and subsequently learned affective and intellectual responses to the image, triggered by instructional devices and squeezing out spaces of uncertainty or ambiguity that the image might otherwise contain. We might think, for instance, of 'canned laughter', which serves as an explicit marker for an expected or predetermined affective response. These responses, which are resolutely sensory-motor, are produced in accordance with broader social imperatives, such that, Deleuze explains:

> TV is, in its present form, the ultimate consensus: it's direct social engineering, leaving no gap at all between itself and the social sphere, it's social engineering in its purest form. For how could professional training, the professional eye, leave any room for something supplemental in the way of perceptual exploration? (N, 74)

In dedicating itself to predetermined perceptual conventions, in other words, television eschews the aesthetic experimentation which might move us beyond sensory-motor images and into the violent reflexivity of thought. In this context, Deleuze continues, returning to his account of the death of the classical cinema with the end of the Second World War:

> Cinema met its first death at the hands of an authoritarian power culminating in fascism. Why does its threatened second death involve television, just as the first involved radio? Because television is the form in which the new powers of 'control' become immediate and direct. (N, 75)[56]

Television, in other words, in deploying perceptual clichés in order to produce a kind of professional spectatorship, is intimately linked to a broader engineering of desire characteristic of control societies, and as such deleterious to the artistic potentials of cinema. 'Even Mabuse changes his method', writes Deleuze, 'and operates through television sets' (N, 71), and this evocation of Fritz Lang's Dr Mabuse – who, across three sprawling films, uses radiophonic, telematic and telepathic techniques to foment social unrest and instigate an 'empire of crime' – serves explicitly to link these mass mediatic techniques to the imperatives of fascism. And while it is certainly true that the Nazi propaganda machine offered up a blueprint for mass media more generally, there are nevertheless a few caveats that we might make around this position, which suggests a certain elitism with which Deleuze has occasionally been charged.

First, these are not his only remarks about the medium, and in essays on the televisual works of both Beckett and Godard, Deleuze suggests that television might nevertheless possess its own unique potentials for a deterritorialisation of thought. Second, Deleuze undoubtedly has a particular kind of television in mind – his frequent example is the game show – and we might object that television, particularly in the years since he was writing, has itself become a complex and self-reflexive artform. Finally, we might note that this picture is further complicated by the fact that Deleuze is undoubtedly best known in France today for his *own* television appearances, and the *Abécédaire de Gilles Deleuze* programme, produced by Pierre-André Boutang in the late 1980s.[57] We will return to these ideas in the final chapter.

For now, we might simply note that Deleuze's claim is not that television is *incapable* of aesthetic invention, but rather that it tends overwhelmingly to avoid it, and this, in itself, is not an unconvincing claim. Importantly, in *Cinema II*, Deleuze seems to suggest that this is likewise a danger immanent to the new, 'numerical' images of computation, which eschew not only aesthetic experimentation, but perception in general, such that:

> the frame or the screen functions as instrument panel, printing or computing table, the image is constantly being cut into another image, being printed through a visible mesh, sliding over other images in an "incessant stream of messages," and the shot itself is less like an eye than an overloaded brain endlessly absorbing information: it is the brain–information, brain–city couple which replaces that of eye–Nature. (*CII*, 274)

The brain–city couplet thus designates a regime of *total* intelligibility, a multidimensional information space where perceptual ambiguities are no longer productive, but rather constitute an obstacle or problem. This, indeed, is the model Flaxman persuasively takes up, suggesting it as emblematic of a 'new idea of cinema'.

Deleuze himself is not strictly or simply pessimistic here, suggesting that certain film-makers are already exploring this new, multidimensional information space for its political and aesthetic potentials. Thus, in his discussion of Syberberg's *Hitler: A Film from Germany* (1977) – which combines invented characters and real testimonies, genuine artefacts and surreal, theatrical framings into an informatic assemblage with more than a passing resemblance to the then-unrealised Internet – Deleuze writes:

> one of Syberberg's originalities is to stretch out a vast space of information, like a complex, heterogeneous, anarchic space where the trivial and the cultural, the public and the private, the historic and the anecdotal, the imaginary and the real are brought close together, and sometimes on the side of speech, discourses, commentaries, familiar or ancillary

testimonies, sometimes on the side of sight, of existing or no longer existing settings, engravings, plans and projects, acts of seeing with acts of clairvoyance, all of equal importance and forming a network, in kinds of relationship which are never those of causality. *The modern world is that in which information replaces nature.* (*CII*, 276; emphasis added)

That cinema has the power to reflect this complex contemporary reality, and further, that it is able to use information itself in the service of this project, suggests an ambiguous and contradictory state of affairs which continues to characterise art in the twenty-first century. Nevertheless, Deleuze is emphatic: 'Syberberg's powerful idea is that *no information, whatever it might be, is sufficient to defeat Hitler*' (*CII*, 276) – which is to say that information *itself* must nevertheless still be animated by aesthetic and political concerns from outside the information space, given its inherent 'neutrality' or 'nullity'.

Indeed, Deleuze will claim that in the context of this dangerous nullity, it is necessary to 'go beyond' information, refusing to take seriously its apparent neutrality and instead asking the cynical and evaluative questions of philosopher or artist. 'Going beyond information is achieved on two sides at once', he writes, 'towards two questions: *what is the source and what is the addressee?*' (*CII*, 276). Information may well be the transmission of 'facts' in a newspaper, or data in a computer or communications system, but for Deleuze, this factuality is at best a banal and uninteresting problem, at worst, the disguise of a repressive configuration of power. The question of the interests and contingencies that these 'facts' express – the subterranean powers they serve and the unconscious desires which they interpolate – remains a fundamentally ethico-aesthetic question of *value*, no matter how stubbornly we might deny it. In this context, Deleuze writes, 'redemption, art beyond knowledge, is also creation beyond information' (*CII*, 277) – and this is the task of both philosophy and art.

This introduction of questions of both origin and intention into the apparently 'neutral' information space is once more conceived, for Deleuze, in terms of creativity and resistance. In a 1990 conversation with Antonio Negri, he returns to the profound schism in his thought between *creation* and *communication*, claiming: 'Creating has always been something different from communicating. The key thing may be to create vacuoles of noncommunication, circuit breakers, so we can elude control' (*N*, 175). A little later he returns to the clutch of political concepts advanced throughout *Cinema II*, suggesting:

> What we most lack is a belief in the world, we've quite lost the world, it's been taken from us. If you believe in the world you precipitate events, however inconspicuous, that elude control, you engender new space-times, however small their surface or volume [...] Our ability to resist control, our submission to it, has to be assessed at the level of our every move. We need both a creativity *and* a people. (N, 176)

Control, in other words, forecloses or wards off the outside by offering up predetermined materials to thought and sensibility, which are domesticated or 'trained' in such a way as to eschew creativity and belief. This belief, as we saw in the previous chapter, is not a belief in any predetermined world or orthodoxy, but rather in the world's infinite and immanent capacity to become other than it is – a situation which revolutionary politics and artistic creation both express.

Information occupies an ambiguous position at this confluence, intimately related to control yet presenting itself as 'factual' or 'neutral'. Art and philosophy, dedicated as they are to questions of value, ought to criticise and render problematic this neutrality – asking questions about the genesis and effects of information, tracing the unconscious desires which it articulates and identifying the hidden masters that it serves. In this context, they might produce sites of 'noncommunication' – ruptures or points of impossibility in information systems, which confront us with their outside. And while Deleuze offers up a few tantalising hints as to how this project might be undertaken in the context of control societies, his own analysis is perhaps limited by a refusal to understand *information itself* as ontogenetic or – what amounts to the same thing – as a complex production of values.

In order to fully grasp this latter claim, however, we must look more closely at information theory itself. In turning to cybernetics and to the cybernetically informed philosophy of Gilbert Simondon, we encounter a concept of information as not simply control or factuality, but rather designating radically undetermined processes – a multivalent ontogenesis which might become the grist of a uniquely digital art.

Notes

1 Quoted in A. Gaudreault and P. Marion, *The End of Cinema? A Medium in Crisis in the Digital Age*, trans. T. Barnard (New York: Columbia University Press, 2015), p. 31.

2 For a thorough history of the advent of sound, and the disparate reactions with which it was greeted, see D. Gomery, *The Coming of Sound – A History* (Abingdon: Routledge, 2005).
3 Gaudreault and Marion, *The End of Cinema?*, p. 11.
4 See W. Benjamin, 'The Work of Art in the Age of its Technological Reproducibility', in *The Work of Art in the Age of its Technological Reproducibility and Other Writings on Media*, ed. M. W. Jennings, B. Doherty and T. Levin (Cambridge, MA: The Belknap Press of Harvard University Press, 2008), pp. 19–55.
5 A. Bazin, 'The Ontology of the Photographic Image', in A. Bazin, *What is Cinema? – Vol. I*, trans. H. Gray (Berkeley, CA: University of California Press, 1967), p. 14.
6 In particular the bourgeois sensibilities of the painter. See A. Bazin, 'An Aesthetic of Reality: Neorealism (Cinematic Realism and the Italian School of the Liberation)', in A. Bazin, *What is Cinema? – Vol. II*, trans. H. Gray (Berkeley, CA: University of California Press, 2005), pp. 16–40.
7 Gaudreault and Marion, *The End of Cinema?*, p. 45.
8 D. N. Rodowick, *The Virtual Life of Film* (Cambridge, MA: Harvard University Press, 2007), p. 7.
9 S. Prince, *Digital Visual Effects in Cinema: The Seduction of Reality* (New Brunswick, NJ: Rutgers University Press, 2012), p. 4.
10 Rodowick, *Virtual Life*, p. 7.
11 G. Balbi and P. Magaudda, *A History of Digital Media: An Intermedia and Global Perspective* (New York: Routledge, 2018), p. 169.
12 Rodowick, *Virtual Life*, p. 8.
13 Ibid., p. 5.
14 I have here adopted the term as it is developed in Manovich's *The Language of New Media*, which in many ways determined the subsequent parameters for the academic study of media after computerisation. Note that Manovich, alongside the likes of Rodowick, ultimately argues that '*new* media' constitutes something of a misnomer, suggesting an idealistic rupture in place of various (actual) technical and cultural continuities. See L. Manovich, *The Language of New Media* (Cambridge, MA: MIT Press, 2001).
15 Gaudreault and Marion, *The End of Cinema?*, p. 11.
16 Rodowick, *Virtual Life*, p. 8.
17 See the exhaustive study by Manuel Castells, *The Rise of the Network Society (2nd Edition)* (Chichester: Wiley-Blackwell, 2010).
18 Flaxman, 'Out of Field', p. 120; M. Hadjioannou, 'In Search of Lost Reality: Waltzing with Bashir', in D. Martin-Jones and W. Brown (eds), *Deleuze and Film* (Edinburgh: Edinburgh University Press, 2012), pp. 104–20.
19 See Balbi and Magaudda, *A History of Digital Media*.

20 The breadth of Flaxman's interests is perhaps best captured in the book *Gilles Deleuze and the Fabulation of Philosophy*, part of a two-volume study dedicated to the 'powers of the false' in art and philosophy. At the time of writing, a second volume, dedicated specifically to the question of cinema, remains in the works. Regrettably, the contributions it will no doubt make to these very debates remain to be seen.

21 Flaxman, 'Out of Field', p. 120.

22 See, for instance, A. Groenstad, 'Back to Bazin? Filmicity in the Age of the Digital Image', *Popular Culture Review*, 13(2) (2002), pp. 11–23.

23 Flaxman, 'Out of Field', p. 120.

24 Ibid.

25 Ibid., p. 127.

26 We might think about this change via recourse to the horror genre. What long trajectory has led horror film from the obscure expressionism of Murnau's *Nosferatu* (1922) or Wiene's *The Cabinet of Dr. Caligari* (1920) to contemporary so-called 'torture porn', and why? Stanley Kubrick's *The Shining*, as we have seen, derives its terror from vast stretches of uncertainty punctuated by sudden, transcribed bursts of information, which impel us into a field of questions: 'What is the Overlook Hotel? What happened here? Is it real or in his head?' In sitting down to watch a film like *Saw* (2004) or *Hostel* (2005), though, there is only one question: 'How much "information" – in the form of moans, torn flesh and dilated pupils – can I take?' Ultimately, however, this distinction relies on a semantic conception of information which will prove inadequate to our aims.

27 Bazin, indeed, claims that from the earliest experiments with phonography and photography, their creators were animated by the idea of an artform that might perfectly replicate reality. The history of cinema therefore becomes less a probabilistic and piecemeal development towards an uncertain end, and more a process pursuant to a 'guiding myth', 'a recreation of the world in its own image, an image unburdened by the freedom of interpretation of the artist or the irreversibility of time'. Bazin, 'The Myth of Total Cinema', in Bazin, *What is Cinema?*, p. 21.

28 As Bazin writes: 'If the origins of an art reveal something of its nature, then one may legitimately consider the silent and the sound film as stages of technical development little by little made a reality out of the original "myth" ... every new development added to the cinema must, paradoxically, take it nearer and nearer to its origins. In short, cinema has not yet been invented!' Ibid.

29 Flaxman, 'Out of Field', p. 128.

30 As Rodowick rightly notes, in the contemporary mediascape, 'theatrical screening of films is a marketing device to enhance video/DVD sales and to promote and sustain franchises in toys, games, and related

sources of revenue ... "filmed entertainment" is just another element in the software chain of diversified media giants, though an important one, since it feeds significantly expanding nontheatrical markets.' Rodowick, *Virtual Life*, p. 27.
31 Flaxman, 'Out of Field', p. 129.
32 Ibid.
33 Ibid.
34 Ibid., p. 134.
35 Deleuze would most certainly have been aware of the metaphysical response to cybernetics advanced by Simondon, particularly in the text *L'individu et sa genèse physico-biologique (L'individuation à la lumiere des notions de forme et d'information)*. We can only speculate as to why he elects not to draw on it in any of his own discussions of information.
36 Deleuze, *Two Regimes*, p. 322.
37 Woodward, *Lyotard and the Inhuman Condition*, p. 41.
38 Ibid., p. 70.
39 See R. Ruyer, *La cybernétique et l'origine de l'information* (Paris: Éditions Flammarion, 1954).
40 See, for instance, the essays 'Matter and Time' and 'Time Today', in J. F. Lyotard, *The Inhuman: Reflections on Time*, trans. G. Bennington and R. Bowlby (Stanford, CA: Stanford University Press, 1991); P. Virilio, *The Information Bomb*, trans. C. Turner (London: Verso, 2005); and J. Baudrillard, 'The Implosion of Meaning in the Media', in *In the Shadow of the Silent Majorities ... or the End of the Social*, trans. P. Foss, P. Patton and J. Johnston (New York: Semiotext(e), 1983).
41 M. Heidegger, 'Traditional Language and Technical Language', trans. W. T. Gregory, *Journal of Philosophical Research*, 23 (1998), p. 141.
42 Deleuze, *Two Regimes*, p. 320.
43 V. Conley 'Order-Word', in A. Parr (ed.), *The Deleuze Dictionary – Revised Edition* (Edinburgh: Edinburgh University Press, 2010), p. 198.
44 See, for instance, the contributions in the collection *Control Culture: Foucault and Deleuze after Discipline*, edited by Frida Beckman.
45 See, in particular, M. Foucault, *Discipline and Punish – The Birth of the Prison*, trans. A. Sheridan (New York: Vintage, 1995).
46 Wiener, of course, had become the best-known proponent of information theory in the twentieth century through his work in cybernetics. The title of his first book dedicated to this nascent field, *Cybernetics: or Control and Communication in the Animal and the Machine*, makes explicit the connection Wiener establishes between processes for the transmission and interpretation of information, and the sensory-motor operations of regulation in living things – what he calls 'control'.

47 P. Patton, 'Philosophy and Control', in Beckman, *Control Culture*, p. 195.
48 See J. T. Nealon, '"The Path is for Your Steps Alone": Popular Music, Neoliberalism and Biopolitics', in Beckman, *Control Culture*, p. 105.
49 The digitally mediated organisation of both student and academic labour in the twenty-first-century university in many ways perfects this form.
50 The Minitel system was a text-based digital service accessible through telephone lines and rolled out across France in 1982 by the state telecommunications and postal administration. This system, which provided each home in France with a small screen that could be used to access various informatic databases and services – stock listings and prices, for instance, the telephone directory, school results and train schedules – was one of the most widely adapted pre-Internet digital communications systems, but was ultimately superseded by the American APRANET model throughout the 1990s. It was finally discontinued in 2012. Its explicitly 'informational' functions, as well as its centralised direction by the French state, clearly influenced Deleuze's conception of the '*image numérique*' and of control societies. For an authoritative treatment of the Minitel system and its history, see Castells, *The Rise of the Network Society*, ch. 5.
51 Guattari had developed his own concept of the machine in an essay dedicated to *The Logic of Sense*, which served to instigate his collaboration with Deleuze. Drawing on his broadly Marxian heritage, Guattari opposes machines to structures, for which they serve as a paradoxical site of simultaneous collapse and instigation. While Guattari intervenes here in terms of semiotics, construing the machine not necessarily in technical terms but as that 'event' which overturns a given structure of signification, his approach is nevertheless rooted in a Marxian-revolutionary approach according to which machines understood in the quotidian sense – for instance the printing press, or the automatic looms of pre-revolutionary France – precipitate the production of an urban proletariat and as such, ultimately, the revolutionary production of an entirely new universe of semiotic reference. See F. Guattari, 'Machine and Structure', in *Molecular Revolution: Psychiatry and Politics*, trans. R. Sheed (London: Penguin, 1984), pp. 111–19.
52 M. Poster, 'Afterword', in M. Poster and D. Savat (eds), *Deleuze and New Technology* (Edinburgh: Edinburgh University Press, 2009), p. 260.
53 Ibid.
54 S. Newman, 'Politics in the Age of Control', in Poster and Savat (eds), *Deleuze and New Technology*, p. 105.
55 F. Beckman, 'Introduction: Control of What?', in Beckman (ed.), *Control Culture*, p. 2.

56 In this context, Deleuze returns to themes that are likewise present in his earlier work with Guattari. In *A Thousand Plateaus*, for instance, they evoke a regime of 'machinic enslavement', in which individuals, once plugged into the mass-media systems of capital, become little more than transmission nodes for predetermined functions and movements of information. As they write, 'one is enslaved by TV as a human machine insofar as the television viewers are no longer consumers or users, nor even subjects who supposedly "make" it, but intrinsic component pieces, "input" and "output," feedback or recurrences that are no longer connected to the machine in such a way as to produce or use it. In machinic enslavement, there is nothing but transformations and exchanges of information, some of which are mechanical, others human.' Deleuze and Guattari, *A Thousand Plateaus*, p. 458.

57 As Tamara Chaplin has argued, consistent televisual coverage of French philosophers has had a profound effect on the practice and dissemination of the discipline in that country throughout the twentieth and twenty-first centuries. See T. Chaplin, *Turning on the Mind: French Philosophers on Television* (Chicago: University of Chicago Press, 2009).

5
Cybernetic Information

We've seen that, for Deleuze, the cinematic frame is like an 'informatic system', but that this system can be said to be artistic to the extent that it opens onto an external 'whole' or 'outside', which is *virtual*, and as such the proper domain of thought. This openness of the image, however, is threatened by an approach which treats the image fully or simply as information – moving away from experiments in perception in favour of a manipulation or processing of data. But what do we mean when we talk about both *data* and *information* – given that these have historically been such contested and multiple concepts? For Deleuze, information is tied to order-words and control, designating an operation according to which 'you are told what you are supposed to believe'.[1] But has he here erred in equivocating semantic and technical senses of the term, neglecting certain philosophical implications of information as a concept?

Such definitional problems have lain at the heart of information theory since its inception. Claude Shannon, the mathematician and electrical engineer whose early work on telecommunications problems would see him regularly dubbed the 'father of information theory',[2] was dubious that the term could be comprehensively defined at all, writing:

> The word "information" has been given different meanings by various writers in the general field of information theory. It is likely that at least a number of these will prove sufficiently useful in certain applications to deserve further study and permanent recognition. It is hardly to be expected that a single concept of information would satisfactorily account for the numerous possible applications of this general field.[3]

While we've established the way in which Deleuze uses the term, Shannon's remarks thus suggest the possibility of other readings, which might help us to think information differently. This chapter is dedicated to such readings, turning to accounts of information in its *technical*, *mathematical* and *ontological* guises – not only those of cybernetics and information theory, but also that of Gilbert

Simondon, for whom information designates the process whereby individuals are ceaselessly *in-formed* by forces from 'outside'. In reading these alternate accounts of information, we equip ourselves with tools for rethinking the contemporary, informatic image, not as a site of closure or control, but rather of radically unforeseen individuations.

The Mathematical Theory of Communication

One of the most systematic and compelling contemporary philosophical treatments of information is that of Luciano Floridi, who draws on the distinction made by Claude Shannon and Warren Weaver in order to bracket as distinct two major senses of information as a term: on the one hand, *semantic*, and on the other, *technical* or *ontological*.[4] Semantic information is perhaps closest to the popular, everyday sense in which the term is used, designating 'well-formed, meaningful and truthful data'.[5] In this context, information is something like fact, constituted through correct adherence to the propositional structures of some kind of language, and referring to an objectively verifiable situation in the world. This kind of information can be discussed in terms of meaningfulness, truth and falsehood, and must meet certain predetermined semantic criteria (the rules of a language) in order to be considered information at all.

Opposed to information in this sense is information we might variously refer to as statistical, technical or ontological – which is to say, information as an a-signifying process which, theoretically, exists prior to any semantic overlay. In this context, Floridi explains:

> Information theory approaches information as a physical phenomenon, syntactically. It is not interested in the usefulness, relevance, meaning, interpretation or aboutness of data, but in the level of detail and frequency in the uninterpreted data (signals or messages). It provides a successful mathematical theory because its central problem is whether and how much data, not what information is conveyed.[6]

And this latter kind of information, importantly, is intimately linked to notions of both uncertainty and indeterminacy. In the 1920s, for instance, statistician and geneticist R. A. Fisher defined information as a measure of the amount of uncertainty which might be removed from the results of an experiment.[7] Leaving aside the specifics of his mathematics, which is rooted in sigma-algebras of probability, we might say simply that for Fisher, the more 'uncertain' the results of an experiment, the larger a distribution of probabilities might be extrapolated from it. As such, the experiment has an amount of potential 'informativeness' commensurate with the initial level of 'uncertainty' it contains (with both terms understood in a rigorously statistical sense).[8]

A similarly probabilistic account of information emerges in the work of Claude Shannon, whose project, like the Deleuzian time-image, has its roots in the Second World War. Shannon worked during the war as a cryptographer, and his subsequent thought is consistently animated by the wartime exigencies of clarity, efficiency and speed in communicating information. After the war, he was employed by Bell Telephone Laboratories, where he was charged with ameliorating the 'noise' accompanying the transmission of telephonic and radio signals.[9] In 1948, as a result of this work, he published 'A Mathematical Theory of Communication' (the MTC), later fleshed out with Warren Weaver into a book of the same name. This key text laid much of the groundwork for subsequent information theory, establishing some of the core conceptual and technical presuppositions which have animated its development. As Susan Ballard explains:

> Shannon's initial brief was to develop efficient telephone lines, and his approach involved breaking down a system into subsystems in order to evaluate the efficiency of the channels and codes. The concern was with signal and the emphasis was on the consistency of transmission and reception of information through any given medium. To increase efficiency Shannon insisted that the message be separated from its components; in particular, those aspects that were predictable were not to be considered information. Furthermore, Shannon was adamant that information must not be confused with meaning.[10]

This distinction is of the utmost importance, and emerges from the fact that Shannon had been charged with optimising communication channels without foreknowledge of the particular messages they might be used to transmit. This amounts to posing the problem of information transmission in terms of the freedom to select among possible messages, and an uncertainty as to what message might actually be received – both of which ought to be maximised for the most efficient and dynamic communication system. As Weaver explains, in his popular introduction to Shannon's more technical piece:

> To be sure, this word information in communication theory relates not so much to what you *do* say, as to what you *could* say. That is, information

is a measure of one's freedom of choice when one selects a message ... the concept of information applies not to the individual messages (as the concept of meaning would), but rather to the situation as a whole, the unit information indicating that in this situation one has an abundant amount of freedom of choice, in selecting a message, which it is convenient to regard as a standard or unit amount [emphasis added].[11]

In the simplest possible terms, this means that information, according to the MTC, designates the statistically measurable amount of uncertainty that is removed from a situation which requires the presence of this uncertainty in order for information to be transmitted at all. To explain via recourse to an example from Floridi: if informee A anticipates a message from informer B, when it is known in advance that B produces only one message (we might think of flipping an unbiased coin with the same symbol on both sides), then A is in a state of 'data deficit' (uncertainty) of zero, and no information, in the MTC sense, will be communicated. If, however, B is capable of transmitting two equiprobable messages (as in the case of an unbiased two-sided coin), suddenly A is in a state of data deficit *greater than zero*. Upon tossing the coin, B therefore produces an amount of information which is equal to the amount of data deficit that it removes for the informee.[12]

Tied to this probabilistic approach to information is the problem of translating messages into the most efficient possible medium for transmission. In the case of a telephone line, this amounts to translating a human voice into variations in electrical current, which can be 'reassembled' as an audible output at the other end of the line. Regardless of the particular medium or content, this is the model which underpins all digital communication systems, whereby an information source provides a *transmitter* with a message which is translated into a *signal* before being sent to a *receiver*, the task of which is to retranslate the signal back into the original message.[13] These technologies are *digital* inasmuch as the most efficient means of effecting these translations – both from the point of view of human engineers and the computers that would increasingly handle most digital labour – is mathematical symbolisation, with disparate media encoded as numbers which can be decoded for reproduction by the receiver. Importantly, the primary technical problem is that of affording each of the links in this chain the maximum potential for transmitting or receiving information. Thus, Shannon explains:

> The significant aspect is that the actual message is one selected from a set of possible messages. The system must be designed to operate for each

possible selection, not just the one which will actually be chosen since this is unknown at the time of design.[14]

In his attempt to model this maximal 'possibility' of messages, Shannon is thus dedicated to the study of probability space distributions which might likewise be maximal. This approach leads him to suggest that information mirrors, in certain respects, the thermodynamic process of entropy – given that, like Fisher, he sees increased uncertainty as commensurate with an increase in information content, and as such, increased 'disorder' within a system (although, as Floridi notes, the term 'randomness' is perhaps less culturally loaded and potentially misleading).[15] In this sense, the more information a system contains, the more 'entropy' it produces.[16] The fundamental unit of this kind of transmissible, entropic 'Shannon' information is the *bit*, which refers to the entropy of a random variable that is, with equal probability, typically either 0 or 1, as in binary systems (or more properly, the information gained when the value of this variable is known). And as Floridi therefore notes, the basic building blocks of information systems are fundamentally – in a rigorously pre-semantic sense – *differences*.[17]

Floridi associates these differences, or *data*, with their etymological roots in Euclid's *dedomena*, or 'the given'. Prior to any semantic or epistemic interpretation, the singular datum can be thought of as an instance of discontinuity or difference which constitutes the 'event' of our – or any other informational entity's – perception. As Floridi explains:

> Dedomena ... are pure data or proto-epistemic data, that is, data before they are epistemically interpreted. As 'fractures in the fabric of Being', they can only be posited as an external anchor of our information, for dedomena are never accessed or elaborated independently of a level of abstraction. They can be reconstructed as ontological requirements, like Kant's *noumena* or Locke's *substance*: they are not epistemically experienced, but their presence is empirically inferred from, and required by, experience ... dedomena are whatever lack of uniformity in the world is the source of (what looks to informational organisms like us) data, e.g. a red light against a dark background.[18]

Importantly, these philosophical linkages derive from an initially technical formulation of information as uncertainty or difference. In seeking to understand problems attendant to the efficiency of communication, Shannon had discovered an *ontological* vocabulary of perhaps unprecedented explanatory power. The birth of cybernetics, a strange and now somewhat forgotten generalised science of information systems,[19] thus quickly built upon Shannon's work in producing a variety of complex, informational accounts of psychology, society and environment.

Paradigmatic is the thought of Norbert Wiener, whose own wartime research dedicated to problems in control and communications engineering was equally influential on the development of information theory. Wiener's work was primarily dedicated to automatic guidance systems for anti-aircraft guns, and in this context he had developed statistical models of what he followed control engineers in calling 'feedback'. This is the process by which a guidance system might 'observe [...] by itself the statistics concerning the motion of the target plane, which then works these into a system of control ... adjusting its position to the observed position and motion of the plane'.[20] And this model, according to which a control centre uses fed-back statistical information in order to maintain certain continuous functions in the face of external perturbations, seemed to Wiener to be an almost ideal model of the perceptual and cognitive functions of complex living things. Combined with Alan Turing's work on mechanised computing, these technologies seemed to suggest a new model of mentation as akin to 'information processing', such as would inform the famous Macey Conferences which birthed cybernetics research throughout the 1940s. As Wiener explains:

> From that time, it became clear to us that the ultra-rapid computing machine, depending as it does on consecutive switching devices, must represent almost an ideal model of the problems arising in the nervous system ... the synapse is nothing but a mechanism for determining whether a certain combination of outputs from other selected elements will or will not act as an adequate stimulus for the discharge of the next element, and must have its precise analogue in the computing machine.[21]

The nervous system, in other words – like the guidance system on an anti-aircraft gun – processes and responds to differences, using this *information* to extend actions and maintain certain variables, as in processes like homeostasis. This is the sense of the oft-quoted formula of second-order cyberneticist Gregory Bateson, who suggests that a *bit* of information is essentially 'a difference which makes a difference'[22] – a discontinuity or variation which is communicated throughout an information system. As Bateson explains, in the context of his ecological approach to mind:

we can assert that any ongoing ensemble of events and objects which has the appropriate complexity of causal circuits and the appropriate energy relations will surely show mental characteristics. It will compare, that is, be responsive to difference ... it will "process information" and will inevitably be self-corrective either toward homeostatic optima or toward the maximisation of certain variables.[23]

And this leads Bateson to conclude that 'a "bit" of information is definable as a difference which makes a difference. Such a difference, as it travels and undergoes a successive transformation in a circuit, is an elementary idea.'[24]

This formulation is striking not just for its apparently Deleuzian resonances. Bateson's project – which is emblematic of the more sophisticated cybernetic interventions – thus seeks to characterise thought itself as informatic. No longer the product of an immaterial or interiorised *cogito*, both thought and mind emerge from their embeddedness in complex systems for the transmission of information conceived as a fabric of differences – instances of discontinuity or disorder which produce or extend affects. These differences are 'perceived' in the context of the maintenance of certain continuous functions, helping complex systems to organise and self-regulate.

Indeed, it is in this context that many cyberneticists would come to imbue information with a metaphysical and even moral status. For Wiener, information conceived statistically represents the measure of a genuine operative principle – irreducible to matter or to energy – through which order is able to crystallise from the generalised disorder of the universe. Against Shannon's entropic information, Wiener characterises information as *negentropic*, writing, in *The Human Use of Human Beings*:

> There are local and temporary islands of decreasing entropy in a world in which the entropy as a whole tends to increase, and the existence of these islands enables some of us to assert the existence of progress ... we ourselves constitute such an island...[25]

Information, in other words, is the means by which certain complex and relatively isolated systems – such as human beings – deploy feedback and control mechanisms to organise themselves against the generalised thermodynamic cooling of the universe. For Wiener, this becomes a means of grasping human history itself, as a gradual proliferation and perfection of information control and communications systems, in a process which might ultimately be taken up and perfected by human-built machines. And while Wiener would ultimately retreat from this somewhat grandiose picture of informatic 'progress',[26] we might observe that his account of information – like those of Fisher, Shannon and Bateson – helps us to conceive of it as no longer strictly semantic, but rather as processual, dynamic, and even ontogenetic.

Cybernetics, however, remains broadly dedicated to a set of implicit ideals deriving from its genesis in certain technical problems, in particular those related to the speeds and logistics of global, mechanised warfare. Shannon's objectives of efficiency and clarity in communication, and Wiener's emphasis on regulation and control in informatic systems, subtly orient the cybernetic imaginary towards a particular set of operative ideals and often unconscious social values. If information is a mechanism *purely* of communication and control, then what it communicates are the imperatives of a particular *status quo* – in keeping with a critique we saw Deleuze making in the previous chapter. But while cybernetics remains dedicated to values inherited from its origins in particular technocratic, martial and state-directed projects, we might now turn to another ontological account of information, such as perhaps overcomes these limitations.

Simondon and Information

Gilbert Simondon's work on information constitutes a protracted response to cybernetics, drawing on its ideas and vocabulary in order to think about his two central and intimately related themes – on the one hand, the *problem of individuation*, on the other, the *meaning of technology*. Simondon's thought, as we saw in the introduction, responds to what he takes to be the profound alienation which results from our inability to properly grasp technical objects and realities. In understanding the technical object as something like a slave, claims Simondon, the Western intellect has inherited a dubious set of conceptual orientations quite directly from the Athenian *polis*, which, in its bracketing as distinct technical and epistemological knowledges, has prevented us from understanding a hominisation which is, in its essence, technical.[27] At the same time, and in the same context, we have inherited a dubious account of the individual, which is based on an untenable distinction between form and content – equally linked to vectors of conceptualisation derived from Athenian society.[28]

It is in this context that Simondon turns to contemporary developments in technical knowledge ignored by mainstream twentieth-century philosophy – most notably in cybernetics and information theory.[29] Simondon is at pains, however, to distinguish his own concept of information from that of cybernetics, which he feels does not go far enough in accounting for the processual and undetermined aspects of ontogenesis. As such, Simondon argues that information should not be understood in terms of *communication*, but rather in terms of *genesis*, an approach commensurate with what he calls a 'universal cybernetics' or 'allagmatics'.[30] In keeping with Simondon's ontological commitments, allagmatics would strive to grasp information not in terms of a probabilistic transmission between static and neutral receivers, but rather as an 'improbable' event which leads to the individuation of new forms. In this context, he explains, information 'must never be reduced to signals or to the supports of carriers of information in a message';[31] rather, information is the condition for emergence and evolution – the radical production of the new.

I do not propose to treat Simondon's philosophy of information in depth here, given that Deleuze himself elects not to evoke it in the context of his critique of information in control societies, and that to do so would be to overspill the limits of the present work. We can only speculate as to why Deleuze decides not to draw explicitly on Simondon's thought in his discussion of the informatic image. Deleuze appears to have understood information in a particular, broadly critical way, and seems to have hoped that an informatic art might still be animated by forces that are ultimately non-informational – in keeping with his broader philosophical and aesthetic tastes.[32] This aspiration, I suspect, emerges from a situation in which the informatic 'revolution' was still an ambiguous and undecided proposition, and a life totally mediated by information technologies and informatic images of thought might somehow still be circumvented. We are not, however, afforded this kind of immaculate approach today, a situation which perhaps explains the recent explosion of Anglophone scholarship dedicated to Simondon's work.[33]

For our purposes, it suffices to say that Simondon, like Deleuze, is dedicated to a project which will think processes of individuation without recourse to already constituted individuals. Rejecting Aristotle's hylomorphic schema – according to which the individual is conceived in terms of a predetermined or ideal form imposed on a brute and receptive matter[34] – Simondon claims that processes of individuation must rather be understood against the horizon of pre-individual 'metastable states' (*I*, 5), which, like the Deleuzian virtual, work to resolve differential energetic tensions through their contingent actualisations.

Cybernetic Information

Simondon takes the concept of metastability from non-equilibrium thermodynamics, where it designates a state within a dynamical system which is simply other than that system's ground state, or state of lowest energy. Simondon adapts this idea to posit a 'metastable system' as that in which there is a potential energy engendered by a disparity between distinct orders of magnitude, such as find themselves in need of resolution. It is this disparity or 'disparation' between discontinuous structural orders which individuation seeks to resolve, actualising an individual as the 'solution' to an energetic tension which is fundamentally 'problematic'. As Simondon explains, in this light:

> Individuation must [...] be considered as a partial and relative resolution that manifests in a system which contains potentials and includes a certain incompatibility with respect to itself, an incompatibility that consists of forces of tension and the impossibility of an interaction between the extreme terms of the dimensions. (I, 4)

In this context, processes of individuation express certain pre-individual structural realities, concretising new dimensions or relations in order to resolve the tensions engendered by their discontinuity.

One of Simondon's preferred examples, as we have already briefly seen, is that of *crystallisation*, which sees a crystal, starting from an initial germ or seed, organise a supersaturated 'mother liquor' through the progressive polarisation of its molecules – as such rendering it solid (I, 81–2). Each layer of crystallised liquid serves as a basis for the crystallisation of further layers, in a series of progressive phases which Simondon will also describe as a process of 'transduction'. Transduction indicates

> a physical, biological, mental, or social operation through which an activity propagates incrementally within a domain by basing this propagation on a structuration of the domain operated from one region to another: each structural region serves as a principle and model, as an initiator for constituting the following region, such that a modification thereby extends throughout the structuring operation. (I, 13)

In its resonances with induction and deduction, transduction also suggests a mode of thought – a means of articulating the simultaneous individuation of thought alongside its objects. At whatever register it is grasped, transduction or individuation is instigated by an initial seed or causal 'event', which Simondon calls a 'structural germ' or 'singularity' (I, 81). The singularity, not to be confused with the individual or the process of individuation itself, designates the catalytic moment at which an element from *outside* the system is inserted, transforming what was a stable, equilibrium state into a metastable state in need of resolution. This germinal event, importantly, acts as *information*, engendering the polarisation or organisation of the system while delimiting both an inside – the process of individuation – and an outside – the metastable state – which are only retroactively perceptible once this process has distributed them. The seed is 'information' in the sense that the particular structural imperatives it brings into the system make it 'the origin of an active orientation that is progressively imposed' (*I*, 79), such that the singularity can be usefully understood as containing a kind of virtual, structural blueprint, progressively actualised through activity in the metastable system.

The implications of this model are multiple and complex, but we might underline just two key dimensions here. First, for Simondon, an individual, or process of individuation, is thus always the 'event' of discontinuity in what was a hitherto stable situation. And second, individuation, at whatever level it is considered – be it physical, biological, psychological or social – is always *ecological*, delimiting both a process of individuation and the metastable state within which it is effected. Considered in this light, matter, far from passively 'receiving' a form, is an active participant in processes of information, undergoing energetic phase-shifts which transform – or rather transduce – being in accordance with a distribution of pre-individual structural imperatives.

Simondon thus develops a concept of information which might multilaterally account for the genesis of individuals conceived in the broadest possible sense, deploying information as a fundamental ontogenetic principle. Bypassing the debates in cybernetics around the materiality or immateriality of information,[35] its human or non-human status, Simondon conceives of information as an operative process in matter, the modality by which matter is able to individuate and in so doing become other than it is. In this context, the cybernetic approach to information is philosophically inadequate, given its dedication to a purely technocratic image of information transmission as between ostensibly static and predetermined individuals, such as might be modelled by the mathematics of probability. The problem with this model from a philosophical perspective is its ontological naivety, and a sense that transmission is not always and irrevocably *transduction* or *individuation*: the creation of an entirely new state of affairs. Or, as Simondon explains:

> Relation can never be conceived as a relation between preexisting terms, since it is a reciprocal regime of information exchange and of causality in a system that individuates. Relation exists physically, biologically, psychologically, collectively as the internal resonance of the individuated being; relation expresses individuation and is at the being's centre. (I, 352)

Information conceived in terms of a communication of probability is not sufficient to account for such geneses, a fact which limits cybernetics to a study of pre-distributed, 'closed' systems of the transmitter/receiver type. For Simondon, indeed, as we have said, information is *improbable* – given its transcendence of a given or actualised state of affairs and its production of a situation which could never have been fully determined in advance.

Certainly, individuations can be more or less homogeneous with their conditions, or the pre-individual domains within which they take place. Some individuations are more dramatic and unexpected than others, which is why probabilistic models work in certain limited situations. In this context, Simondon proposes a vocabulary of the 'tension' of information, which might account for the qualitative or differential intensity of a particular process of individuation or transduction, its potential for propagation throughout 'increasingly varied and heterogeneous domains'. As Simondon explains:

> The difference between this hypothesis and that of information theory is the fact *that a theory of the tension of information is proportional to a schema's capacity to be received as information by receivers that are not defined in advance.* Thus, while a probabilistic theory can be applied to the measurement of the quantity of information in the prediction of an exchange between emitter and receiver, a measurement of the tension of information could hardly occur except through experimentation...
> (I, 689)

This amounts to a suggestion that purely statistical accounts of information as a probabilistic category neglect certain speculative and aesthetic dimensions of conceptualisation which are more properly those of experimental science, philosophy or art. The 'tension' of information in a particular system can only be grasped through an experimentation with the parameters and materials of that system, in a movement which understands its potential individuations as radically indeterminate.

While Simondon's concerns therefore extend far beyond information *technics*, they are nevertheless essential to his thought as a kind of expressive material. Information technology provides us with a new vocabulary with which to build concepts, but this boon depends upon philosophy's reciprocal embrace of a style of thinking which is attentive to the unique meaning of technical objects and realities. In *On the Mode of Existence of Technical Objects*, Simondon turns to communication technics explicitly, suggesting that information theory engenders a kind of paradox here, given that it depends upon the maximisation of an aleatory ground (the field of possible messages) yet constitutes information which is *meaningful* to the extent that it is systematised. As he explains:

> Information is, in a sense, that which can be infinitely varied, that which, in order to be transmitted with the least possible loss, requires a sacrifice of energy efficiency so as to avoid any reduction of the range of possibilities... But information, in another sense, is that which, in order to be transmitted, must be above the level of pure random phenomena, such as white noise or thermal agitation; information is then that which possesses a regularity, a localisation, a defined domain, a determined stereotypy through which information distinguishes itself from pure chance.[36]

In this context, information can be understood as a 'third way' between form – as systematised, meaningful content – and pure chance, understood as the variability to which individuals are open at the level of pre-individual metastable states. Or as Simondon explains, 'information is not form, nor is it a collection [*ensemble*] of forms; it is the variability of forms, the influx of variation with respect to form'[37] in a model which cybernetics has failed to properly grasp.

For Simondon, as we have seen, this approach offers up a vocabulary which might help us to think the processual ontogenesis of individuals, conceived in the broadest possible sense. Information is variation or difference in the process of structuration – a process which is never fully completed given that individuation is always ecologically situated. But Simondon is also interested in distinguishing processes of *vital* and *psychological* individuation from those which are strictly physio-chemical, such that he will posit living beings as a particular kind of informatic 'transducer'.[38] While all individuation is transduction, the term also has a particular, noetic sense, indicating the creativity via which the living thing takes *itself* as a source of information, self-regulating as a kind of 'metastable system', and as such a rich theatre for further individuations. As Simondon explains:

> Indeed the living thing is not exactly a transducer like those that can be found in machines; it is that and something more; mechanical transducers are systems with a margin of indeterminacy; information is that which adds determinacy. But this information must be given to the transducer; it cannot invent it; it is given to it by a mechanism that is analogous to that of perception in the living... On the contrary, the living thing has the capacity to give itself information, even in the absence of all perception, because it possesses the capacity to modify the forms of the problems to be resolved; for the machine, there are no problems, only data that modulate the transducers...[39]

This latter contention is key, inasmuch as it establishes the unique characteristics of the 'informatic machine' that is the living being – that is, a being possessed of a capacity to *problematise*. In significant passages, Simondon thus advances a distinctly Bergsonian account of problematisation, which sees the living being, unlike the machine, derive information temporally, or rather from the *virtual*.[40] As Simondon explains, for the machine,

> there is no modification of forms that would be oriented by the presentiment of a problem to be resolved; the virtual does not act upon the actual, because the virtual, insofar as it is virtual, cannot play a role for the machine. It can only react to something that is positively given, actually done. The living thing has the faculty to modify itself according to the virtual: this faculty is the sense of time, which the machine does not have because it does not live.[41]

As such, and as we have seen via recourse to Deleuze's three syntheses of time, problematisation requires a noetic movement *beyond* the actual, into the virtual, such as serves to confront the empirically given with its limits and contingency, propelling us to think the given in such a way that it might become *other than it is*. The cybernetic model, according to which the processing of actualised differences – *data* – might give an account not only of computational functions, but also the synaptic and electro-chemical operations of 'thought', neglects this properly temporal character of thinking, such as splits the subject, forcing it to become *other than itself*.

This is not to return to a kind of anthropocentric valorisation of human mentation as a privileged metaphysical site, nor to retreat into vitalism in the face of a 'machinic' cybernetics of thought. The problem, indeed, for Simondon as for Deleuze, is that the cybernetic model retains a *distinctly human* – which is to say pre-philosophical and *doxic* – model of thinking as a sensory-motor process of 'transmission' between already recognised terms. Philosophical thought, however, in order to consummate its project of breaking with *doxa*, must rather be *creative* – which is to say, it involves engendering transductive processes between terms which are *not* pre-distributed, which must rather be created or described by the very movements of transduction. This kind of noetic individuation is not guaranteed, and we might recall Simondon's vocabulary of the *tension* of information – the extent to which a given process of information might produce heterodox and unexpected individuations, describing radically unforeseen 'receivers'.

If the question of the tension of information is not statistical, this is because it is ultimately *aesthetic*, such that it might be meaningfully explored from the perspective of the 'experiments' of art. Here, we find a similar concept operating under a different name, and designating the productive interpolation of 'pure chance' such as dislocates form or meaning, producing hitherto unthinkable individuals. Interestingly, this concept is also articulated by information theory, albeit here as a deleterious environmental presence which communication systems need to be protected against. In these contexts, it is called *noise* – the chaotic and a-signifying content which disrupts a given semantic system. But in turning to accounts of noise in both the mathematical theory of communication and modern art, we find a means of reconceiving communication *as individuation*, and as such, perhaps, of approaching a uniquely digital outside.

Noise in the MTC

We've seen that systems modelled in terms of the MTC require the presence of 'uncertainty' in order to transmit information. This uncertainty is conceived in terms of probability space distributions, which is to say, of *possibility*, a term both Deleuze and Simondon will follow Bergson in criticising. For a system to communicate information in terms of the MTC (as reduction of data deficit), this system depends upon a pre-distribution of possibilities, paradigmatically a 'shared alphabet' which informer and informee might use to encode and decode signals respectively. The maximisation of 'uncertainty' pursued by Shannon and Weaver is thus a maximisation of possible combinations of this shared alphabet or vocabulary, at every point in the communication system's architecture. This shared or pre-distributed ground of possible messages thus determines the nature and limits of the content a communication system is able to transmit – which is to say, the types of individuals it is able to engender.

We may recall though that the *possible* – according to a critique which Deleuze takes up from Bergson – is a concept of dubious philosophical worth, the source of false problems, given its retroactive derivation from the actual. As Deleuze explains in *Bergsonism*:

> the possible is a false notion, the source of false problems ... we give ourselves a real that is ready-made, preformed, pre-existent to itself, and that will pass into existence according to an order of successive limitations. Everything is already *completely given*: all of the real in the image, in the pseudo-actuality of the possible.[42]

It is this dimension of the possible which obscures the intensive and unthinkable processes which determine *becoming* – occluding a thought of genuine novelty or difference. Rather than the real resembling the possible, Deleuze claims that it is the possible that retrospectively resembles the real, 'because it has been abstracted from the real once made, arbitrarily abstracted from the real like a sterile double'.[43] But what is given is not the possible, nor is it the real, at least not in its entirety. Rather it is the *actual*, which must be opposed not to the possible but to the virtual that it actualises. While the possible resembles the actual, the virtual, as we have seen, can bear no such resemblance, given that this amounts to something like an organism resembling its own DNA. As such, Deleuze will claim, under the arid rubric of the possible, 'we no longer understand anything either of the mechanism of difference or of the mechanism of creation';[44] nothing, in other words, of time conceived as actualisation of the virtual.

But is the MTC really dedicated exclusively to 'possible' and as such predetermined messages, rendering it inextricable from an image of information as control, or the replication of certain highly formalised individuations? In what follows I'd like to suggest that the MTC articulates its own image of the unthinkable, or outside – albeit in a form that it tries actively to suppress. Information theory's account of *noise*, I claim, not only suggests the inevitable presence of certain unthinkable materials – transforming probabilistic 'uncertainty' into radical, albeit sensible, indeterminacy – but also renders problematic the distinction between semantic and purely technical information, drawing out the limits of information theory's ostensible 'neutrality'.

For in spite of their insistence on the distinction between semantic and technical problems confronted by information theory, Shannon and Weaver's formulation of information does indeed evoke normative semantic criteria. The entwined 'freedom' and 'uncertainty' identified by the MTC abide only in specific and predetermined ways, as Weaver reveals in his introduction of the idea of signal noise:

> If noise is introduced, then the received message contains certain distortions, certain errors, certain extraneous material, that would certainly lead one to say that the received message exhibits, because of the effects of noise, an increased uncertainty. But if the uncertainty is increased, the information is increased, and this sounds as though the noise were beneficial![45]

The technical problem of information transmission is thus inextricably linked to a semantic problem, whereby 'some information is spurious and undesirable and has been introduced via the noise. To get the useful information in the received signal we must subtract out this spurious information.'[46] The concept of noise thus introduces an ambiguity into the MTC's account of uncertainty, given that there is both 'desirable' uncertainty (freedom of choice in selecting a message) and 'undesirable' uncertainty (interposed by errors and noise).[47] And this 'undesirable uncertainty' may well point us back in the direction of virtuality and the outside.

As Shannon and Weaver acknowledge, there can be no information without noise. The very technicity of information technologies, which imply temporal and kinetic dimensions, means that they are constantly, to varying degrees, 'open' to the presence of noise.[48] All technology generates noise – in the form of dust, tics and glitches, the thermodynamic functioning of machines, the accumulated loss of fidelity as signals travel down wires and through computational-mechanic processes of encoding and decoding. The presence of noise, however, rather than being merely an undesirable operative remainder in information transmission systems, opens the otherwise rigorously technical posing of the problems of the MTC onto the semantic register. As we have noted, via Weaver, noise may still be conceived as information, but it is 'unwanted' information, in the sense that it does not accord with the original content of the message (or the intentions of the informer). Noise is *unintentional*, and is produced as an empirical consequence of the spatio-temporal transmission of data. But data, in the pre-semantic terms we have encountered in Floridi, Bateson et al., need not have any predetermined systematisation – referring simply to instances of difference or discontinuity which might be subsequently interpreted *as information*. As such, noise – or undesirable information – is still data at the ontological level, the informational 'difference which makes a difference', to return to Bateson's phrase.

In this sense, information theory affords us two forms of information, one, 'desirable' according to the predetermined parameters of the transmission system, the other, 'undesirable' and undetermined, the 'infinite variation' of form which Simondon associates with ontogenesis. In this context, it is as if information theory has spooked – opening itself, via probabilistic statistics, onto the infinite variation or becoming of the pre-individual plane of immanence, before closing up again and retreating into a kind of sensory-motor paradigm. The semantic understanding of information returns to adjudicate between two forms of information, the one 'wanted' and useful, the other 'unwanted' and as such meaningless.

Indeed Shannon's project, dedicated as it is to practical applications in communications engineering, is squarely oriented around the identification and mitigation of this latter kind of information, which he is able to calculate in the case of known signals, and as such, to ameliorate with the subsequent addition of *redundancy*.[49] The requirements and parameters of a given informatic system, however, and as such the semantic decision as to which aspects might be considered useful and which are unwanted, remain both contestable and contingent. Indeed, as Peter Krapp has noted, perhaps the only discernible difference between noise and signal is that of intentionality, as he explains via an intuitive example: 'Though arguably musical, an orchestra tuning up is generally considered to be noise, but the clapping of an audience, a form of white noise, is taken to be meaningful and, hence, signal.'[50] And while the intentions of both information theory and cybernetics have thus formed a particular image of information – such as attempts to exclude aleatory or environmentally produced differences in signals – they also open up a way of thinking about information as an unintentional phenomenon, such as we find valorised in art.

Art indeed, and modern art in particular, has long been dedicated to questions of intentionality, and to opening up the syntax of a given semiotic system to disordering and aleatory processes in a reciprocal movement of deterritorialisation and reterritorialisation. In this context, the mixture of noise and signal is no longer a *problem* – at least not in the quotidian sense of that term – but rather a productive and genetic encounter such as we see valorised by Simondon or Deleuze. Modern art and philosophical aesthetics have increasingly turned to this connection between noise and information, using it to rearticulate a long-standing idea of aesthetic experience as that which overspills the intensions or interiority of any given subject. Umberto Eco, for example, has explored the parallels between poetics and information theory, writing, in *The Open Work*:

> This phenomenon, the direct relationship between disorder and information, is of course the norm in art. It is commonly believed that the poetic word is characterised by its capacity to create unusual meanings and emotions by establishing new relationships between sound and sense, words and sounds, one phrase and the next – to the point that an emotion can often emerge even in the absence of any clear meaning.[51]

Likewise, John Cage, whose experiments constitute perhaps the best-known project to redraw the limits of music through its admixture with noise, outlines his objective thus:

> Invade areas where nothing's definite (areas-micro and macro-adjacent the one we know in). It won't sound like music – serial or electronic. It'll sound like what we hear when we're not hearing music, just hearing whatever wherever we happen to be. But to accomplish this our technological means must be constantly changing.[52]

Cage's long-standing project – alongside others like Pierre Henry, Karlheinz Stockhausen, La Monte Young, and non-musicians like Artaud and Yves Klein – was to thoroughly problematise any auditory demarcation between noise and music. And indeed this experimentalism has been replicated throughout the twentieth century in more popular forms like rock and jazz, with their gradual movements into amplified and a-tonal dissonance. From Jimi Hendrix to The Stooges, Miles Davis to Alice Coltrane, popular musicians have probed the expressive potentials of noisy materials, often in the context of a politicised incredulity towards 'official' or hegemonic semiotic systems. As the experience of modern music suggests, *noise* can indeed be deployed to simultaneously dislocate and redistribute such systems, articulating their contingency and limits. It is via recourse to such practices, and an aesthetic conception of noise, that we will therefore now proceed, before returning to the digital image.

The Art of Noise

Emerging from the Latin *nausea* – via a Middle English connotation of 'quarrelling' or dispute – the word noise has historically designated a certain 'failure to communicate',[53] resulting from an unintentional or unwanted a-signifying content present in a message or signal (understood in the broadest possible sense). And while noise has thus tended to be understood as undesirable or unpleasant, certain aesthetic practices begin to valorise it with modernity. The reasons for this development are multiple and complex, but we might identify two key factors here: first, a generalised crisis in traditional forms of legitimation or 'order', which opens up a new idea of art as experimentation and novelty – a movement that we might follow Lyotard in articulating as a transition from an aesthetics of the *beautiful* to one of the *sublime*;[54] and second – in an intimately related evolution – the development of mechanical reproducibility, which calls into question the privileged agency or intentionality of the artist.

In this context, modern art begins to articulate a new relationship between formalised systems and empirical or environmental factors, which increasingly feature in works as an irreducible and even traumatic presence destabilising a habitual (formal) order. Douglas Kahn has written that 'noise can be understood in one sense to be that constant grating sound generated by the movement between the abstract and the empirical',[55] and indeed, in understanding noise as a kind of indeterminacy between abstract – which is to say, systematised – content and empirical, random and environmental forces, we begin to grasp the role it plays in the modern aesthetic paradigm. As Kahn explains:

> Imperfections in script, verbal pauses, and poor phrasing are regularly passed over in the greater purpose of communication, yet they always threaten to break out into an impassable noise and cause real havoc. As a precautionary measure, such local impurities are subsumed under a communication presumed to be successful, even if many important details and larger associations are lost in the process. The process of abstraction itself, what is lost, is thereby involved in the elimination of noise. Noise in this way is the specific, the empirical...[56]

To transpose this claim into the terms of the MTC, we might say that intentional messages always require a certain abstraction, in accordance with a pre-distributed realm of 'possibilities' which constitutes 'good', or 'common sense'. But noise, as an empirical, singular and aleatory environmental presence, consistently menaces this good sense, threatening predetermined possibility with the potential for new and aberrant messages, external to all intentionality on the part of the transmitter.

Futurist painter Luigi Russolo offers us one of the richest accounts of this schism between 'abstract' sound and 'empirical', singular noise in his 1913 manifesto 'The Art of Noises', composed as a letter to his friend and fellow futurist Francesco Balilla Pratella. Russolo, in the spirit of twentieth-century avant-gardism – which in the forms of dada, surrealism and art brut had turned increasingly to aleatory and non-intentional forms of creativity – argues that industrialisation calls for new creative practices commensurate with the phenomena of mechanisation, urbanisation and the demise of a traditional bourgeois artist-subject. Noise, Russolo suggests, arrives at just this juncture, constituting a new phenomenon which might help us to rethink the very function and origins of art.

Apart from very rare events like storms and avalanches, and aside from circumscribed and ritualistic instances of music, Russolo claims that the pre-industrial world was essentially noiseless, writing: 'Ancient life was all silence. In the nineteenth century, with the invention of the machine, Noise was born. Today, Noise triumphs and reigns supreme over the sensibility of men.'[57] The industrial revolution, claims Russolo, caused noise to proliferate everywhere, and music, in its gradual movement towards dissonance and atonality – as practised by contemporary composers like Schoenberg, Prokofiev and Bartók – is itself moving towards the raw principle of a 'noise music', as Russolo explains:

> At first the art of music sought and achieved purity, limpidity and sweetness of sound. Then different sounds were amalgamated, care being taken, however, to caress the ear with gentle harmonies. Today music, as it becomes continually more complicated, strives to amalgamate the most dissonant, strange and harsh sounds. In this way we come ever closer to noise-sound. This musical evolution is paralleled by the multiplication of machines, which collaborate with man on every front. Not only in the roaring atmosphere of major cities, but in the country too, which until yesterday was normally silent, the machine today has created such a variety and rivalry of noises that pure sound, in its exiguity and monotony, no longer arouses any feeling.[58]

And despite its emergence from an industrial milieu, Russolo is at pains to identify noise with a certain organic primacy, such as has been obscured by 'institutional' art and cultural formalisation. In its immediacy and irreducibility, noise, he claims, is at odds with the transcendent and elitist objectives of 'sound'. As he explains, in a passage which is not un-Deleuzian:

Cybernetic Information

> Noise [...] has the power to conjure up life itself. Sound, alien to our life, always musical and a thing unto itself, an occasional but unnecessary element, has become to our ears what the overfamiliar face is to our eyes. Noise, however, reaching us in a confused and irregular way from the irregular confusion of our life, never entirely reveals itself to us, and keeps innumerable surprises in reserve.[59]

This distinction – between the abstractions or calcifications of an institutional *art* and the productive and multiple cacophony of *life* – maps onto the Deleuzian injunction that thought should seek its provocations in the unexpected and differential intensities which we are as yet incapable of thinking. Importantly, Russolo is responding to the same set of techno-historical factors which render a particular mode of signification problematic, and which will ultimately give birth to the cinematographic image: the birth of photography – which forces visual art to abdicate its 'representational' function and turn to the question of its own idiosyncratic ontogenesis. More than this, the 'art of noises' is industrial in the same way as cinema – massively reproducible and proliferating to ever larger publics disjunctive events in sensibility and thought.

Russolo remains a key reference for an avant-garde tradition dedicated to letting processual, aleatory and environmental factors (co)determine the structure of artworks. Examples are plentiful, but perhaps one of the most illustrative in this context is Alvin Lucier's sound work *I am Sitting in a Room* (1969), in which the artist records himself reading a short text before replaying this recording back into the room. The text spoken is as follows:

> I am sitting in a room different from the one you are in now. I am recording the sound of my speaking voice and I am going to play it back into the room again and again until the resonant frequencies of the room reinforce themselves so that any semblance of my speech, with perhaps the exception of rhythm, is destroyed. What you will hear, then, are the natural resonant frequencies of the room articulated by speech. I regard this activity not so much as a demonstration of a physical fact, but more as a way to smooth out any irregularities my speech might have.[60]

This last remark, a reference to Lucier's own stutter, constitutes a wry nod to the 'non-intentional' slippages and dislocations which reside at the heart of speech, and which are passed over in the interest of communication. As promised, this replay is itself re-recorded, the process repeating again and again until, after around fifteen minutes, the words have become unintelligible and all we are left with is the strangely beautiful resonant harmonies of the room. Given that all enclosed areas have unique resonant characteristics, which in this case are reinforced by each subsequent replay of the recording, we might say that in effect, Lucier – via the recording technology at his disposal – plays the room itself as an instrument, opening the semantic content of his message onto the entropic processes immanent to the signal's transmission through a circumscribed space-time. Symbiotically, the a-signifying, entropic noise of the universe is folded back into the signifying practice of Lucier's art, *in-forming* a new 'individual' in the form of the work – to which a plurality of other artists have since responded.[61]

Indeed, as Eco rightly notes, it is not sufficient to establish a simple dualism between information-as-indeterminacy and 'meaningful' structures or semantic formalisation. Artistic practices, even those which take as their materials the noisy content that lies beyond pre-established signifying regimes, work to incorporate and organise these materials, subjecting them to what Eco describes as a 'new kind of organisation'. As he explains, in the context of literature and poetry:

> The concept of information is useful here only to clarify one of the directions of aesthetic discourse, which is then affected by other organising factors. That is, all deviation from the most banal linguistic order entails a new kind of organisation, *which can be considered as disorder in relation to the previous organisation, and as order in relation to the parameters of a new discourse.*[62]

It should be noted, however, that the 'ordering' principles of contemporary art differ from those of classical art, inasmuch as they maintain an essentially parasitic relationship with the previous order – enacting a bipolar movement between disordering practices and the order of the system which gives birth to them. As Eco continues:

> In fact, one might say that rather than imposing a new system, contemporary art constantly oscillates between the rejection of the traditionally linguistic system and its preservation – for if contemporary art imposed a totally new linguistic system, then its discourse would cease to be communicable. The dialectic between form and the *possibility* of multiple meanings, which constitutes the very essence of the "open work," takes place in this oscillation.[63]

We might here recall Simondon's postulation of information – understood in an ontogenetic sense – as offering a kind of 'third way' between systematised content and pure chance or variation; a process

Cybernetic Information

via which new organisations or individuations take place. Indeed the 'open work'[64] to which Eco gestures constitutes an aesthetic assemblage which might render this image of ontogenesis explicit – producing a high 'tension' of information in its ambiguous capacities for connecting with all manner of as-yet-indeterminate receivers. Central to such an aesthetic practice is a production and foregrounding of *noise*, which becomes a key concept that we might use to think becoming or individuation across media, from poetry and music to digital and cinematic images.

And indeed, twentieth-century avant-garde film-making is replete with 'noisy' experiments, like the short films of Stan Brakhage and Marie Menken, both of whom deploy aleatory, non-intentional and environmental elements to 'co-produce' their work. Brakhage's films *Mothlight* (1963) and *Dog Star Man* (1961–64) incorporate over-exposures, negative scratching, blurring, and various physical degradations of film stock in order to depict the fallible and bodily elements of consciousness and memory. Menken's play with superimposition, over- and under-exposure, fast and slow motion, blurring and wavering hand-held camera – revolutionary at the time of her early films – constitutes a lilting fabric of quotidian imagery, reified as impressionistic time-images across films like *Go! Go! Go!* (1962–64) and *Lights* (1966). But such films, we might argue, depend upon their bodily presence as film stock, and a direct, indexical relation to environmental factors that leave their fingerprints. How might we conceive of images which use digital means and media in a similar way? What does noise look like in the *digital image*, and how might this noise serve to provoke and displace our thinking? To answer these questions, we must turn to *Inland Empire*, where we encounter both a new, digital time-image, and an informatic outside.

Notes

1. Deleuze, *Two Regimes*, p. 320.
2. L. Floridi, *Information: A Very Short Introduction* (Oxford: Oxford University Press, 2010), p. 6.
3. Quoted in ibid.
4. Floridi, *Philosophy of Information*, p. 42.
5. Ibid., p. 80.
6. Ibid., p. 31.
7. K. Faucher, *Metastasis and Metastability: A Deleuzian Approach to Information* (Rotterdam: Sense Publishers, 2013), p. 7.

8. I have elected not to treat in-depth the mathematics of information, given not only the limits of my own abilities in this space, but also the central focus and interests of this work, which ultimately lie elsewhere. I refer the interested reader to clear, authoritative treatments of the mathematics underpinning both Wiener and Shannon's work in J. R. Pierce, *An Introduction to Information Theory: Symbols, Signals and Noise (Second Edition)* (New York: Dover, 1980).
9. S. Ballard, 'Information, Noise, et al.', in M. Nunes (ed.), *Error: Glitch, Noise and Jam in New Media Cultures* (New York: Continuum, 2011), p. 61.
10. Ibid., p. 61.
11. Shannon and Weaver, *Mathematical Theory*, p. 9.
12. See L. Floridi, 'Semantic Conceptions of Information', in *Stanford Encyclopedia of Philosophy* (summer 2019 edition), ed. E. N. Zalta, https://plato.stanford.edu/archives/sum2019/entries/information-semantic/
13. Shannon and Weaver, *Mathematical Theory*, p. 7.
14. Ibid., p. 31.
15. Floridi, *A Very Short Introduction*, p. 43.
16. Although for this perhaps confusing association we may well have mathematician and physicist Jon von Neumann to thank, given his advice to Shannon that: 'You should call it entropy for two reasons: first, the function is already in use in thermodynamics under the same name; second, and more importantly, most people don't know what entropy really is, and if you use the word *entropy* in an argument you will win every time.' Quoted in ibid., p. 42.
17. Ibid., p. 62.
18. Floridi, *Philosophy of Information*, p. 86.
19. Cybernetics, indeed, is a relatively niche discipline today – a fact that is perhaps surprising given the massive proliferation of the kinds of human–machine assemblages it initially emerged to theorise. As D. A. Novikov has noted, however, a proliferation of subdisciplines and particular applications in diverse fields of study has systematically deflated the vision of a unified systems theory immanent to 'golden-age' cybernetics of the 1950s–60s. In this sense, the 'failure' of cybernetics has also been its immense success, with key concepts like information, control and feedback taken up by a bewildering diversity of research paradigms and disciplines. See D. A. Novikov, *Cybernetics: From Past to Future* (Cham: Springer, 2016), pp. 13–20.
20. Wiener, *The Human Use*, p. 62.
21. N. Wiener, *Cybernetics: or Control and Communication in the Animal and the Machine* (Cambridge, MA: MIT Press, 1985), p. 14.
22. G. Bateson, *Steps to an Ecology of Mind* (New York: Ballantine Books, 1978), p. 315.

23 Ibid.
24 Ibid. In order to explain this association of 'bit' and 'idea', Bateson evokes the example of someone felling a tree with an axe, whereby feedback loops help to adjust this person's motions commensurate with changes in the face of the tree. Thus, explains Bateson, in the context of this circuitry of person–axe–tree: 'we should spell the matter out as: (differences in tree) – (differences in retina) – (differences in brain) – (differences in muscles) – (differences in movement of axe) – (differences in tree), etc. What is transmitted around the circuit is transforms of differences. And, as noted above, a difference which makes a difference is an *idea* or unit of information.' Ibid., p. 318.
25 Wiener, *The Human Use*, pp. 36–40.
26 Wiener was well aware that his work on the technics of command-and-control systems was intimately related to the interests of the American military-industrial complex and the looming prospect of global nuclear war. His own participation in the war effort must be understood in the context of his fervent opposition to fascism, an attitude that he was unwilling to extend to Soviet communism. In a 1947 open letter to *The Atlantic Monthly* entitled 'A Scientist Rebels', Wiener thus responded to a request for his work from a scientist working on guided missiles: 'When [...] you turn to me for information concerning controlled missiles, there are several considerations which determine my reply. In the past, the comity of scholars has made it a custom to furnish scientific information to any person seriously seeking it. However, we must face these facts: The policy of the government itself during and after the war, say in the bombing of Hiroshima and Nagasaki, has made it clear that to provide scientific information is not a necessarily innocent act, and may entail the gravest consequences. One therefore cannot escape reconsidering the established custom of the scientist to give information to every person who may inquire of him. The interchange of ideas which is one of the great traditions of science must of course receive certain limitations when the scientist becomes an arbiter of life and death.' N. Wiener, 'A Scientist Rebels', *The Atlantic Monthly*, January 1947, p. 46.
27 As Simondon writes, in his introduction to *On the Mode of Existence of Technical Objects*: 'The technical object, taking the place of the slave and being treated as such across relations of property and custom, has only partially liberated man: the technical object possesses a power of alienation because it is itself in a state of alienation, one more essential than economic or social alienation. The importance of technical objects in contemporary cultures requires philosophical thought to make the effort of reducing technological alienation by introducing into culture a representation and scale of values adequate to the essence of technical objects.' Simondon, *Mode of Existence*, p. xiii.

28 Simondon claims that this distinction is linked to the division of labour according to which free men or citizens are responsible for a kind of formal knowledge which is communicated to the class of slaves, who implement this knowledge in the context of various material substrates. While there are some accomplished treatments of Simondon's political philosophy (see, for instance, A. Bardin, *Epistemology and Political Philosophy in Gilbert Simondon: Individuation, Technics, Social Systems* [Dordrecht: Springer, 2015]), the theme of slavery in his work has remained relatively underexplored, particularly as it might relate to contemporary projects dealing with the legacies of trans-Atlantic slavery in critical race theory, Afro-pessimism and so on. There remain important connections to be made in this space, given what we might characterise as a broader tendency in Western thought to fabricate concepts through classed, gendered and racialised mechanisms of exclusion.

29 The reasons for Simondon's relative obscurity – both during his working life and after his death – are complex and multiple, but arguably stem from his dedication to relatively unfashionable questions related to both technicity and ancient metaphysics, in a French intellectual milieu dominated first by existentialism and phenomenology, and later by Marxism and psychoanalysis.

30 Simondon defines allagmatics as a 'theory of operations', able to account for the qualitative transformations or translations already present in information theory. But whereas information theory remains dedicated to relatively simple translations like, for instance, that of light waves into symbolic and as such spatial media, a universal theory of operations would need to account for translations or *transductions* between multiple and reciprocally determining temporal processes and spatial structures. As Simondon explains, 'allagmatics must be related to information theory, which contemplates the translation of temporal sequences into spatial organisation or vice versa; yet, since it proceeds on this point like Gestalt theory, information theory instead contemplates the already given sequences or configurations and can hardly define the conditions of their genesis. On the contrary, what must be contemplated is absolute genesis, like the mutual exchanges of forms, structures, and temporal sequences. Such a theory could then become the shared foundation of Information theory and Gestalt theory in Physics' (*I*, 263).

31 Quoted in Faucher, *Metastasis and Metastability*, p. 41.

32 For a thoughtful discussion of the ways in which Deleuze's approach to information – alongside his broader aesthetic modernism and a sense of art as that which short-circuits intellectual response – renders his thought perhaps incompatible with subsequent trajectories in contemporary art (in particular conceptual art), see S. Zepke, 'A Work of

Art Does Not Contain the Least Bit of Information', in S. van Tuinen and S. Zepke (eds), *Art History After Deleuze and Guattari* (Leuven: Leuven University Press, 2017), pp. 145–64.

33 Recent years have seen a huge amount of interest in Simondon's work in the Anglophone world, where translations of his work had not been forthcoming. The short pieces 'Technical Mentality' and 'Techno Aesthetics' were translated by Arne De Boever, and published in *Parrhesia* in 2009 and 2012 respectively. 'The Essence of Technicity' appeared, translated by Ninian Mellamphy, Dan Mellamphy and Nandita Biswas Mellamphy, in *Deleuze Studies* in 2011. The collection *Gilbert Simondon: Being and Technology*, edited by De Boever, constituted the first book-length study of Simondon published in English, in 2012. It was not until 2017 that *On the Mode of Existence of Technical Objects*, translated by Cécile Malaspina and John Rogove, became the first of Simondon's major works to be published in full, in English.

34 According to this theory, matter (*hyle*) and form (*morphe*) pre-exist their entanglement, and as such, partake in the same mode of being as the individual which they constitute. Simondon, however, claims that this model neglects not only the alternate form that matter takes prior to a given individuation, but also the materiality involved in any given form. For Simondon, the formation of an individual is thus properly understood via recourse to the differential energetic conditions which constitute a metastable state.

35 For more on this, see Faucher, *Metastasis and Metastability*, p. 42.

36 Simondon, *Mode of Existence*, p. 148.

37 Ibid., p. 150.

38 In the broadest possible terms, a transducer is a device which converts energy from one form into another – for example an amplifier, which translates variations in electrical current into sound vibrations.

39 Ibid., p. 156.

40 Simondon's explicit engagements with Bergson are generally critical, and amount to a claim that the latter's thought privileges temporal 'operations' over discontinuous and spatially discrete elements of structure, paradigmatically the disparate orders of structural magnitude which call for resolution in the form of a new individual. Nevertheless, we find a number of striking conceptual resonances right throughout their *oeuvres*, not least among them a clear articulation of Simondon's project to think processes of individuation over already 'achieved' or temporally circumscribed individuals in the early stages of Bergson's *Creative Evolution*. It should not be forgotten that Simondon, like a whole generation of French 'epistemologists', grew up in an intellectual landscape fundamentally coloured by Bergson's thought. See *Creative Evolution*, pp. 12–13.

41 Simondon, *Mode of Existence*, p. 157.
42 Deleuze, *Bergsonism*, p. 98.
43 Ibid.
44 Ibid.
45 Shannon and Weaver, *Mathematical Theory*, p. 19.
46 Ibid.
47 Ibid.
48 Ballard, 'Information, Noise, et al.', p. 60.
49 Leaving aside the technicalities of informatic 'redundancy', we might say simply that redundancy designates the inclusion of an excess of intended data (message) in the context of noisy or limited channels, in order that the proliferation of 'unwanted' information is counterbalanced by a greater proportion of 'desirable' information, as such making the reception and translation of the originally intended message more likely. As Floridi explains: 'We are more likely to reconstruct a message correctly at the end of the transmission if some degree of redundancy counterbalances the inevitable noise and equivocation introduced by the physical process of communication and the environment. Noise extends the informee's freedom of choice in selecting a message, but it is an undesirable freedom and some redundancy can help to limit it.' Floridi, *A Very Short Introduction*, p. 40.
50 P. Krapp, *Noise Channels: Glitch and Error in Digital Culture* (Minneapolis, MN: University of Minnesota Press, 2011), p. 55.
51 U. Eco, *The Open Work*, trans. A. Cancogni (Cambridge, MA: Harvard University Press, 1989), p. 52.
52 J. Cage, *A Year from Monday: New Lectures and Writings by John Cage* (Middletown, CT: Wesleyan University Press, 1967), p. 27.
53 M. Nunes, 'Error, Noise, and Potential: The Outside of Purpose', in M. Nunes (ed.), *Error: Glitch, Noise and Jam in New Media Cultures* (New York: Continuum, 2011), p. 3.
54 See J. F. Lyotard, 'The Sublime and the Avant-Garde', in C. Cazeau (ed.), *The Continental Aesthetics Reader – 2nd Edition* (New York: Routledge, 2017), pp. 585–97.
55 D. Kahn, *Noise, Water, Meat: A History of Sound in the Arts* (Cambridge, MA: MIT Press, 2001), p. 25.
56 Ibid.
57 L. Russolo, 'The Art of Noises' (excerpts), trans. C. Tisdall, in U. Appollonio (ed.), *Futurist Manifestos* (London: Tate Publishing, 2009), p. 74.
58 Ibid., p. 75.
59 Ibid., p. 85.
60 A. Lucier, *I am Sitting in a Room*, Lovely Music Ltd, New York, 1981.
61 Indeed, Lucier's work has been appropriated in the context of the digital media ecology, with a YouTube user re-enacting the piece in

order to reveal the subterranean architectures of digital encoding – recording himself reciting a text derived from Lucier's, posting the video on YouTube, ripping it from YouTube in mp4 format and reposting it. The user repeats this process 1000 times, until all we are left with is an indistinct collage of digital shapes and sound. As his own script explains: 'what you will see and hear, then, are the artefacts inherent in the video codex of both YouTube and the mp4 format...' 'Ontologist', 'I am Sitting in a Video Room 1000', YouTube, 28 May 2010, https://www.youtube.com/watch?v=8qKz5YW5J-U.

62 Eco, *The Open Work*, p. 60.
63 Ibid.
64 For Eco, the 'open work' is a resolutely contemporary development, indicating an artwork which is essentially unfinished, and as such invites or provokes a kind of creative participation on the part of its performers, readers or spectators. While all artworks arguably invite a kind of free, collaborative apprehension, the open work of the twentieth century is characterised by an artistic practice which tries deliberately to inculcate this 'openness' throughout the work. See ibid., pp. 3–13.

6

Inland Empire

In this chapter, we explore David Lynch's 2006 film *Inland Empire*, treating it as a counterpoint to some of the claims made by both Deleuze and Flaxman about new forms of informatic image. Rather than effecting operations of closure or control, I claim that *Inland Empire* produces a uniquely *digital outside* – forcing us into a series of noetic encounters which simultaneously unground and provoke our thinking. The film achieves this in several key and interconnected ways, first, by foregrounding its own informatic materiality, such that the digitisation of cinema becomes a central conceptual and aesthetic motif. In rendering explicit not only certain new possibilities, but also the aesthetic limits of its own digital form, the film thus enacts experiments analogous to those Blanchot identifies in poetic language – drawing to the surface of the image irreducible, singular and inhuman technical events. These components of the image constitute a kind of digital 'noise', which Lynch works actively to proliferate. Lynch does this at both the semantic *and* the technical registers of his composition, using this noise to produce unthinkable situations and materials.

Second, the film returns to the kind of auto-criticism Deleuze identifies with the cinema of the time-image, foregrounding the problematic facts of contemporary film production, and centralising what Robert Sinnerbrink has called a story about 'Hollywood in trouble'.[1] In producing a nightmarish vision of contemporary Hollywood – its descent into corruption and violence intimately tied to its encounter with new media – Lynch articulates a contemporary politics of information, which, while often oriented by the imperatives of control, tends equally towards overinflation and excess, opening up spaces of chaos and dysfunction. We've seen Deleuze claim that in order to avoid the closure of information systems – opening them up to their outside – we might pose contextual, critical and speculative questions which are the remit of both art and philosophy. 'Going beyond information is achieved on two sides at once', he writes, 'towards two questions: *what is the source and what is the addressee?*' (CII, 276).

Inland Empire

And *Inland Empire*'s protracted criticism – not only of Hollywood as a menacing centre for the distribution of information, but of a whole new media ecology within which it is situated – works towards just these questions. And while the film is not sparing in its depiction of these new mediatic images, its own genesis as a series of fragments intended for Lynch's website suggests that this is what Adorno might call *immanent critique*,[2] a politicised use of contemporary digital aesthetics to explore possibilities for their own overcoming.

Finally, the film uses digital technology to produce 'incompossible' loops of a-chronic temporality, 'splitting' its characters in a mechanism which suggests new forms of informatic subjectivity. The film's characters are dissolved across these temporal loops in various modes of performativity, fantasy and multiple identity, in such a way as impels us to think forms of digital subjectivity which might elude the operations of neoliberal subjectivation and control. This is because these subjects – primarily the complex assemblage composed by and around Laura Dern – ultimately *affirm* this splitting, becoming the agents or authors of this very situation, and suggesting the possibility of a dividual and resistant 'people to come', in a model commensurate with Deleuze's account of the three syntheses of time. On these key and interrelated registers, the film opens up fresh philosophical territories from which we might think *with* digital media, yet *against* tendencies towards control and closure in the informatic image. This dual movement, I claim, is that which might characterise a digital outside.

Synopsis

Before embarking on a discussion of the film, however, we must carefully note the difficulty of any such 'analysis'. As Sinnerbrink has noted, the film actively resists interpretation, 'communicat[ing] an experience of thinking that resists philosophical translation or paraphrase...'.[3] To encounter the film is to encounter *kino-thought* – the outside – and a fragmentary and chaotic structure hostile to theoretical systematisation. As such, the discussion in this chapter does not hope to provide a definitive 'reading' of the film's thematic or aesthetic components. Even if we entertain the idea that the film is able to make some kind of contribution to philosophical thought, we must acknowledge the fact that any attempt to (re)articulate these contributions in the context of written philosophy risks ironing out their specificity and eliding what was valuable about them in the first place.

Deleuze, indeed, acknowledges this very problem in the final pages of *Cinema II*, noting that theoretical works on cinema have always been a fraught proposition. Responding to Godard's remark that the film-makers of the New Wave only ever wrote theoretical texts which were ancillary to their *creative* practice as film-makers, Deleuze suggests that 'this remark does not show a great understanding of what is called theory. For theory too is something which is made, no less than its object' (*CII*, 287). And inasmuch as I hope to argue that the film contributes something to philosophical thinking, it is in the context of an idea of philosophy itself as 'creative practice', commensurate with Deleuze's own methods. As he explains:

> For many people, philosophy is something which is not "made," but is pre-existent, readymade in a prefabricated sky. However, philosophical theory is itself a practice, just as much as its object ... a theory of cinema is not "about" cinema, but about the concepts that cinema gives rise to and which are themselves related to other concepts corresponding to other practices ... it is at the level of the interference of many practices that things happen, beings, images, concepts, all the kinds of events. (*CII*, 287)

As such, my discussion of *Inland Empire* in this chapter does not constitute an 'analysis' in the strict sense. Instead, this chapter responds to the film as a noetic *event* – as an assemblage of both thinkable and unthinkable materials, capable of producing various 'interferences': between art and philosophy, but also between itself and its spectators – as such effecting rhythms and displacements in thought which would not have been possible without such an encounter.

Inland Empire tells the 'story' – though we may not ultimately be justified in using this term – of fading Hollywood actress Nikki Grace (Laura Dern), who hopes to make a comeback by embarking upon a film called *On High in Blue Tomorrows*, which, in typical Lynchian style, we soon learn to be cursed. The film charts the movement by which Nikki becomes gradually indiscernible from the role she is to play – 'Susan Blue', a Southern Belle trapped in an apparently abusive relationship. In a key early scene, Nikki and her co-star Devon Berk (Justin Theroux) sit down with the film's director, Kingsley Stewart (Jeremy Irons) and his laconic assistant Freddy (Harry Dean Stanton), on a vast, empty soundstage for a preliminary read-through of the script. Shortly after beginning their reading, Freddy notices a presence lurking in the shadows of the half-finished set. Running to investigate, Devon hears receding footsteps, and chases the apparent intruder into a corner of the soundstage where they seem to have disappeared, inexplicably, 'where', in Devon's words, 'it's hard to disappear'.[4]

This unsettling event provokes Stewart to disclose his knowledge that *On High in Blue Tomorrows* is fact a remake of an unfinished German feature entitled *47*, whose two lead actors were murdered. The script, he informs us, is apparently the subject of an old Polish gypsy hex, a fact the studio has kept from those involved. As Stewart explains, gesturing to his right-hand man:

> Now, Freddy is purposefully out and about gathering what in this business is the most valuable commodity ... *information*. Information is indispensable. You probably know this from your own lives ... we all have people who gather, agents, friends, producers, and sometimes they share ... sometimes not... Now, Freddy has found out that our producers know the history of this film and have taken it upon themselves not to pass on that information to us.

Later, Nikki walks down an alleyway, and noticing a door marked *Axxon N*,[5] she enters, finding herself in the shadows at the back of the same soundstage. Peering out, she sees the impossible sight of herself in rehearsal, with the previous scene now shot from a different angle. Horrified, as Devon runs towards her, she flees through a door in the unfinished set. Whereas in the previous version of this scene, Devon encountered the door as the flimsy façade of a dummy house, in this reality (or *temporality*) Nikki emerges into an *actual* house in another part of the world.

From this point on, the fragments of narrative begin to fall away, in favour of a series of dark, recurrent and almost imperceptibly connected images. Nikki appears to be living, suddenly, in a suburban house with an abusive husband, apparently 'becoming' Sue Blue. She encounters a group of sex workers, the 'valley girls', who share stilted, sexually charged and incoherent dialogue. We see images of Polish sex workers in 1930s Lodz, and a backyard gathering of circus performers. With a man wearing glasses in a shadowy office, Nikki/Sue discusses stories of her abuse at the hands of men, dating back to childhood. Interspersed at regular intervals is footage of a group of actors in sinister rabbit costumes, occupying a set reminiscent of classic 1950s sitcoms, and accompanied by an incongruous laughter track.

Nikki/Sue eventually walks down Hollywood Boulevard at night, and, shortly after once more seeing the 'sign' *Axxon N* scrawled in chalk across a door, is stabbed with a screwdriver by Devon's wife – who has come to believe that the two on-screen lovers are having an affair in the 'real world'. She dies an agonising, slow death, vomiting blood, and falls on to the pavement beside a group of homeless people. At this point, after having disappeared from the film for over an hour, we hear Kingsley Stewart call out 'cut', and the camera zooms out to reveal that Nikki has been on a film set. Further surreal images follow – Nikki wanders trance-like into a projection room where her performance is already on the screen. She is pursued by a terrifying 'red-lipped man' whom she shoots, causing his face to change into a distorted copy of her own. Finally, Nikki is at home again, apparently happy, while the end credits roll and a group of dancers mime and perform to Nina Simone's *Sinnerman*.

A Semantic Outside

The first thing we might therefore say about *Inland Empire* is that it is, in a certain sense, unwatchable. We might recall Robert Musil's account, in *The Confusions of Young Törless*, of his protagonist's attempt to read Kant's *Critique of Pure Reason*: 'When he stopped reading in exhaustion after half an hour he had only reached page two.'[6] And it is with a similar sense of despair that we realise, upon reaching the one-hour mark of this labyrinth of images, that there remain over two hours of the film ahead. Indeed, what makes the perceptual and noetic experience of *Inland Empire* so difficult – a characteristic that it perhaps shares with Kant's critiques – is the sustained hostility it offers to any habitual exercise of thought. Central to this difficulty is *information*, which Lynch deploys in various ways throughout the film. In the early scenes – the most conventional 'movement' or 'action-images' – we are drip-fed just enough semantic information to orient our subsequent perceptual experience. This is a story about the production of a Hollywood film, starring an actress whose career is on the wane. However, these plotted elements are quickly problematised with the introduction of noisy semantic materials in the form of non sequitur and non-sense.

In an important early scene, Nikki is visited at her home by a mysterious older woman, who claims to be her neighbour. The visitor (Grace Zabriskie) approaches Nikki's house, followed by the ubiquitous, wavering hand-held camera. On being admitted by Nikki's butler, she and Nikki are seated at a small table. In a thick

Inland Empire

Polish accent, the visitor explains that she has been visiting all of her 'new neighbours'. Their subsequent exchange exemplifies the film's consistent operation – at both the semantic level of dialogue and narrative, but also, as we will see, at that of its technical-aesthetic texture – to disrupt all systematisation, embracing a disjunctive openness to content which does not accord with any pre-distributed syntax or sensibility.

'Which house are you living in?', asks Nikki, to which the visitor replies, enigmatically, with a hint of contempt, '... just down the way ... tucked back in the small woods...' And already we find ourselves implicated in the film's 'play' with information: the visitor refuses to communicate in any clear or coherent way; her obscure comments instead comprise a free association of dark and disconnected images.

The scene unfolds as an uncomfortable game at the level of semantic information, with Nikki probing nervously for some kind of concrete identification from the visitor, something the latter consistently resists. This indeterminacy is replicated aesthetically: Nikki is shot in a standard close-up, her face well-lit and centred. The visitor, while initially shot in a similarly neutral way, is gradually – through the imposition of shot and counter-shot – drawn inexorably closer to the camera, which begins to produce an uncomfortable 'fish-eye' effect, the frame cropping her face in a style reminiscent of Dreyer. Framed in this way, the visitor continues her oblique dialogue:

> 'So ... you have a new role to play I hear...'
> 'Up for a role ... but, uh, I'm afraid, far from getting it.'
> 'No no ... I definitely heard that you have it.'
> 'Oh?'

Here, the 'game' of information begins to take on its critical dimensions, with the introduction of the key motif of Hollywood as a kind of sinister nexus for the selective distribution of information – an information which consistently implies mysterious and *withheld* information – such as forces both characters and spectator into a speculative and critical mode. It appears as if this strange visitor has access to some kind of portentous information concerning Nikki, ultimately predicting the 'brutal fucking murder' with which the film within the film will end. The visitor also appears to possess a strange mastery over the film's disjunctive temporal structure, which she evokes in a passage of dialogue before appearing to become the very agent of its 'splitting':

Yes. Me, I ... I can't seem to remember if it's today, two days from now, or yesterday. I suppose if it was 9:45, I'd think it was after midnight! For instance, if today was tomorrow, you wouldn't even remember that you owed on an unpaid bill. Actions do have consequences. And yet there is the magic. If it was tomorrow, you would be sitting over there.

The visitor points, and in the subsequent first-person shot we encounter the first of a series of temporal 'splittings' which punctuate the film: we now see Nikki, inexplicably sitting in another chair, at another time, talking and laughing with her friends. Nikki's butler returns holding the telephone – it's her agent, and Nikki has got the part in *On High in Blue Tomorrows*.

The 'magic' to which the visitor refers – and which she appears to enact with her pointed finger – is clearly that of cinema, which, as we have seen, articulates temporal formations which are 'impossible' from the perspective of sensory-motor action. The ostensibly systematised narrative we have so far encountered is likewise rendered problematic by this sudden, inexplicable shot, which interpolates a temporality that is meaningless, noisy, in its non-coherence to an initially coherent informatic system. Indeed this scene, and the sudden temporal shift with which it concludes – the visitor is gone, her warnings forgotten, the film continues with Nikki preparing for her role – is indicative of the increasing uncertainty which permeates the film. On the semantic register, there is the 'game' of information, such that we identify with Nikki in seeking desperately to extrapolate meaningful content from the crumbs of information we are fed. And this uncertainty at the semantic level is replicated in the film's visual aesthetics, with the obscure, cropped framing of Nikki's visitor denying us, in certain key respects, coherent visual content.

We will recall that for Weaver, in the context of the MTC, 'greater freedom of choice, greater uncertainty, greater information go hand in hand'.[7] Weaver is here referring to the 'desirable uncertainty' which he associates with a maximal possibility of meaningful messages being transmitted by a given communication system. But as we have seen, we might also understand this uncertainty as 'undesirable', and as such fundamentally entwined with information in an a-signifying, ontological sense. We might also, in this context, return to Deleuze's account of a 'thought without image', which depends not upon a 'recognition' of pre-distributed terms (good sense), but rather on an encounter with the fundamentally *unthought*, which paradoxically forces us into the act of thinking. And these two formulations provide a helpful mechanism with which we might grasp the noetic complications that characterise this scene. In opening its systematised informational content to information in this other sense – as a-signifying data or difference – the scene works to force us, like Dern's character, beyond habitual cognition and into thought as a violence of invention. No longer simply spectators to an unfurling narrative, we are confronted rather with the problem of a collapse in narrativity, such that we must begin the difficult task of *thinking* the form of the film upon which we have embarked. In terms of Simondon's account of information as transduction, we might say that the film's use of uncertainty thus dramatically increases its *tension of information* – which is to say, its potential to engage and to articulate radically unforeseen receivers.

Lynch himself appears to be thinking along these lines, interested less in provoking predetermined affective or intellectual responses than in generating images which are fundamentally indeterminate. In his book, *Catching the Big Fish*, he calls the relation between spectator and film 'the circle',[8] indicating a kind of differential circuitry which produces unanticipated feelings, thoughts and impressions in the audience. As he explains:

> There is a circle that goes from the audience to the film and back. Each person is looking and thinking and feeling and coming up with his or her own sense of things... So you don't know how it's going to hit people. But if you thought about how it's going to hit people, or if it's going to hurt someone, or if it's going to do this or that, then you would have to stop making films ... you never know what's going to happen.[9]

Clearly, then, Lynch's directorial practice is a far cry from the meticulous determinations of *Avatar*. But might we not identify these same functions in the Deleuzian time-image, and the *auteur* cinema of the twentieth century? None of these devices depend upon the film's specifically digital technics, which I claim are integral to the particular outside Lynch constructs. It is to these technics/techniques of the image, then, that we must now turn.

A Technical Outside

Leaving aside the intractable character of the film's narrative, *Inland Empire* also produces and plays with information at the levels of both perception and technicity. In the most immediate terms, the film is *dark*, not only conceptually, but also quite literally – with the majority of scenes dimly lit and indistinct – a situation which engenders a constantly strained spectatorship. Likewise, the clarity of the film's image-scape is muddied at a more fundamentally technical level, with frequent instances of pixelation, consistent slippages of camera focus, and the ubiquitous wavering movements of hand-held cinematography. In fully embracing this primitive, glitchy aesthetic, *Inland Empire* returns to the gritty aesthetic of Lynch's breakout film *Eraserhead* (1977), which used both its film stock and its black and white palette to explore various strata of its own materiality – from the speckled flesh of its prosthetic monsters through to a multilayered and distinctly tactile sound design.

But the material dimensions of *Inland Empire* constitute less the meticulous constructions of *Eraserhead* – Lynch and Alan Splet spent around a year, for instance, producing the latter's sound-effects alone[10] – than a deferral of certain aesthetic decisions to algorithmic, computational and aleatory processes immanent to digital technics. Lynch himself neatly summarises the film's haphazard genesis in *Catching the Big Fish*, where he explains:

> When we began, there wasn't any INLAND EMPIRE, there wasn't anything. I just bumped into Laura Dern on the street, discovering that she was my new neighbour. I hadn't seen her for a long time, and she said, "David, we've got to do something together again." And I said, "We sure do. Maybe I'll write something for you. And maybe we'll do it as an experiment for the Internet." And she said, "Fine." So I wrote a fourteen-page monologue, and Laura memorised all fourteen pages and it was about a seventy minute take.[11]

This typically brief and unassuming account of his directorial practice gives us some key axioms via which we might understand the assemblage of Lynch's film. First, its genesis is quite literally found in a chance encounter between two individuals, whose relationship will generate a new individual in the form of the work. Such an openness to chance, which interposes undetermined and productive forms of information at all levels of the film's production, constitutes one of the key themes to which we will return throughout this chapter.

Furthermore, this precis suggests that Lynch, always interested in new forms,[12] had determined to produce a work for the Internet. Indeed, it was only after filming began that Lynch realised, in his words, '[that] I couldn't release it on the Internet because it was too good…'[13] and determined to produce a film fit for theatrical presentation. After shooting the initial 70-minute take with Dern, Lynch

Inland Empire

assembled the rest of the film himself over a period of three years, filming with a low-tech Sony PD-150 hand-held camera, and editing the footage with the widely available editing program Final Cut Pro. It was Lynch's first film shot entirely on digital video, a technical device which features prominently not only in the film's look, but in its very structure, as largely improvised and performance-driven – a situation Lynch and his actors have attributed to the efficiency and dynamism afforded by digital shooting.[14]

Importantly, Lynch explicitly uses this digital aesthetic to evoke a variety of other, non-cinematic screen forms – various scenes suggest the aesthetics of pornography, online meme culture, amateurish home movies and other 'user-generated' content. Furthermore, these disparate images are assembled in such a way as to suggest a network of multilaterally related images, juxtaposed according to a scrambled or inaccessible logic, closely resembling the disordered and proliferating informatic relations we often experience online. Indeed, Lynch's conviction that these forms have, in some sense, rendered obsolete a traditional directorial practice informs his (perhaps polemical) claim that it is the last feature film he intends to make.[15] Thus in its very technical gestation, *Inland Empire* is indicative of the interconnected, multi-platform character of new media, emerging from the networked informatic images which Deleuze had greeted with some mistrust.

These aesthetic decisions, as I have suggested, are consistently complicated by the mechanical determinations of digital technics, which form a fundamental aspect of the film's visual texture. Throughout the film our perception is consistently drawn to the operations of the PD-150 camera, which struggles to autofocus on faces or sets which are shot too closely, or to adapt to changes in lighting beyond its aspect capacity. Frequent pixelation of movement and of shadow, fish-eye effects resulting from extreme close-ups, along with the movement of the hand-held camera, all contribute to make the *limits* of digital materiality a key dimension of the film. While we are thus confronted with a distinctly digital aesthetic, the film's images are far from the totalising, overdetermined 'money shots' of *Avatar*, such as we encountered in Chapter 4. Indeed, rather than the lavish intentionality of spectacular Hollywood productions, the images here suggest our haphazard experience of the digital in a plurality of more quotidian contexts – as user-generated content viewed on smartphones, feature films warped to be viewed on the back of aeroplane seats, or video-chats conducted with the pixelated faces of distant loved ones – the obscure, private and contingent modes in which we experience digital images daily.

We might turn to a particular scene late in the film, selecting it almost at random, in keeping with the film's aleatory, hyperlinked structure. Here both Nikki and the hand-held camera slowly move down a hallway, so dimly lit as to provide only snatches of decipherable visual content. In the background we hear the high-pitched, almost ineffable whirr of the digital camera's mechanics. Lamps dotted along the hallway are shot so closely as to overwhelm the camera's brightness aspect, becoming abstract shapes and pools of colour. Nikki, her dirtied face shot with inquisitorial closeness, is suddenly approached by an aggressor – 'the Phantom' – a sinister male figure who has appeared sporadically throughout the film. Drawing a gun she fires on her attacker, whose face is suddenly and harshly lit with torches, the brightness of which again overwhelms the aspect functions of the camera, constituting a pixelated blur of light. Nikki fires again, and the face of her attacker – through a cheap-looking superimposition effect – becomes her own, contorted by a nightmarish, clown-like grimace. Finally, the face becomes a bizarre digital mosaic, centred around the sole discernible feature, a cavernous open mouth, gushing with a blood-like substance.

The scene is by turns vaguely comical and distinctly unpleasant, and at no point do we fully grasp what is happening in terms of the logical progression of narrative. Indeed, it exemplifies the film's consistent and performative refusal to communicate meaningful or 'probable' information – be it at the level of narrative or at the perceptual level of sight – in any clear or determinate fashion, instead producing flows of information-as-noise which overwhelm any determinate interpretative structure. The special effects in this sequence – the nightmarish, clown-like visage of Dern's character, followed by the terrifying, bloodied collage of the Phantom's face – thus offer up a distinct counterpoint to the excesses Flaxman rightly identifies in *Avatar*. Here, the effects do not tend towards some idealised or total 'virtual reality'. Rather, they are excessive inasmuch as they are gratuitous, hyperbolic, distinctly unreal. Dern's face, with its too-large mouth and pinched, strained eyes, is clearly altered by the cheap post-production effects, foregrounding their algorithmic determinations. These more distinct facial features are situated in a desert of obscure flesh, its only texture the imperfect rendering of the DV camera's software, struggling with the imperative of the harsh torchlight.

Inland Empire

In this image, Lynch has opened up an anti-representational space such as we find in non-figurative and abstract art more generally. However, despite its continuity with these forms, Lynch also attains productive forces commensurate with the new, information image specifically. Dern's face as much resembles Munch's paintings as it does the kind of primitive facial alteration software deployed on smartphone applications and designed to age, beautify or otherwise alter the user's photograph. And the inclusion of such an image in the context of a work of artistic cinema – as well as the deferral of aesthetic control or intentionality on the part of the *auteur* to algorithms – suggests a democratisation of certain 'problematic' functions of the image which might constitute a model of aesthetic production moving into the digital age. These glitchy, noisy slippages of intended digital functioning appear, in the context of mass digital media, to be in the process of proliferating as the experience of ever larger publics. And like Deleuze's time-image, these 'problematic' events at the level of digital materiality might thus constitute a mass production of noetic encounters, provided we are properly able to identify those tendencies in the image which escape from predetermined control. I will return to this claim in the final chapter.

For now, it suffices to say that Lynch's foregrounding of the digital *as digital* – not in the service of a representational schema of spectacularly 'believable' images, but rather as an irreducible technical presence, with operations of its own, over and above the explicit intentions of the *auteur* – thus evokes the autonomous material dimensions of language with which Blanchot begins to sketch the space of literature. And much like Blanchot's account of language, the import of Lynch's intervention derives from the fact that this imperfect technical modality is one through which we conduct our very lives. By refusing to communicate predetermined information and allowing the relatively uncontrolled interpolation of irreducible technical operations and materials, the film draws out the fundamentally inhuman dimensions of digital technics – which, in their irreducibility and excess, efface the 'I' as much as anything we find in Kafka. We might recall Foucault's characterisation of the outside as 'the movement of the speaker's disappearance',[16] and it is just this tendency towards the autonomous, aleatory and material dimensions of the digital 'communication system' which precipitates the disappearance of Lynch as *auteur*, in supreme command of each aesthetic detail.

But as we have seen in our exploration of the works of Blanchot, Foucault and Deleuze, the outside is not simply entangled with the 'death of the author', or the emergence of a particular artistic style. In Foucault's terms, the outside constitutes 'the essential hiding place of all being',[17] the pre-discursive condition of speech and silence, truth and falsehood, with which certain art forms might afford us contact. In the context of literature, the outside is thus 'the giant murmuring upon which language opens',[18] an impersonality which is, for Blanchot, ultimately *ontic*. In the twentieth-century cinematic movement-and-time-images, it will become an 'out-of-field', proliferated through irrational cuts and intolerable optical and sonic situations. In *Inland Empire*, we encounter a new outside: no longer out-of-frame but *within* the frame, in an excess of computational materiality which is properly informatic.

As I've suggested, we might better understand the ontological implications of this outside by turning to information theory itself. If we take seriously the conceptual implications of the theory underpinning these digital technics – whereby predetermined semantic structures constitute the only means via which we might distinguish a-signifying, empirical data (noise) from 'information' conceived as meaningful or desirable – we discover in the film a profound expression of information in its inhuman, aleatory and productive guises. As we have seen via Simondon, once we abandon a concept of information as intrinsically linked to communication – as a 'neutral' transmission between static and predetermined transmitter/receivers – we can conceive of information as *ontogenetic*: the condition for new individuals that articulate energetic disparities and that are distributed by the very process of information, conceived as the transduction of a qualitatively new situation.

The noetic value of Lynch's film is to render this model sensible, articulating a high 'tension' of information through its interpolation of aleatory and technical devices. From the algorithms of the camera's computational (re)composition of data to the wavering of the director's physical presence in the form of hand-held cinematography, the film's images deploy noisy materials which undermine communicative intent on the part of the *auteur*, as such multiplying potential 'messages' which might be subsequently extrapolated. This productive disparity – as we've suggested – plays a role at various levels of the film: in terms of our response as spectators, but also throughout its production, during which systematised, signifying and intentional processes are constantly disrupted – which is to say *in-formed* – by the 'noise' of random events.

Inland Empire

We might turn to another scene from the film, set in what Lynch calls 'the little house', in order to illustrate this movement from 'noisy' events in production through to noetic events in spectatorship. Here, Nikki – having entered the soundstage's dummy door and now ensconced in an apparently suburban existence as Sue – stands in the backyard of a run-down home, where she is confronted by a man (Krysztof Majchrzak), who emerges from behind a tree with a lightbulb in his mouth. The lightbulb's presence, Lynch explains, was the result of an aleatory process which exemplifies the creative ethos operative during production. Preparing to shoot the scene at Lynch's house, Majchrzak had arrived wearing a pair of 'goofy' glasses which he intended to wear in character. Lynch, however, felt that the glasses weren't right, at which point Majchrzak asked for an alternative prop around which he might orient his performance. As Lynch explains:

> So I went to my cupboard and saw a little piece of broken tile, I saw a rock, and I saw a red lightbulb, but very transparent like a Christmas light. I took these things out and offered him a choice ... and he picked up the bulb.[19]

For Lynch, these aleatory and experimental moments are invariably productive, taking place, in his terms – which emerge from his practice of transcendental meditation – in the context of a 'unified field'[20] which might situate disparate images and their relations. As he continues:

> I really had this feeling that if there's a Unified Field, there must be a unity between a Christmas tree bulb and this man from Poland who came in wearing these strange glasses. It's interesting to see how these unrelated things live together. And it gets your mind working. How do these things relate when they seem so far apart? It conjures up a third thing that almost unifies those first two.[21]

This 'third thing' – the equal parts menacing and absurd image of a man emerging from behind a tree with a lightbulb in his mouth – constitutes, in our terms, a *new individual*, which, in its ambiguity and multiplicity, will in turn produce new noetic individuals or ideas on the part of its receivers. This image is noise in the sense of its being unwanted or unintentional information, conforming to no predetermined system of signification. And as such, it might serve as the information for new systems – new regimes of signs, ideas or images – as it has, indeed, in informing my own approach throughout this book.

It is important, however, that we do not understand noise in absolute terms, as something like the totality of pre-systemic content. Noise must be conceived in perspectival terms, in the context of a systematisation that it disrupts, but of which it is simultaneously the condition. Music is 'made' of noise, but a noise which music strives to contain through its systematisation of notes, scale and metre. Or, as David Lapoujade has written, in the context of language:

> it is not a matter of "leaving" language by invoking an experience of limits that would be a silence, a cry, or music – as if the latter were outside language – but rather of recognising that the latter constitute the outside of language, an outside that works on language from within. They are the other side of language, a non-linguistic material whose intensive, chromatic variations work on language from the inside and, in so doing, disarticulate it.[22]

In this sense – and here we might think once more of Eco's 'open work' – what prevents Lynch's film from slipping into 'an empty aestheticism' (*CI*, 18) are the shifting and parasitic relations between systematised, meaningful content, and pure chance – which is to say, the variation and difference which is the paradoxical condition of all systems. Lynch encourages interference between these 'two sides' of every system at various levels of his production – semantic, technical and compositional – producing an extremely differentiated or 'open' system, which is as such highly charged with chaotic potentials for confronting or exciting thought.

Hollywood's Outside

These operations are thus also political in the idiosyncratic terms we encountered in Chapter 3. Here we saw that the time-image reinjects questions of disparity and overinflation into a capitalist logic of equivalence, revealing intolerable situations and forcing the subject – be it character or spectator, individual or collective – to become *other than it is*. And indeed, *Inland Empire* marries these functions with its less obviously political experiments, enacting an immanent critique of the new, informatic image as *dispositif* of social individuation. Importantly, this critique is tied to the film's origin in a particular psychogeography, and to major centres for the production of both contemporary images and subjectivity. The film's title, *Inland Empire*, refers to the metropolitan area inland of Los Angeles, comprising the cities of Riverside County and San Bernadino. In keeping with the film's meditation on the contemporary status of film, it is telling that this locale is not Hollywood, but rather 'Hollywood adjacent'. This is American suburbia: landlocked, fraying and without obvious *raison d'être* – the 'any-space-whatever' which, even in California, has been so profoundly altered by ever wider post-industrial and informatically mediated networks of production. This is where a Trumpian 'Middle America' begins, in the living rooms, duplexes and tract housing which constitute the latter part of *Inland Empire*'s *mise en scène* – an America which chooses television over cinema, or, more importantly, which increasingly experiences the globalised culture of images through smartphones, tablets and laptops.

Lynch's exploration of suburbia – and of its surreal, subterranean and incongruous dimensions – has been the source of frequent critical commentary.[23] Lynch himself articulates this aspect of his work in an interview with Chris Rodley, where he tells us:

> My childhood was elegant homes ... green grass, cherry trees. Middle America as it's supposed to be. But on the cherry tree there's this pitch oozing out – some black, some yellow, and millions of red ants crawling all over it. I discovered that if one looks a little closer at this beautiful world, there are always red ants underneath.[24]

Lynch here evokes the opening scenes of *Blue Velvet* (1986), in which the idyllic fields of suburban childhood are transfigured into the Daliesque locale of severed, ant-covered ears. This passage also suggests a practice of 'viewing' which causes interference between different perceptual schemes – a reorientation of our gaze such that an official surface of images (the American Dream) is placed in contact with the 'noise' it strives to exclude (following Wiener, we might say the 'evil' of disordered, entropic nature – of ants, pitch and blood).

The suburbia of *Inland Empire* is of an altogether different order; however, this operation of interference recurs. This is digital suburbia – a world of interpenetrating flows of information: of informatic socialising (social media), informatic sex (pornography), informatic labour (Silicon Valley is only six hours away), all combined in such a way as to produce lives half-lived in virtual space. *Inland Empire*'s 'ants' are not only the technical glitches this space engenders, but also the material violence upon which these 'virtual realities' depend: violence against women (domestic abuse, the film's trafficked sex workers), economic exclusion (the drifters among whom Nikki/Sue eventually 'dies' on Hollywood Boulevard), and the fractious pressures this new culture of images places on more archaic dimensions of human subjectivity.

These auto-critical mappings of contemporary screen culture's conditions of possibility are likewise expressed in the film's exploration of Hollywood's European heritage, which constitutes another important aesthetic dimension. The creativity of Hollywood, of course, has long been driven by the European avant-garde's diaspora – its most fertile periods the direct result of war and dispossession on the Continent. *Inland Empire* might well explore the underbelly of American life, but its simultaneous extension of deep roots into a European *mise en scène*, both in the form of scenes set in the Balkans and Poland and in terms of a constellation of explicit references to European art film (we encounter devices from *Persona*, *Last Year at Marienbad*, *Pierrot le Fou* and *Un Chien Andalou* to name just a few), establishes a continued trajectory of 'problematic', temporally experimental cinema from the twentieth century into the twenty-first.

But Lynch's project, as we have suggested, has long been dedicated to marrying these more rarefied experimental traditions with a surrealism and unease altogether closer to home. As we've seen, the film contains images which evoke such diverse screen forms as pornography, user-generated video, surveillance footage and sitcom – all of which are combined into a nightmarish melange. In this way, the film traverses the ecology of contemporary digital media, which has exploded since the film's release in 2006. Indeed, in this marriage of a European avant-garde tradition with popular screen aesthetics, Lynch perhaps opens up critical territories which elude Deleuze's own analysis. As Mark Poster observes, in the context of a critique of Deleuze's predilection for 'high art' works of cinema, such an approach does not necessarily orient one towards an efficacious study of contemporary media. 'One cannot come near the problem of media with a view of the everyday as degraded, debased and baleful', Poster writes,[25] and while this criticism may be a little heavy-handed – particularly given Deleuze and Guattari's interest in certain forms of 'minor' creative practice – it perhaps helps us to differentiate Deleuze's approach from that which we find in *Inland Empire*.

Lynch is fascinated by pop-cultural and low-brow screen forms, as demonstrated by the success of his surrealistic 'soap opera' *Twin Peaks* (1990–91), to which we will return in the final chapter. More recently, in addition to reviving *Twin Peaks*, he has produced diverse content for his website and for YouTube, including a series of sardonic reports on the weather in LA, and a series of videos called

Inland Empire

Today's Number Is... which sees him pick a numbered ping-pong ball out of a jar each day.[26] This compulsive engagement affords Lynch a proximity to new, informatic images which is absent from Deleuze's analysis, enabling him to paint them not only with some admiration, but in the full richness of their horror. Key to this approach is a profound awareness of their slippages and surrealisms, what we might call the semantic and technical noise which is one of their richest affects. The absurd non sequiturs of overwrought, multi-writer soap opera dialogue; the stilted, zombielike acting of Hollywood's straight-to-video products or of 'narrative' pornography; the obscure pace of late-night television, with its whirl of infotainment, evangelism and advertising – all are reworked by Lynch, not merely into a kind of self-aware cultural critique, but into strange moments of beauty and sublimity.

Lynch, as we have seen, acknowledges this capacity to cause 'interference' between disparate perceptual schemas – different forms of 'viewing' – which is symbiotic, in the sense that while it might reify the mundane and even the ugly, it serves likewise to problematise the 'beauty' of an official or institutional surface, for instance the American Dream. In *Inland Empire*, this tendency to experiment with some of the surrealisms immanent to both everyday life and popular forms emerges in the 'Rabbits' sequences which pepper the film. These scenes, adapted from a 2002 series of web films, feature three humanoid rabbits who share disjointed dialogue in a shabby living room. Lynch's tagline for the series, which, with typical irony, he refers to as a sitcom, runs: 'in a nameless city deluged by a continuous rain ... three rabbits live with a fearful mystery'.[27] The dialogue shared by the rabbits is, like that of Nikki's Polish visitor, comprised entirely of non sequiturs ('I am going to find out one day', 'When will you tell it', 'Who could have known?', 'What time is it?').[28] Each of these fragments, subtracted from a series which might meaningfully contain it, serves to 'communicate' according to an apparently random distribution, establishing new, and no longer sensory-motor, connections. These new relations of (non)sense are overlaid with a canned laughter track which likewise appears to bear no relation to the image's semantic content, producing a disjunction between sounds, as well as between sound and vision, in a mechanism reminiscent of *Last Year at Marienbad* or Duras's *La Femme du Gange* (1974).

The rabbits' 'fearful mystery' is thus perhaps that of communication itself, which teeters on the verge of incoherence, particularly under the strain of capitalism's vast process of semiotic deterritorialisation. This process – the compulsive removal and recombination of signs from their traditional 'territories' or substances – begins with forms of mechanical reproduction like writing, but reaches ubiquity with online, networked and digitally encoded images. The rabbits, indeed – in their anthropomorphic animality and soundbite utterances, imbued with an indeterminate affectivity both menacing and droll – are evocative of online memes, which depend upon an abysmally ironic play with these chaotic (re)distributions of sense. For our purposes, these sequences constitute a kind of multidimensional machine producing information in the a-signifying, Shannon sense: a tissue of 'bits' of aleatory and entropic data which resists ready-made systematisation or meaning. In their determination *not* to communicate, but rather to extend these flows of entropic information into various undetermined intellectual and affective responses – Lynch's 'circle' – these sequences likewise contaminate the audience with their 'mystery', which is to say the ambiguous possibility of communicating at all.

This coming apart of traditional semiotic affectivity in the context of Hollywood – as in sitcoms, memes and pornography – accords with the immanent Marxism we traced through Deleuze's account of the time-image. The resistance to new forms of machinic enslavement or control must take place, to quote Guattari again, 'not through a politics of return to archaic territorialities, but through the crossing of an additional degree of deterritorialization'.[29] If, under capitalism, 'all that is solid melts into air', as Marx and Engels once famously wrote,[30] indicating a catastrophic liquidation of traditions, borders and sensibilities, the properly revolutionary task is to understand this process as ambiguous and contestable, and the condition for radically unforeseeable individuations in thought, sensibility and society. For Deleuze and Guattari, this process is inhibited by a sophisticated machinery of reterritorialisation and recoding, such that capitalism's immense energies are corralled back into repression, banality and misery. But a properly revolutionary deterritorialisation is possible, provided this former tendency escapes and overflows the latter – as in Lynch's film, which hints at the increasing pressures faced by traditional semiotic and cognitive apparatuses of 'capture'.

It is not, however, sufficient to simply let capitalism continue to proliferate (which is to say, destroy life on the planet), trusting in forms of semantic non-sense and narrative breakdown alone in order to posit new and 'revolutionary connections'.[31] These developments require, to slip explicitly into Deleuze's terms, the continued intervention not only of philosophy – which might use them to fabricate concepts – but also art – which might use them to produce new arrangements of affects and percepts in the context of sensible materials. Lynch's film, and the disjunctive assemblages it uses in order to generate information in its aleatory and excessive guises, constitutes just such a project, and arrives with an imperative that philosophy should follow suit, creating new concepts with which we might continue to engineer the always endangered species that is thought.

These themes aside – we will return to them shortly – we must also recall that the agent which might enact this kind of revolutionary thought – a thought from/of outside – does not pre-exist this process, but must likewise be *created* in the context of an encounter with the intolerable, in the world and at the very heart of thought. In this context, we will turn, finally, to *Inland Empire*'s sketch of a new form of 'incompossible' digital subjectivity. This subjectivity, I claim – personified in Dern's 'split' character – draws on performative and technical elements of identity, simultaneously problematising these dimensions through a consistent foregrounding of their functionality and limits. This digital subject, as it emerges throughout the film, suggests the proliferation of such subjectivities far beyond the rarefied air of cinema or art, orienting us towards the possibility of a 'people to come', who might emerge in and through the new, informatic image.

Digital Incompossibility

In one of the film's very first scenes, shot in black and white, we encounter a man and a woman, their faces blurred, speaking in Polish. 'Do you know what whores do?', asks the man. 'Yes', replies the woman, 'they fuck.' This sequence – the first of many featuring sex workers throughout the film – with its indistinct faces and robotic sexual dialogue, is the clear restaging of a similar scene at the beginning of Godard's *Weekend* (1968). The blurred aesthetic and nihilistic eroticism of the scene are also obvious evocations of pornography. *Inland Empire*'s persistent motifs of sexual exploitation – in the form of pornography, sex trafficking, and indeed popular cinema – are interwoven into what Lynch has claimed is the film's central premise: '[a story] about a woman in trouble'.[32] Importantly, this thematic element is profoundly entangled with digital media, which appear, at least initially, to constitute the next in a long line of image technics used to control and to exploit the female body.³³

But Lynch deploys these digital technics in a complicated way, such as perhaps renders problematic this very operation. We've already seen how shooting with a hand-held digital camera determined the film's raw material: a powerful lead performance from Dern, effected in part by the efficiencies and flexibility of digital recording. As Dern has said:

> We were shooting constantly ... there were no large lights to put up, and we had no need to wait between setups for coverage, because David was holding the camcorder – he could cover an entire scene in 20 minutes or an hour. The luxury was incredible shorthand on the set. There was never any downtime.³⁴

This 'shorthand' results in an excoriating performance from Dern, a mammoth undertaking marbled throughout the film's almost three hours, which re-establishes an indexicality with specifically digital contours. The visceral affective aspects of Dern's performance, her tiredness, the hoarseness of her voice, the tics and twitches of her face – which the camera follows with an almost cruel insistence – suggest the demands and traumas inflicted upon women not only in the context of Hollywood 'performance', but through gendered performance generally.

In this sense, the film takes up one of Hollywood's oldest and most problematic tropes, foregrounding an intimate connection between the screened image and a feminised object of desire. However, its self-aware exploration of this tradition, which resonates with immanent critiques like those of Wilder or von Trier, works towards the critical questions that Deleuze argues are essential if we are to 'go beyond' information considered as control or a proliferation of order-words. We might recall here the film's fictional director Kingsley Stewart, and his claim that in the context of the movie business, the most important commodity is *information*. And indeed, the film's identification of the Hollywood studio system as a nexus for the distribution of information as control – which is to say, as an ordering function attendant to specific forms of subjectivation – becomes a key theme throughout Lynch's assemblage. We might return once more to Deleuze's claim, in the context of the ascendance of informatic images: '[to go] beyond information is achieved on two sides at once, towards two questions: *what is the source and what is the addressee?*' (CII, 276). And indeed, the film moves repeatedly towards just these questions – evoking the marketised and misogynistic imperatives of Hollywood as producer of certain highly interested flows of information. These flows, far from 'communicating' in any platitudinous sense, communicate violently, as one communicates a physical force or imperative.

In Nikki's case, we encounter a sexualised imperative to *perform*, to become a subject through subjection to the realities of the various screen worlds through which the character moves and is interpolated. Throughout the production of the film within a film, Hollywood communicates this imperative to Nikki, who is gradually 'split' into simultaneous and mutually interfering personalities – Nikki the actress, and Susan Blue, the 'battered wife' she is to play in *On High in Blue Tomorrows*. Gradually, through Dern's equal parts extreme and subtle performance, Nikki becomes increasingly impossible to distinguish from this 'second' character. She embarks upon an affair with Devon; however, the film's dense, allusive nature means that we are never able to fully distinguish on which level of reality this affair is taking place. The Hollywood universe appears to enact a profound and consistent violence against Nikki, who, in a series of non-linear and disjunctive scenes, variously becomes a trafficked sex worker, a woman trapped in a violent suburban relationship, and ultimately, in a role the film suggests is laterally related – with particular resonance in a post-Weinstein world – a female movie star.

The implication of digital technics in this process, in terms of the way in which Nikki/Sue is subjectivised through her constant 'capture' – not only by recording technologies but ultimately by the disorienting network they constitute – is indeed commensurate with the screen-based mechanisms of control that Deleuze has suggested might supplant the creativity of cinema. But the film's assemblage is also suggestive of a potential mode of *resistance* to these very functions, given their destruction of a habitually circumscribed experience of space-time. We have already introduced a key scene, early in the film, in which Nikki and co-star Devon are startled by a presence in the shadows at the back of a vast soundstage. On running to investigate, Devon is mystified to find nobody there, the intruder having apparently disappeared into thin air behind a dummy door. It's only later, as we follow Nikki's descent into the madness of her role, that we emerge to view this same scene from the shadows. This looping of time obviously calls into question the film's 'realism': we have entered a temporality which is multiple and as such irreducible to sensory-motor action, as in the Deleuzian time-image.

'Time is out of joint' (*CII*, x), Deleuze writes, quoting Hamlet, and the non-linear and disjunctive trajectories of the time-image likewise dislocate truth – contaminating it with the false in a dynamic cross-pollination. As Deleuze explains, in the 'crystalline' descriptions of the time-image:

> narrative ceases to be truthful, that is, to claim to be true, and becomes fundamentally falsifying ... it is a power of the false which replaces and supersedes the form of the true, because it poses the simultaneity of incompossible presents, or the coexistence of not-necessarily true pasts. (*CII*, 136)

The notion of 'incompossibility' refers us to Leibniz, and an idea Deleuze introduces via the Aristotelian paradox of contingent futures.[35] Leaving aside the specifics of this discussion, it suffices to say that Deleuze here recruits Leibniz into the service of his own cine-metaphysical project, to understand actual realities as contingent resolutions of pre-individual disparities or intensities. As we have seen, actualised states emerge only as the contingent contractions of differential virtual structures, the operations of which are excluded or obscured by the interests of habitual perception. With the notion of incompossibility, Deleuze reactivates this mutant Bergsonism, suggesting a complication of the interested reductivity of actualisation via a multiplication of 'presents' which coexist in the art object.

These presents are not, after all, 'impossible', but rather 'incompossible', in the sense that they cannot coexist in terms of an actualised sensory-motor horizon. But they can indeed coexist in the *artwork*, such that Dern's character can confront herself through the temporal loops of *Inland Empire*. In this context, art replaces Leibniz's God as the adjudicator of an ultimately 'compossible' world. In his stead, we encounter a mechanical-artistic process which passes through various incompossibilities, causing them to coexist in all of their chaotic discord. Time, in the post-war cinema, thus emerges as a Borgesian labyrinth of interwoven temporal trajectories, confounding laws like that of the excluded middle, and creating radically inhuman space-times. These space-times, in keeping with Deleuze's rigorously immanent account of the artwork and its affects, are perfectly real, producing affective and noetic individuals of the most concrete order. They may indeed be 'false', but in keeping with the 'powers of the false', which Deleuze takes up from Nietzsche, they serve to generate new modes of thought and life, as real as anything conceived under the arid rubric of the truthful.

Inland Empire

This production of mutually incompossible realities is one of the time-image's richest philosophical effects, but *Inland Empire* suggests a more generalised form of incompossibility which is constituted through contemporary information networks. To be 'captured' in the network of contemporary information – as biometric data, surveillance footage, or through more subtle forms of social media 'confession' and 'performance' – is increasingly the experience of everyday life under control-mediated capitalism. To return to Deleuze's vocabulary, we might say that the subjects of this capture are *dividual* – 'split' as an effect of the unique retentional capacities of recording techniques, which the digital paradigm has proliferated beyond cinema into all walks of life. And while such 'split' personalities, *Inland Empire* suggests, have long characterised the female pop-culture icon – we might think of a whole tradition of 'doomed' starlets, from Jean Harlow and Marilyn Monroe right through to Britney Spears – it appears that the pressure of being digitally arrested in various idealised contexts, while living in a fractious 'reality' which leaves each of these retained temporalities behind, is increasingly the experience of anybody who maintains a curated, online identity on social media.

The entwined role of both capital and control here is perhaps self-evident. As Rob Horning has noted, in conversation with the artist Amalia Ulman,[36] social media identities are constructed in response to market forces, which depend upon the unpaid labour of 'self-creation', in the form of a consumption of branded commodities:

> Consumer culture relies on the ideological fiction that self-expression brings personal fulfilment and "self-actualisation," so that the injunction to reveal oneself is not a burden, but bliss. This makes us both consume more – the self is articulated through branded commodities that have ever-shifting signifying potential – and provide more undercompensated labor (often the sort of "immaterial" labor that invests commodities with their signification capacity, giving brands their "meaning").[37]

This undercompensated labour – the 'liking' of certain images which as such generates value; the production of online 'content' which keeps users engaged and as such brings them into contact with more advertising, itself inter-bleeding with ostensibly non-commercial 'content' – is equally the labour involved in the construction of a 'self' through dividual relationships with these various commodities.

But these dividual functions, in keeping with an anexact use of the term throughout Deleuze's *oeuvre*,[38] perhaps open onto alternate modes of subjectivation that are altogether less amenable to the imperatives of capital and control. While this might appear a bleak portrait of digital subjectivity – a discharge of our responsibility to be self-critical or genuinely self-creative in favour of a commodity fetishism which might relieve us of these burdens – this kind of impossible, 'split' subjectivity might also be thought in terms of the creative 'splitting' we encountered in Chapter 1. Here we saw that a certain temporal disparity – such as Deleuze elaborates with reference to the third synthesis of time – likewise 'splits' the subject, impelling it to become other than it is. Rather than a process of 'prosumer'[39] self-creation, this is the site of a genuine creativity, immanent to temporality once it is properly understood as the interplay of intensive forces across the virtual–actual axis. The subject, conceived as a temporal 'event', must constantly become *other than it is*, incorporating the trauma of an intolerable encounter into the creative actualisation of a new individual. And indeed, this is exactly the movement we witness throughout *Inland Empire*, in the context of the digital image space.

Dern's character does not, after all, meet with an unhappy ending. Something *happens* throughout the film, such that the dividual 'splitting' of Nikki/Sue, albeit the result of malevolent forces immanent to both Hollywood and to an ecosystem of contemporary control technics, is ultimately recuperated into a kind of victory. After the bloody trauma of the film's later scenes – Nikki/Sue's descent into madness, her ultimate 'death', and the killing of 'the Phantom' – Nikki returns to her home, and smiles warmly at her Polish visitor, whom we have not seen since the beginning of the film. A one-legged woman, using crutches, walks slowly across the following shot, and looking around, at what we soon realise is Nikki's opulent house, smiles and whispers 'sweeeeet'. The camera pans across to an unnamed character (Laura Harring), who blows Nikki a kiss. Nikki returns the kiss, and serenely looks on as a group of women dance and mime to Nina Simone's *Sinnerman*, while the film's credits roll.

This final scene, replete with references to Lynch's other films,[40] is one of the most complex and arresting in the movie, and consummates an operation whereby *Inland Empire*'s characters, while 'split' through their participation in a network of digital images, appear to emerge victorious and happy, having refashioned themselves in an active self-creation. Nikki, in killing 'the Phantom', has also destroyed *herself*, but this self was always-already problematic – a clutch of sexuated sensory-motor habits trapped by the circuitries of

Inland Empire

a relentlessly *actual* space-time. In confronting her *digital* self – which is to say, by simultaneously *becoming* this self, and no longer viewing this simulacrum as an external malevolence which might threaten a predetermined individual – Nikki has opened up potentialities for a genuinely creative participation in digital space-times, a *becoming digital*, no longer the reactive function of control, but rather the creative eschewal of any predetermined individuality.

Of course, we must distinguish between simply 'opening up' a potential and actualising it in a new and radically unforeseen form. Alongside an 'openness' to new forces, we require a noetic model informed by an ethics of affirmation, which sees us embrace an encounter with that which we cannot yet think in all of its problematic – and potentially painful – dimensions. The thinker, in order to become the *agent* or *author* of such an event, must embrace the forces of the outside, deploying them in the service of a creativity which might bring about new modes of thought and life. In this context, we might say that our experience of the ecology of digital images is indeed both intolerable and impossible – 'splitting' us across disparate, simultaneous and aberrant technically mediated space-times. But the impossible and intolerable, as we have seen, are those conditions which impel us beyond the actual, and into the creative and resistant activity of thought. *Inland Empire*, and Dern's trajectory through it, not only stages the trauma of this new situation, but suggests that our path to genuine creativity – cinematic, philosophical and beyond – might be to throw ourselves into these new incompossibilities, such that we might fully experience their tensions, errors and noises – emerging with 'new weapons' and as new processes of (*in*)dividuation.

We might begin to think the reality of this evolution by returning to Deleuze's claim that both the brain and the screen are analogous sites for the recomposition of images, understood in Bergson's metaphysical sense. In this context, the loops of incompossible digi-time laced throughout *Inland Empire* afford us an opening onto a thought, which is to say, a mode of *life*, freed from the straitjacket of the sensory-motor schema. These hyperlinked, glitchy images exemplify Deleuze's contention that:

> A flickering brain, which relinks or creates loops – this is cinema ... everything can be used as a screen, the body of a protagonist or even the bodies of the spectators; everything can replace the film stock, in a virtual film which now only goes on in the head, behind the pupils ... a

disturbed brain-death or a new brain which would be at once the screen, the film stock and the camera, each time membrane of the outside and the inside... (*CII*, 221)

As I have argued throughout this book, this amounts to a claim that for Deleuze, the cinema affords us a thought which is no longer strictly human. Rather it is *inhuman*, multilaterally implicated with an outside of unthought materials and virtual potentials, comprising in turn an indeterminate and shifting 'inside' which might recombine and redeploy their energies. And while Deleuze is wary of new forms of telematic and informatic images, our reading of *Inland Empire*, in concert with a rereading of information theory, suggests that we may be justified in extending this model to engage the digital image, in all of its problematic excess.

This digital outside, as I have said, need not be strictly cinematic. Indeed, the images which comprise *Inland Empire* constitute a mosaic of disparate media which suggests a wider context for this noetic model. As Justus Nieland has written:

> The film's media ecology (projection, phonography, the performing body, radio, television, the Internet) is wildly impure, upping the ante on Marshall McLuhan's axiom that media always take as their content another medium, and embedding its characters in a vast digital *combinatoire*, a network of fractal worlds...[41]

This 'impurity' calls into question the hitherto circumscribed world not just of cinema but of art, a concept which may no longer serve us. As Matthew Fuller has written, in the context of a generalised aestheticisation of global consumer culture since the mid-twentieth century, 'art is no longer only art. Its methods are recapitulated, ooze out and become feral in combination with other forms of life.'[42] Fuller's contention, that there has been a proliferation of what he provisionally terms 'art methodologies' into all walks of life, from popular music and television to self-reflexive productions of the self through erotic subcultures, social media and fitness regimes, indeed appears to problematise a modernist-inflected Deleuzian account of 'art' as it is developed across his *oeuvre*.[43] As Fuller writes, in the context of what he describes as the 'media ecologies' of the twenty-first century:

> A diffusion is occurring in which art methodologies can pop up unexpectedly, not even recognising themselves as art, indeed possibly not even having that filiation in a genealogical sense, but connecting to it by means of arrival via a different phylogenetic route...[44]

Inland Empire

Contemporary examples abound. There is pop music, which since the 1960s has often presented itself as 'high art'.[45] There are contemporary 'cinematic' television series, which, abiding in the long shadow of *Twin Peaks*, take cues from surrealist, New Wave and experimental cinema. More recently, there are social media practices like Instagramming which – in its structural emulation of a retro, square photographic image, complete with filters to degrade image quality – evokes the polaroid experiments of Andy Warhol and David Hockney, its content oscillating between the landscapes of Ansell Adams and the eroticism of Helmut Newton or Maripol. The algorithmically determined aesthetic of Dern's 'clown face', suggesting as it does popular digital image manipulation practices more generally, might be read in just this context. Its aesthetic and affective dimensions suggest a broader theme which emerges from our encounter with *Inland Empire* – that we may no longer be justified in locating the outside in the rarefied productions of high art, be they those of cinema, literature or painting. Rather, the outside – as an ungrounding condition of thought – might better be located in the circuitries that abide between an ever more aesthetically literate public[46] and ever more mutant consumer-capitalist-art objects. We will return to these objects in the final chapter.

For now, as I have argued, a helpful concept we might bring to bear in this context is that of noise, which constitutes not a totalising but rather a perspectival designation, engendered in the context of a relatively closed information system which confronts disruptive forces from 'outside'. What must therefore be developed – and *Inland Empire*, although in many ways an *auteur* work in the traditional sense, suggests this – are more generalised practices which precipitate this kind of interference, deploying noisy materials from outside in such a way as to change qualitatively the individuals a given system is able to produce. We might return, in this context, to our refrain: 'going beyond information is achieved on two sides at once, towards two questions: *what is the source and what is the addressee?*' (*CII*, 276). Lynch's complex exploration of the singular potentials of digitality enacts a movement towards just these questions. In *Inland Empire*, the information source is Hollywood, or more properly, a fissure or break in Hollywood, caused by its encounter with new media. The question of an addressee is more difficult, but is perhaps tied to the notion of a 'people to come', and a kind of spectator or subject of the digital image that we are yet to properly understand or realise. In this context, the film might constitute, in Deleuze's words, 'not the myth of a past people, but the story-telling of a people to come' (*CII*, 229).

A (Digital) People to Come

As we saw across previous chapters, the problems of informatic control and of a potentially resistant noise stretch beyond cinema or art, which we have used as a relatively circumscribed ground on which to stage them. That informatic techniques of the image are the harbinger of profound changes in subjectivity *tout court* is a commonplace, and has been the source of no shortage of popular commentary. We have already spoken of interventions like that of Nicholas Carr, for instance, who suggests that the hyperactivity of networked information is deleterious to human capacities for critique and depth reflection. But this spectre of 'too much information' assumes, as I have suggested, a particular kind of information, which is to say, an information which is hyperactive only along pre-distributed channels of transmission and exchange. But what if, following Simondon, Floridi and the other thinkers of information we have encountered, we were to begin to conceive of this information overload in terms of its being a-signifying, chaotic and indeed ontologically productive?

This amounts to thinking a kind of information which might *inform* new individuals, or processes of individuation, perhaps even at the level of mass social movements, constituting what Deleuze calls a 'people to come'. While Deleuze associates the informatic image primarily with subjectivation in control societies, the 'people' who populate *Inland Empire*, like Dern in her final, serene surveillance of the chaos crowding her ballroom, give us a hint of what this might look like, suggesting a new and chaotic form of post-digital subjectivity. Subjected to a series of dividual 'splittings' and traumas, they are ultimately – through a process of affirmative creation within the digital milieu – the site of new and radically undetermined processes of individuation. We might articulate the implications of this development in a passage we have already encountered, in which Deleuze writes:

> The forces within man enter into a relation with forces from the outside, those of silicon which supersedes carbon, or genetic components which supersede the organism, or agrammaticalities which supersede the signifier... What is the overman? It is the formal compound of the forces within man and these new forces. It is the form that results from a new relation between forces.[47]

Inland Empire

This process need not constitute the uncritical embrace of an 'accelerationism' whereby new forms of humanity defer their noetic operations to cybernetic networks – we might think, here, of the strange trajectory of Nick Land.[48] As we saw in Chapter 5, such an 'image of thought' indeed continues to evoke an all-too-human model, according to which thought constitutes a computational transmission between already pre-distributed terms or actualities.

This 'overman', or rather woman, might instead constitute a processual being – capable of problematising both its existence and its *milieu* in terms of an affirmative openness to virtuality and the outside. As Deleuze has suggested, such developments might take place through human noetic participation in the cinematic image, which causes brain and screen to occupy a plane of shifting and indeterminate relations. But this screen might also be the *digital screen*, which, in the ruinous yet unbridled desiring-production with which Deleuze and Guattari associate capitalism, remains irreducible to any given reterritorialisation or mechanism of control. That such individuals would lack 'revolutionary' consciousness in any party-political, twentieth-century sense is a fact which animates Deleuze and Guattari's entire project in the 'cold years' after May 1968.[49] Deleuze's work on cinema, and his elaboration of the themes of 'belief in the world' and 'a people to come', stems from just this situation, and a conviction that revolutionary thought must be articulated in an altogether new way.

We might then ask what 'world', or rather what 'link with the world', does *Inland Empire* impel us to believe in? I'd like to suggest that this is a world in which the universe of networked digital images might be other than simply a mechanism of marketing or control. It might rather be a universe redolent with intensive differences and virtual potentials, such as bubble in a metastability just beneath the skin of each image, ready to be provoked into the revolutionary production of the genuinely new. This would not be the quantitative 'new' of capitalist overcoding – of prosumer self-creation or an 'innovation' in consumer technics – rather this would be the *qualitatively* new, the as-yet unthinkable, the forces of the outside.

We saw Deleuze claim that 'a work of art does not contain the least bit of information...' *Inland Empire*, however, overflows with information, saturating us in its overwhelming affectivity. In combining dual senses of noise – conceived both as an empirical presence in information technologies, and as a chaotic grist which guarantees the 'openness' of art – *Inland Empire* works to problematise any simply technocratic, coercive or predetermined informatic operation. It achieves this by making a virtue of its noise, articulating noisy materials which consistently and explicitly refer to themselves *as information*. The film's use of digital technology – the shaky, hand-held camera, the glitchy, autonomous operations of software – constitutes a technical riposte to the charge that digitisation necessarily equates to a clarification or simplification of the image. The images of *Inland Empire* in fact undergo a constant complication, tending towards obscurity, proliferation of noise and, in Simondon's terms, an increased tension of information. And while we may well object that a film like Lynch's occupies a rarefied and relatively esoteric place in the ecology of contemporary information images, it gestures towards those 'shifting, slipping, dislocations, and hidden emissions' (N, 7) to which Deleuze attributes the source of his own philosophy, and out of which new forms of thinking and of acting might still, even now, emerge.

Notes

1. R. Sinnerbrink, *New Philosophies of Film: Thinking Images* (London: Continuum, 2011), p. 144.
2. Without wading into the complex specifics here, what distinguishes our own concept of critique from that of Adorno is the central role of negation or negativity in the thought of the latter, such that critique depends upon a trans-historical perspective which might 'enter' a given text in order to draw out its internal contradictions. As Adorno writes, 'criticism retains its mobility in regard to culture by recognising the latter's position within the whole. Without such freedom, without consciousness transcending the immanence of culture, immanent criticism itself would be inconceivable: the spontaneous movement of the object can be followed only by someone who is not engulfed by it.' T. W. Adorno, 'Cultural Criticism and Society', in *Prisms*, trans. S. Weber and S. Weber (Cambridge, MA: MIT Press, 1988), p. 29. Our own approach, following Deleuze and ultimately Spinoza, is dedicated to the proposition that we are not afforded this immaculate and transcendent perspective, and must face the far more difficult prospect of a criticality immanent only to the field in which it operates.
3. Sinnerbrink, *New Philosophies*, p. 142.
4. *Inland Empire*, dir. David Lynch, Absurda/Studio Canal, 2006.
5. The term is first introduced in the film's opening sequence, accompanying the black-and-white image of a record spinning on a gramophone. Here, a voice-over tells us that we are listening to 'Axxon N ... the longest running radio show in history ... continuing, in the Baltic

region: a grey winter day in an old hotel'. This strange semiotic recurs throughout the film, at several points scrawled in chalk on doorways and featuring an arrow indicating the direction Nikki is to follow. At each point when this device recurs, it immediately precedes a 'splitting' of the character: the first time immediately prior to her discovery of herself, viewed from the shadows of the soundstage. The second time, Nikki sees the sign on Hollywood Boulevard, immediately before noticing herself across the street, flashing a mocking grin. While Simon Critchley and Jamieson Webster have described Axxon N. as 'the axiom of the unintelligible' (S. Critchley and J. Webster, 'What is the Hole Inside the Hole: On David Lynch's Inland Empire', *Bedeutung*, 3, 'Life and Death', http://www.bedeutung.co.uk/magazine/issues/3-life-death/critchley-webster-lynch-empire/), Sinnerbrink argues that 'one can more fruitfully approach the resonances of "Axxon N." as a cinematic "axon" or brain/nerve cell linking multiple layers of consciousness … a topologically linked series of nested narrative filmworlds…' (Sinnerbrink, *New Philosophies*, p. 151). Clearly, as the harbinger of the film's various 'doublings' of Nikki's character, the term is related to the 'splitting' of the subject through its participation in various networks of retentional/recorded images (gramophone, film image and so on).

6 Quoted in M. Weigelt, 'Introduction', in I. Kant, *Critique of Pure Reason*, trans. M. Weigelt and M. Muller (London: Penguin, 2007), p. xv.
7 Shannon and Weaver, *Mathematical Theory*, p. 18.
8 D. Lynch, *Catching the Big Fish: Meditation, Consciousness and Creativity* (New York: Tarcher Perigee, 2016), p. 20.
9 Ibid.
10 J. Hoberman and J. Rosenbaum, *Midnight Movies* (Cambridge, MA: Da Capo, 1991), p. 234.
11 Lynch, *Big Fish*, p. 82.
12 Important to note is that Lynch's artistic practice is far from limited to film production, comprising written works, recorded music, and in particular visual/conceptual art, in which he was originally trained. Lynch's very first experiences with film emerged, indeed, from his work as a visual artist ('I began to wonder if film could be a way to make paintings move', ibid., p. 16); as such, his sensibility is inevitably conditioned by the same 'disruptive' concerns with which Eco associates the 'open work' of modern art, which would have formed a significant conceptual component of his training.
13 Ibid., p. 82.
14 A. Dawtrey, 'Lynch Invades an Empire', *Variety*, 11 May 2005, http://variety.com/2005/film/markets-festivals/lynch-invades-an-empire-1117922566/.

15 M. Idato, 'David Lynch on the Return of *Twin Peaks* and Why He Will Never Make Another Film', *Sydney Morning Herald*, 16 April 2007 (updated 5 May 2017), http://www.smh.com.au/entertainment/tv-and-radio/david-lynch-on-the-return-of-twin-peaks-and-why-he-will-never-make-another-film-20170416-gvlr60.html.
16 Foucault, 'Maurice Blanchot', p. 18.
17 Ibid., p. 57
18 Blanchot, *Space of Literature*, p. 27.
19 Lynch, *Big Fish*, p. 83.
20 The term refers both to 'unified field theory' in physics – according to which the functions of gravitation and electromagnetism might be understood as different manifestations of a single field (as first theorised by Einstein) – and also to what Maharishi Mahesh Yogi describes, in the context of transcendental meditation, as the 'unified field of consciousness', a consciousness of the universe itself, to which practitioners of transcendental meditation might cultivate access. Lynch has been a practitioner of TM since the early 1970s.
21 Lynch, *Big Fish*, p. 83.
22 Lapoujade, *Aberrant Movements*, p. 287.
23 See, for instance, Todd McGowan's analysis in *The Impossible David Lynch* (New York: Columbia University Press, 2007), pp. 90–109.
24 Quoted in M. Chabon, 'David Lynch's Night Truths', *The Paris Review*, 20 March 2018, https://www.theparisreview.org/blog/2018/03/20/david-lynchs-night-truths/.
25 Poster, *Deleuze and New Technology*, p. 261.
26 D. Lynch, 'David Lynch Theatre', YouTube, 1 February 2020, https://www.youtube.com/c/davidlynchtheater.
27 C. Marshall, 'David Lynch Made a Disturbing Web Sitcom Called "Rabbits": It's Now Used by Psychologists to Induce a Sense of Existential Crisis in Research Subjects', *Open Culture*, 30 May 2018, http://www.openculture.com/2018/05/david-lynch-made-a-disturbing-web-sitcom-called-rabbits.html.
28 Lynch, *Inland Empire*.
29 Guattari, *Machinic Unconscious*, p. 227.
30 K. Marx and F. Engels, *The Communist Manifesto*, trans. S. Moore (London: Penguin, 2002), p. 223. Note that Marx and Engels are here referring explicitly to *bourgeois culture*, as opposed strictly to a capitalist mode of production (which is nevertheless the engine of the former). This distinction is significant inasmuch as a contemporary shift into what the likes of Yanis Varoufakis has called 'techno-feudalism', tied equally to the trajectory of Sino-capitalism, suggests that the capitalist mode of production is in many ways *more* effective once it abandons bourgeois values of individualism and liberty, to which it was long believed intrinsic. This development is reflected in my own wording in the text.

31 Deleuze and Guattari, *A Thousand Plateaus*, p. 473.
32 Dawtrey, 'Lynch Invades an Empire', para. 4.
33 For what is undoubtedly the authoritative exploration of this theme, see L. Mulvey, 'Visual Pleasure and Narrative Cinema', *Screen*, 16(3) (1975), pp. 6–18.
34 Quoted in N. Kadner, 'Lynch Goes Digital with *Inland Empire*', *American Cinematographer*, 88(4) (2007), https://theasc.com/ac_magazine/April2007/PostFocus/page1.html.
35 For Aristotle, propositions about states of affairs in the future seem to transgress the law of non-contradiction inasmuch as they are contingent, and neither true nor false. Thus the propositions 'a sea-battle will be fought tomorrow' and 'a sea-battle will not be fought tomorrow' have the same contingent status until one is realised or actualised to the exclusion of the other. Leibniz attempts to solve this essentially semantic problem with his metaphysical notion of *compossibility* – the idea that God does not actualise all possibilities because not all possible substances are *com*possible, or capable of existing simultaneously. These possibilities nevertheless have a semantic and divine reality in other 'possible worlds'. See G. W. Leibniz, *Discourse on Metaphysics*, trans. G. Rodriguez-Pereyra (Oxford: Oxford University Press, 2020), pp. 18–23.
36 Ulman's widely publicised Instagram work *Excellences and Perfections* (2014), in which the artist took and posted 175 photos – of her brunch, selfies in lacy underwear, getting apparent (but ultimately fake) breast implants among a range of other social media clichés, before revealing the entire enterprise as a staged work – suggests the kind of practice that problematises distinctions we might make between art and non-art in the context of what Matthew Fuller has described as contemporary 'media ecologies'.
37 R. Horning and A. Ulman, 'Perpetual Provisional Selves: A Conversation about Authenticity and Social Media', *Rhizome*, 11 December 2014, https://rhizome.org/editorial/2014/dec/11/rob-horning-and-amalia-ulman/.
38 Dividuality, in addition to being a form of subjectivation immanent to the societies of control, is also a characteristic of the cinematic image. Deleuze writes, for instance: 'The cinematographic image is always dividual. This is because, in the final analysis, the screen, as the frame of frames, gives a common standard of measurement to things which do not have one – long shots of countryside and close-ups of the face, an astronomical system and a single drop of water – parts which do not have the same denominator of distance, relief or light. In all these senses the frame ensures a deterritorialization of the image' (*CI*, 18). As is usual with Deleuze, in other words, a single concept thus becomes the site of a polyvocal complication designed to engineer thought.

39 Alvin Toffler's term, developed from the work of Marshall McLuhan and Barrington Nevitt, designates a consumer whom, in the context of mass production and automation, is deployed in various processes of 'production' (customisation, value creation and so on) in order to continue the expansion of profit margins after basic consumer demands have been met. See A. Toffler, *Future Shock* (New York: Bantam Books, 1971).
40 In the centre of the room, for instance, a lumberjack saws a log in time to the music, a reference to the persistent motif of logs and logging in Lynch's work (*Twin Peaks*, *Blue Velvet*, *Industrial Symphony No. 1*).
41 J. Niedland, *David Lynch* (Urbana, IL: University of Illinois Press, 2012), p. 137.
42 M. Fuller, 'Art Methodologies in Media Ecology', in S. O'Sullivan and S. Zepke (eds), *Deleuze, Guattari and the Production of the New* (London: Continuum, 2008), p. 45.
43 Ibid., p. 46.
44 Ibid., p. 45.
45 Notable in this respect is the reception of both The Beach Boys' *Pet Sounds* (1966) and The Beatles' *Sgt Pepper's Lonely Hearts Club Band* (1967) as 'works of art', alongside the Velvet Underground's late 1960s collaboration with pop artist Andy Warhol.
46 As Fuller notes, at the very least, a huge proliferation of fine arts degrees means that, 'to take the British Isles, if we assume that most graduates from art schools since the 1960s are largely still alive, that means that there are several tens of thousands of people around with some kind of art training. Clearly not all of them are now artists or designers in a way that is recognised by art systems' ('Art Methodologies', p. 46). This institutionalised aesthetic literacy, however, is merely the tip of the iceberg, with greater numbers of people than ever afforded material means of access to galleries, cinemas, public art events and recorded music. The exponential increase of this trend, since the advent of the Internet and its easily accessible glut of archived cultural materials, is perhaps self-evident.
47 Deleuze, *Foucault*, p. 131.
48 See N. Land, 'Circuitries', in R. Mackay and A. Avanessian (eds), *The Accelerationist Reader* (Falmouth: Urbanomic, 2014), pp. 251–74.
49 For a clear elaboration of Deleuze's work in relation to the 'problem' of May '68, see the introduction to Colebrook, *Understanding Deleuze*, pp. xxxi–xliv.

7

Art and the Digital

'Art is dead. Godard can't do anything about it.' – graffiti, May '68[1]

In the last chapter, I argued that David Lynch's *Inland Empire* suggests a use of information technologies which might elude operations of control, opening digital media onto the 'outside' of thought, such as Deleuze associates with the cinematic image. But are we able to extend these claims about Lynch's film into an analysis of new media more generally? Despite its implication with digital technics, *Inland Empire* is in many ways, after all, a *time-image* in the twentieth-century sense: directed by an *auteur*, in dialogue with the history of artistic and experimental film, and primarily intended – whether consciously or not – for a particular, aesthetically literate public. *It is art*, in some sense of that term, and as such its entanglement with new and digital media implicates this perennially contested notion.

But we also saw that *Inland Empire* troubles art as a strict category, intersecting with image practices which bear no direct genealogical filiation with artistic canons or traditions. The film evokes the logic and aesthetics of hyperlinked URL environments, of memes and online pornography, home movies and sitcoms – connecting up with images which concretise both affects and percepts but which are not produced by artists or with any particular artistic intent. We saw that Lynch's deferral of creative authority to algorithmic and associated technical operations renders problematic a traditional image of the artist as being in command of every aesthetic detail. The aesthetic of *Inland Empire*, far from being meticulously constructed from the imagination of a particular subject, is rather improvised and chaotic, allowing the autonomous operations of widely available digital technics to co-determine the content of the image. This approach, I've suggested, perhaps complicates a traditional image of both art and of the artist – as the genius creator of rarefied aesthetic objects.

In this chapter, we turn to the question of art, and its relation to the broader ecology of digital images which constitutes twenty-first-century life. While we saw Deleuze claim that the 'essence of cinema' is concerned with effecting new and aberrant movements and individuations in thought, it achieves this *inasmuch as it is art*, and in keeping with a broader valorisation of artistic creation which recurs throughout Deleuze's *oeuvre*. But is Deleuze's modernism – which takes as its touchstone a transgressive noetic 'event' modelled on the Kantian sublime – sufficient to account for the informatic aesthetics which determine both the production of images and the (re)production of social relations in the first decades of the twenty-first century?

In what follows, I'd like to suggest that the contemporary ecology of digital images requires a further renovation of Deleuze's concepts, as well as a move beyond his thought and into that of his collaborator, Félix Guattari, who helps us to conceive of digital media as the site of contradictory impulses: on the one hand, a profound impoverishment in styles of thinking and of living, on the other, immense potentials from which new forms of thought might emerge. In extending Deleuze's idiosyncratic account of television, and in turning to Guattari's fragmentary theorisations of a 'post-media society',[2] we thus acquire tools which might help us to think the relationship between art and mass media in the information age, and the processes of aesthetic, noetic and social individuation they are capable of engendering.

Deleuze on the Box

Deleuze, as we have seen, is broadly critical of mass and popular media, a position exemplified in his infrequent remarks about television. In Chapter 4, we saw Deleuze associate television with the powers of 'control', and the production of a 'professional spectatorship' which eschews philosophically valuable aesthetic experimentation. In this context, his thought is perhaps contiguous with a significant body of theoretical work – from the Frankfurt School to Clement Greenberg[3] – that associates TV with a kind of sedative or infantilising effect, commensurate with its role in the architecture of global consumer capitalism. I'd like to suggest, however, not only that Deleuze's own position is somewhat more ambiguous than this initial precis suggests, but that the medium itself is hospitable to the kinds of resistant noetic 'events' which are the objective of his philosophy. 'Something in the world forces us to think' (*DR*, 139), we've seen Deleuze claim, and in the first part of this chapter I want to draw out some of the ways in which the televisual image might precipitate this creative and catalytic process.

Art and the Digital

In this way, we might better understand contemporary media more broadly, given that television is, in many ways, a prototype for the ecology of digital images. Its gradual infiltration of homes throughout the mid-twentieth century, bringing with it a complex and multivalent set of affects – a homogeneous national and then global image culture, an intimate combination of commercial and ostensibly non-commercial content, an intensification of various forms of audience participation, present, but not essential to other media (the effect of ratings, but also 'everyman' characters and situations) – are all tied to profound anxieties about the new medium's consequences for thought, social mores and possibilities in aesthetic creation. Perhaps most importantly, for our purposes, television emerges as a particular kind of 'flow',[4] extending the cinematographic mechanism for the communication of time and movement and disseminating it in a form which is both constant and programmable. And while broadcast television is on the wane[5] – in the process of losing its hegemonic position to streaming, social media and user-generated content – in many ways these more recent and recognisably digital practices thus continue an evolution which began, in earnest, with the 1950s televisual 'revolution'.

In order to fully grasp this trajectory – which has seen screens proliferate first to homes and then to individual prosumers – we must be attentive to a particular configuration of capitalism, which increasingly takes the (re)production of subjectivity as one of its fundamental objectives. We've already seen how so-called 'consumer culture' deploys subjectivity as both control mechanism and product, displacing the base–superstructure distinction in a dual movement which sees aesthetic production massively increased while institutions like those of education take on the commodity form. In this context, mass media embraces what Bernard Stiegler has called 'a new aesthetics', such as *'functionalis[es] the affective and aesthetic dimensions of the individual so as to produce a consumer'*.[6] In rendering social control fundamentally an affair of aesthetics, contemporary capitalism thus grants the libidinal investiture of signs a perhaps unprecedented importance, replacing bayonets with images. Deleuze and Guattari initially theorise these developments in terms of 'social production',[7] though the latter will increasingly speak of the 'production of subjectivity',[8] indicating a process which sees carefully calibrated semiotic 'machineries' manufacture subjectivity just as factories turn out aluminium, user electronics or cars.

In its capacity for directing movements and associations in cognition, the screened image plays a central role in this process, which is nevertheless fragile and ambiguous, inasmuch as it depends upon the forms of creativity and self-reference which render subjectivity a fundamentally volatile proposition. Indeed, the essentially Freudian notion that subjects are not innate or essential, but rather characterised by artificial and contingent modes of enjoyment, opens up the thought of a subjectivity which might be constructed otherwise – perhaps Guattari's ultimate theme. As he writes in *Schizoanalytic Cartographies*:

> The subjectivity of power does not fall out of the sky; it is not inscribed in the chromosomes that the divisions of knowledge and of labour must necessarily lead to the atrocious segregations that humanity experiences today. The unconscious figures of power and knowledge are not universals… Today, subjectivity remains massively controlled by apparatuses of power and knowledge which place technical, scientific and artistic innovations at the service of the most retrograde figures of sociality. And yet, other modalities of subjective production – those that are processual and singularising – are conceivable.[9]

Indeed, this process, as we saw in Chapter 3, is complex and contested, and the intensive and experimental engineering of desire which is characteristic of what Guattari will call Integrated World Capitalism is liable to produce all manner of haphazard and potentially uncontrollable events. Such, indeed, is a potential of television, and of a subsequent 'post-media' culture, once we bear in mind that their multiple and interfering images come into contact with far more singular and disparate situations globally than do the rarefied films of the post-war New Wave.

But before turning to these latter claims, we might return to some of Deleuze's own remarks about television, which, as I've suggested, are in some sense typical of a broader philosophical hostility towards the medium. The sources of this attitude are complex, but stem at least in part from demographic factors, as Lorenz Engell has noted:

> The easiest and most obvious reason for this circumstance is that the people who are actually responsible for the formation of theory and who are trained for this kind of theoretical work – academics, media scholars, intellectuals, critics, philosophers, and columnists – are simply not interested in television. As a form of mass culture, television is largely commercial and therefore necessarily trivial.[10]

This apparent triviality, Engell explains, combined with television's immense technical complexity, has made detailed theorisations of the medium rare – a neglect which does not take place in isolation. Indeed as Nöel Carroll has argued, a philosophical distaste for 'mass art' more generally can perhaps be explained by the discipline's inheritance of concepts rooted in Romanticism and Kantianism, and an implicit valorisation of 'natural' aesthetic experience over the urban, techno-industrialised world and its vulgarities.[11] Commensurate with this approach – which is closely tied to a notion of art as the product of rare, 'genius' creators – philosophers have been systematically reluctant to theorise both popular culture and new aesthetic technologies until their noetic implications are simply no longer deniable.[12]

Deleuze, it should be said, inherits elements of this reactivity, albeit complicated by his abiding aesthetic modernism. Art, for Deleuze, is generally avant-garde art – in some sense of that term – and his aesthetic tastes run consistently towards experimental and abstract compositions which are in some way disruptive of convention. At the same time, he makes occasional, intriguing remarks, which suggest that his project is in some ways contiguous with broader developments in popular culture. In one of his 'dialogues' with Claire Parnet, for instance, he claims that:

> the good ways of reading today succeed in treating a book as you would treat a record you listen to, a film or a TV programme you watch [...] There's no question of difficulty of understanding: concepts are exactly like sounds, colours or images, they are intensities which suit you or not, which are acceptable or aren't acceptable. Pop philosophy.[13]

Leaving aside, for now, the question of a 'pop philosophy', we might also note that Deleuze's own engagement with film must be understood in the context of a long-standing theoretical hostility to the notion that cinema itself was art, related to both its mechanical reproducibility and its popularity with the masses.[14]

At the same time, and in spite of these remarks, Deleuze is elsewhere decidedly elitist, dismissing popular culture in an offhand way which is perhaps commensurate with the 'aristocratic' impulse critics have attributed to his thought more broadly.[15] In a conversation with Antonio Negri, for instance, he claims, 'we can feel shame at being human in utterly trivial situations [...] in the face of too great a vulgarisation of thinking, in the face of TV entertainment, of ministerial speech, of "jolly people" gossiping' (*N*, 172). Or again, in *Cinema II*, in the context of his discussion of the potential 'death' of cinema:

> because television abandoned most of its own creative possibilities, and did not even understand them, it needed cinema to give it a pedagogical

lesson; it needed great cinema authors to show what it could do and what it would be able to do; if it is true that television kills cinema, cinema on the other hand is continually revitalising television... (*CII*, 252)

This is because television, as we have seen, abrogates or misunderstands the noetic potentials of the image, abandoning aesthetic experimentation in favour of a purely social function. But this passage also suggests the complexity of Deleuze's position, inasmuch as television does indeed possess creative possibilities – albeit those which it has tended to abandon. What might these possibilities be, exactly, and how might they help us to think through digital media? It is in the very notion of the possible, indeed, that we begin to sketch an answer to this question, in a movement which takes us back once more to the virtual, and the outside.

An Art of Exhaustion

In brief discussions of the televisual works of both Samuel Beckett and Jean-Luc Godard, Deleuze gives us a sense of what he feels television might achieve, once it 'stops being bad', and embarks upon its own idiosyncratic experiments with the image. In Godard's 'extraordinarily animated solitude' (*N*, 37), and Beckett's systematic *exhaustion of the possible* (*CC*, 163), Deleuze articulates a vision of television not as socialisation or control, but as precipitating noetic events in a mechanism commensurate with his account of cinema, literature or painting. In this sense, the approach here is typical of his broader aesthetic tastes – television is only philosophically valuable in the hands of *auteurs* taken from his preferred, high-brow canon. At the same time, Deleuze's remarks provide us with some intriguing tools for thinking through the televisual image more generally, provided we are able to extend his ideas beyond a treatment of these circumscribed and avant-garde experiments.

In 'The Exhausted' – a late essay published as the postface to Beckett's collected televisual works – Deleuze describes these works as a '"visual poem," a theatre of the mind that does not set out to recount a story but to erect an image', adding, 'according to Beckett, only television is able to satisfy these demands' (*CC*, 171). Here, Deleuze returns to themes developed in the cinema books, and the idea that the disconnected images of the New Waves escape narrativity, as such attaining a kind of 'purity' in their eschewal of sensory-motor interests. Beckett achieves something similar in his televisual

Art and the Digital

works, each of which centres on a disconnected and isolated image, a space bereft of context or ecology which Deleuze again calls the 'any-space-whatever' (*espace quelconque*), and which habitual mentation cannot fully integrate. In *Quad* (1981), with its white square set against a black void, *Ghost Trio* (1976), with its featureless room, haunted by a Nosferatu hunchback, and ... *but the clouds*... (1977) with its central pool of luminesce:

> it would seem that an image, inasmuch as it stands in the void outside space, and also apart from words, stories, and memories, accumulates a fantastic potential energy, which it detonates by dissipating itself. What counts in the image is not its meagre content, but the energy – mad and ready to explode – that it has harnessed, which is why images never last very long. The images merge with the detonation, combustion, and dissipation of their condensed energy. (CC, 161)

We must be attentive to this difficult formulation, which invites easy misreading. It is not so much that the image *accumulates* energy, but rather that it *exhausts* this energy that renders it significant. For Deleuze, indeed, Beckett's is an art of exhaustion – of aimless characters and intractable situations which open up hitherto unthinkable terrains through their systematic exhaustion of possibility.

We've already encountered Deleuze's critique of the notion of the possible, which, following Bergson, he suggests is a poorly formed concept, given its status as a retroactive derivation from the actual. The possible is the source of false problems, given that it is simply the actual plus or minus preformed, already-actualised components, which 'pass into existence according to an order of successive limitations',[16] in a model which has very little to tell us outside of certain artificial or highly formalised systems. In this context, Deleuze follows Bergson in opposing the possible to the virtual, which, as the structural condition for actualisation, does not resemble the actual at all. But Beckett's televisual image, importantly, expresses not possibility but its *exhaustion*, as such moving beyond the actual and opening onto virtual potentials as the proper domain of thought.

Thus, in *Quad*, which sees four hooded characters traverse the central square in a set of highly choreographed sequences, each following one of four rotationally symmetric paths and alternating their entrances and exits:

> it is a question of exhausting space. There is no doubt that the characters will become tired, and will drag their feet more and more. Yet tiredness

primarily concerns a minor aspect of the enterprise: the number of times one possible combination is realised (for example, two of the duos are realised twice, the four trios twice, the quartet four times). The protagonists become tired depending on the number of realisations. But the possible is accomplished, independently of this number, by the exhausted characters who exhaust it. (CC, 163)

Quad, in other words, 'exhausts possibility' twice over: on the one hand staging each possible combination of the singularities comprising its isolated and highly formal system, on the other – and in continuity with Beckett's broader *oeuvre* – instigating a theatre of exhausted bodies, centralising abject dramatic personae for whom all further movement seems impossible.

For Deleuze, indeed, the exhausted body is a literal time-image, expressing as it does the limits of purposive action and a pure physicality into which thought might 'plunge' (*CII*, 195), and experience as both productive violence and singular constraint. In this way, exhaustion marks the site of a rigorous empiricism, a victory of the local, singular and embodied over the transcendent aspirations of the sensory-motor paradigm. When exhausted, the body is divested of all purpose or intention, and as such is open to an experience of a pure temporality, no longer contracted by sensory-motor interests. 'Only an exhausted person can exhaust the possible', explains Deleuze, 'because he has renounced all need, preference, goal, or signification. Only the exhausted person is sufficiently disinterested, sufficiently scrupulous' (CC, 154), in a mechanism which returns to a practice of thought as the forced dislocation of our habituated goals and exigencies. When exhausted, writes Deleuze, 'one remains active, but for nothing [...] everything divides, but into itself; and God, who is the sum total of the possible, merges with Nothing, of which each thing is a modification' (CC, 153).

Beckett's *exhaustion-image*, in other words, is the site of a radical atheism – returning the transcendent aspirations of thought to their origins in the unthinkable materiality of bodies and their limits. That Beckett achieves or instigates this philosophical inversion – which is simultaneously a dislocation of the personal and communicative pretensions of language[17] – is tied to his idiosyncratic use of the image, which 'emerges in all its singularity, retaining nothing of the personal or the rational' (CC, 158) as a pure perceptual intensity which is sensible, but not yet thinkable. This is the *Beckettian outside* – a composition of sensible materials which articulates an experience of limits: the limits both of the highly constrained and ultimately exhausted systems which comprise the image itself, and of a thought forced to account for these systems without recourse to the arid theology of the possible. Such a thought – in keeping with our account in Chapter 1 – must therefore reach beyond actuality, drawing on the structure of virtual singularities in order to produce counteractualisations, adequate to an image encountered as 'problem'. The question, however, is whether we are able to extend this model to think through television more generally, given the decidedly esoteric character of these experiments. Beckett, we will recall, claims that 'only television [can] satisfy these demands...' and we might turn to the specificity of the televisual form, in order to understand why.

One of the most frequent means of distinguishing the televisual from the cinematic image is in terms of *seriality*,[18] and we might note that the televisual image is often serially or episodically composed until certain possibilities are exhausted, be they creative or commercial.[19] This, combined with what are historically smaller budgets in television production – McLuhan's 'coolness'[20] – means that the televisual image tends to eschew wide-ranging aesthetic experimentation in favour of a highly constrained repetition – a play with the (re)combination of finite elements, which often 'resets' at the beginning of each episode. Deleuze identifies this logic as it is schematised in Beckett's televisual images, returning to the vocabulary of a musical semiotics developed with Guattari. In *Quad*, he writes, 'the form of the ritornello is the *series*, which in this case is no longer concerned with objects to be combined, but only with journeys having no object' (CC, 162, emphasis added), and while this is an apt description of Beckett's highly formal composition, I'd like to suggest that it can be meaningfully extended to account for the televisual image in its more popular articulations.

Thus, the four characters in *Seinfeld* (1989–98) – confined either to Jerry's apartment or to their local diner – exhaust the minutiae of everyday life, successively probing situations, ideas and relations in order to draw out their meaninglessness and futility. This exhaustion evolves, through *Curb Your Enthusiasm* (2000–), into the crawling embarrassment of Larry David's life in LA, and its moral: by the twenty-first century, even a life of wealth and fame is empty and annoying. The characters in *Sex and the City* (1998–2004), meanwhile – through their endless recombination of sex acts, partners and scandals – systematically exhaust liberal American visions of hedonism, in a trajectory which washes them up each week for the same mid-morning brunch. From the gauche hotel of *Fawlty Towers*

(1975–79) to the claustrophobic flat in *Peep Show* (2003–15), the sitcom in particular deploys the serial form to engender an ambience of simultaneous exhaustion and constraint – a sense of stasis and banality which frees the image to explore all manner of a-centred and apparently insignificant circuitries.

The formal continuities between these popular televisual images and those of an *auteur* like Beckett may seem forced or arbitrary, but they begin to make sense once we understand each as *symptomatic*: the product less of local genius than of impersonal 'problems' in modern thought, life and sensibility. Television, indeed, responds to an exhaustion of possibilities which is both localised and general. On the one hand, there is the exhausted body of the viewer, who turns to the screen with the explicit aim of outsourcing cognition. On the other, there is the exhaustion of the narrative form itself, which Deleuze will diagnose in both literature and cinema, and which the artificially isolated 'situations' of turn-of-the-century TV embrace as one of their key axioms. There's no salvation from the mindless tedium of *The Office* (2001–03), which as such becomes the habitat for a menagerie of strange monads, like the tragicomic David Brent. Indeed, what Fukuyama called the 'sadness' of the end of history[21] is particularly clear in serial television, which, by the end of the twentieth century, abandons the *telos* of narrative to become self-consciously about 'nothing' – being stuck in an apartment foyer, waiting endlessly in a Chinese restaurant, or attending the same birthday party for eternity.

Understanding these serial exhaustion-images as possessing a genuine philosophical content – or more properly, as concretising an aesthetic material which philosophy might experience as provocation – requires the suspension of bourgeois notions of the artistic which have frequently obscured the genius of popular culture. This suspension allows us to intuit an inventiveness in television analogous to the more 'sophisticated' experiments of theatre, literature or cinema. Indeed, when Deleuze writes that Beckett's televisual images are '[concerned] only with journeys having no object' (CC, 162), he could well be describing *The Simpsons* (1989–), whose five singularities begin each episode by arriving at the object of so many exhausted trajectories through the inferno of post-industrial labour: the family's grubby couch. It's no accident that the Simpsons begin each week with a fumbling effort to arrive at this same point of commencement, and that this any-space-whatever is the couch, in a mirror image which explicitly interpolates the televisual spectator.[22]

It simply doesn't matter how they arrive in front of the TV each week, or even if they arrive at all – the success of the image depends upon the audience's recognition of their own situation, and a transcendental immobility as profound as any of Beckett's grubbers.

Of course, an image predicated on mechanisms of both recognition and identification will be antithetical to Deleuze's own account of art, which is always valorised as the site of something we don't yet recognise. And indeed, the function of identification lies at the heart of TV as 'social engineering', as critics like Adorno have also noted.[23] In addressing the viewer *as exhausted*, the televisual image thus seeks to engender a particular kind of comfort, affirming the audience's immobility, failures and abjection. But this identificatory comfort is tenuous, given that it must be augmented with sufficient excitative mechanisms to prompt both continued engagement and an attendant consumption of product displays. It's the delicate and often imperfect balancing of these imperatives which renders the 'social engineering' of TV a fundamentally volatile proposition, particularly once we consider the disparate and unpredictable situations into which its flow is broadcast. Televisual production, like all capitalist production, must *innovate* – deterritorialising traditional semiotic investments and capturing desire through circuitries of novelty and transgression – and this fact engenders an avant-gardism which deploys these exhaustion-images in complex and unexpected ways.

This situation becomes particularly clear in the transition from broadcast television to streaming technics, and the arrival, via cable, of the so-called 'post-network' era.[24] The decentralisation of audiences characteristic of this paradigm prompted the second so-called 'Golden Age of Television',[25] and a widely remarked increase in aesthetic experimentation – with new images combining cinematic techniques with potentials immanent to the televisual medium specifically. While the series that emerge from this paradigm thus eschew the aridly formal repetition characteristic of *Seinfeld* or earlier, single-set sitcoms, they are nevertheless tied to determinate and repeated situations in a mechanism designed to engender a kind of 'familiarised complexity'.[26] This methodical (re)composition of finite elements is combined with the serial-narrative form, with its origins less in cinema than the modern novel and radio – though we may ultimately be justified in tracing its roots to certain conventions in myth and popular storytelling.[27]

While ostensibly narrative, these are no longer action-images in the classical sense, subordinating a *richesse* of apparently irrelevant details to a central teleological structure. Indeed, the series characteristic of the so-called 'Golden Age' return to something like the polyphony of modern literature, deploying narrative in an instrumental or secondary way, as a skeleton around which to develop ecosystems of tangential scenes, situations and characters. In this way, the dividual episodic structures of series like *The Sopranos* (1999–2007), *Mad Men* (2007–15), *Breaking Bad* (2008–13) and *The Wire* (2002–08) produce a complex multi-temporal assemblage, in many ways characteristic of the informatic image-space more broadly. The dilation of narrative allows for a horizontality analogous to URL environments, replacing both hierarchies of significance and centralised, purposive movement with time-slices populated by multiple and polyrhythmic ritornellos.

While I don't intend to weigh into the somewhat tired and fastidious debates as to the 'cinematic' status of these productions, I do believe they should cause us to think twice before we consider television as simply control, ideology or distraction. Again, these are often prodigious exhaustion-images, articulating a profound incapacity to narrativise, and frequently returning thought to the impersonal singularity of bodies. It's no accident that *The Sopranos* begins with the event of Tony's first panic attack, which launches the therapeutic encounter which beats at the series' heart. The halting, associative exploration of Tony's psyche – which becomes an exploration of America's – emerges from a traumatic encounter with the body experienced as limit, and a desire for an animal re-embodiment (Tony's ducks and horses), which leads to all manner of crystalline time-images.[28] Before being an affair of language – which, in *The Sopranos*, is always oblique, ironic and vernacular, a 'minor language' as apt to fail and collapse into rage as to communicate discretely – the series stages a ballet of exhausted corporealities; from Tony's binge eating to Paulie and Michael's pointless ordeal in the snow, to the profusion of corpses chopped up or crammed in trunks and freezers.

We risk passing over the noetic potential of these images if we understand them only in terms of social engineering. That Tony's own exhaustion is simultaneously America's, which systematically envelops the show's characters in a morass of overconsumption and violence, is as much the product of irrepressibly 'problematic' social forces as the careful mechanisms of a culture industry. Certainly, the success of these images depends upon the viewer's recognition of their own situation – though this is not a criticism we feel compelled to make today of Visconti's images of bourgeois decay and alienation. My claim is that there is nevertheless *another content* in the image, an irreducible presence of traumatic materiality – such as dislocates habituated norms of signification and comportment, like Walter White's cancer: a black cloud spreading out to abolish possibility. This presence, which in the previous chapter I called *noise*, is the unsayable at the heart of all that is said: the impersonal and unthinkable insistence of bodies, pre-individual forces and intensities. And while Beckett articulates this presence in the context of a familiar regime of avant-garde expression, I'd like to suggest that we might encounter it in the most everyday images of the televisual apparatus – provided we watch carefully.

Twin Peaks: *The Return of the Repressed*

Of course, it goes without saying that the televisual image is so thoroughly implicated with the imperatives of control that we are unable to enact the somewhat sweeping dismissal of 'social' factors with which Deleuze begins his cinematic taxonomy.[29] Indeed, the decentralisation and multiplicity characteristic of the so-called 'Golden Age' is paradigmatic of post-disciplinary societies generally, which, as Paul Virilio has observed, substitute control through stasis and confinement with forms of openness, motion and 'democratic' complexity.[30] Central to these developments is the digital image, which, as Alexander Galloway writes:

> is a question of multiplicity, nay an infinity, of points of view flanking and flooding the world viewed [...] the CCTV meshes deployed across cities; the multiple data points involved in data mining; the virtual camera or "fly-through mode" in CAD software; or crowd-sourcing swarms that converge on a target.[31]

And indeed, this 'reverse panopticon'[32] is replicated in the multiple perspectives of contemporary television, which are just as likely to squeeze out sites of indeterminacy and error as confront thought with an 'out-of-frame' or outside.

At the same time, as Dennis Broe has argued, the 'Golden Age' is linked to new forms of both production and consumption, with streaming services replacing broadcast technics in order to ensnare 'a beleaguered workforce that must simply grab bits of time when it can',[33] turning leisure time into another kind of labour. For Broe, the practices of 'binge watching' which these dividual episodic structures are designed to encourage are intimately tied to a logic of 'engagement' characteristic of both new media and informatic production generally, whereby the *quantities* of information consumed become an important control mechanism. At the level of human subjects, this amounts to 'new accelerated forms of acceptable addiction centred on the mode of delivery [...] and promotion of a social autism that devalues social relations and overvalues pure productivity'.[34]

As Bernard Stiegler has argued, in his own work on control societies,[35] this systematic liquidation of sociality is tied to mediatic techniques which seek to regulate and homogenise the particular aesthetic investments (or sublimations) with which Freud had distinguished singular *desire* from blind and undifferentiated *drives* – a situation the former will link to all manner of violent and impulsive archaisms. In rendering previously heterogeneous experiences of temporality, in particular, industrial and homogeneous, Stiegler argues that the televisual apparatus and its digital successors work to erase our capacity to form aesthetic attachments to singular objects, in favour of a free-floating (or de-cultured) libido receptive both to the shifting imperatives of the market and the standardised objects of industrial production. Stiegler follows Simondon in describing this process as a form of proletarianisation,[36] inasmuch as it liquidates unique and embodied experiences, knowledges and 'arts of the self' – engendering an impoverishment which is no longer strictly speaking economic.

In our terms, we might observe that we are once more in the realm of images which appear to have no outside, working as they do to ward off the experience of singular and unthinkable compositions of sensible materials. The new televisual image – like those of social media, online pornography or the 24-hour news cycle – deploys a compulsive dividuality in the service of an addictive flow which is both incessant and globalised; the first percepts the dividual subject encounters on waking, if she's lucky enough to have slept. But does this amount to a claim that these are the only effects of which the digital image is harbinger?

In the final part of this chapter, I'd like to explore some of the ways in which the digi-televisual assemblage – *when it stops being bad* – might rearticulate these powers of hyper-connectivity, exhaustion and addiction, using them to generate unthinkable images which disturb hegemonic logics of consumption and production. In this context, I'd like to return to the figure of David Lynch, this time focusing on his works for television. Again, my discussion of Lynch's work, and in particular his 'soap opera' *Twin Peaks*, should not be understood as textual analysis in the strict sense – which is to say, as elucidatory or hermeneutic. Rather, my conviction is that *Twin Peaks* can be experienced as a provocation to think televisuality in new ways, just as *Inland Empire* prompts us to think information and the digital image differently. As such, my aim is less to resurrect *la politique des auteurs* than to use a particular aesthetic object 'like a telescope', to use an appropriate image from Proust,[37] which might help us bring into focus some of the slippages and surrealisms of the televisual assemblage generally.

Lynch's work, as we saw in the last chapter, is characterised by an ethic of affirmation, which sees haphazard, experimental and technically overdetermined elements integrated into the composition of images. Network-era television, with its rigorously commercial imperatives, might seem an unlikely habitat for this compositional ethic, but I'd like to suggest that the unexpected success of *Twin Peaks* tells us as much about the televisual sensorium generally as it does about Lynch's own particular artistry. The 'flow' of broadcast television, after all, combines disparate images whose frequent incongruity is only barely masked by the imperatives of commerciality. Hunter S. Thompson once wrote of Las Vegas that 'psychedelics are almost irrelevant in a town where you can wander into a casino any time of the day or night and witness the crucifixion of a gorilla',[38] and indeed, we might say the same of TV, which pre-empts that other hyperactive metropolis of capitalist desire, the Internet, in its surreal melange of advertising, art, televangelism and sexuality. This bizarre assemblage is complicated by the interactivity of the viewer, who anticipates the undulatory 'surfer' of both control and the online image space in her restless participation in this flow's (re)composition.

Lynch's work, as I've suggested, is the product of an analogous form of 'viewing' – such as refuses the normalisation of these mediatic assemblages, traversing them in order to draw out the perverted complexity of banal or everyday images. As David Foster Wallace once suggested, in a tentative definition of the *Lynchian*, 'the very macabre and the very mundane combine in such a way as to reveal the former's perpetual containment within the latter',[39] and indeed, *Twin Peaks* exemplifies this uncomfortable disjunctive synthesis. In more Deleuzian terms, we might say that Lynch's practice articulates a perpetual interference between signifying semiotics and the traumatic and a-signifying content upon which they depend, a content which is *sensible*, yet which hegemonic regimes of signs strive ceaselessly to ward off or render insensible. Importantly, as we've seen, Lynch's staging of this 'return of the repressed' takes the form not of a categorical hostility towards new and popular media, but rather an embrace of non-cinematic image techniques in terms of their singular potentials. In this way, I claim, Lynch's project prompts us to think television itself as a potential source of strange new individuations in thought and in the image – helping us to move from a politics of *auteurs* towards an ecology of images.

At its heart, *Twin Peaks* is, after all, a *soap opera* – something that Angelo Badalamenti's haunting yet melodramatic score consistently affirms. As Robert Loyd has written, the soap opera form – named for the feminised products it was initially intended to market – is characterised by an expansiveness and dilation which troubles coherent or centralised narrativity:

> Although melodramatically eventful, soap operas [...] have a luxury of space that makes them seem more naturalistic; indeed, the economics of the form demand long scenes, and conversations that a 22-episodes-per-season weekly series might dispense with in half a dozen lines of dialogue may be drawn out [...] for pages. You spend more time even with the minor characters; the apparent villains grow less apparently villainous.[40]

We have already seen this kind of dilation in the more recent so-called 'Golden Age of Television', of which the original *Twin Peaks* was in many ways a harbinger. And indeed, while the first two series, set in the eponymous Washington town, are organised around a central narrative mystery – the killing of school Homecoming Queen Laura Palmer – the murder is ultimately a lure, the pretext Lynch and co-creator Mark Frost use to pursue their true objective: the bizarre personalities and surreal social fabric of the town, Twin Peaks itself.

The original series – which aired to ratings success and critical acclaim on the ABC network throughout 1990 and 1991[41] – transplants Lynch's surreal cinematic explorations from the metropolitan centres of the 'old media' paradigm to the televisual heartland of America. Here, Lynch uses both the conceit of the outsider new to town (Kyle MacLachlan's FBI special agent Dale Cooper) and the sprawling structure of the soap opera form as a staging-ground for his own affirmative compositional ethic. Not only is *Twin Peaks* characterised by an almost compulsive addition of characters, subplots and visions which increasingly bear no clear relation to the series' central mystery, but at the level of its production Lynch is again directed by unexpected and aleatory aesthetic 'events'. The show's central villain, the demonic killer BOB, is played by set dresser Frank Silva, who Lynch happened to spot alone on the set and who he felt projected the right menacing aura.[42] His inclusion of motifs from Tibetan Buddhism is linked to an incidental encounter with the Dalai Lama, which took place during filming.[43] Lynch attributes the genesis of other scenes – like the infamous 'red room' – to a combination of unconscious images and bodily affects, which coalesce and cause ideas to 'leap' into his mind.[44]

At the same time, the original *Twin Peaks* was determined by commercial imperatives which give it an austerity and restraint that *Inland Empire* eschews. The show ultimately remained wedded to the narrative arc with which Frost and Lynch had sold it to executives, as to the central mystery which guaranteed its ratings.[45] Lynch shot the series on 35mm film stock, and mixed the sound down from a cinema sound-system, giving it a distinctly cinematic ambience and aesthetic.[46] Indeed, the series is in many ways exemplary of a situation in which the conservatism of the televisual medium is perhaps 'revitalised' by a cinematic sensibility. It's only in the context of *Twin Peaks: The Return* – the fruit of a 25-year interval which takes in Lynch's encounter with the digital – that we discover a uniquely digi-televisual aesthetic, and an intensification of mechanisms of both disjunction and exhaustion which might help us to think a specifically digital outside.

If *Twin Peaks* is in some sense about TV, then *Twin Peaks: The Return* – which ran for eighteen episodes in 2017 – is about *Twin Peaks* itself, as transformed by both digitisation and its own resonant effect on popular culture. Indeed, *The Return* can be meaningfully understood as constituting a fresh node in the feedback loop carefully established between the show and its audience, enacting as it does a wry exploration of its own peculiar cult status. In scenes such as that which sees Audrey Horne – mysteriously returned from her apparent death at the end of season two – enact her sultry, iconic dance across the dancefloor at the Roadhouse, or Ed and Norma embrace to the soundtrack of Otis Redding's 'I've Been Loving You Too Long', after years of silent longing, *The Return* enacts a self-conscious tracing of the circuitries of both diegetic and spectator desire, in a movement spanning decades. As Dennis Lim has written, '*Twin Peaks* was a mass-culture text that called for communal decoding, a semiotic wonderland of clues, symbols, and red herrings',[47] and while *The Return* certainly responds to and reactivates this immense pop-cultural hermeneutics, it is also characterised by a newfound starkness and brutality, which consistently displaces the quaintness of the show's first two seasons.

Indeed *The Return* – which expands the series' *mise en scène* to include events taking place in New York, Las Vegas, South Dakota and elsewhere – is marked by a far *colder* ambience and aesthetic, commensurate with a shift from analogue specificity into the vastness of digital networks. While the initial series alternated menacing shots of the forests surrounding Twin Peaks with the wooded cosiness of the town's various interiors, *The Return* eschews this sense of place in favour of an apparent infinity of impersonal any-spaces-whatever: the warehouses, hotel rooms, prison cells and vacant display homes of post-GFC America. These blank, disjunctively connected locales become the site of a violence which is both far more explicit and decidedly more casual than that of the original series – in the first episode alone we see two young lovers suddenly hacked to death, while the police discover a corpse which has been beheaded (or more properly *re*-headed) – and these sudden bursts of horror are accompanied by a near-ubiquitous semantic breakdown, with characters frequently and inexplicably failing to communicate.

This semantic collapse is replicated at the level of spectatorship, with scenes consistently failing to make any sense in terms of coherent narrative arcs or sensory-motor connections. In a characteristic sequence – which begins as a discussion between characters Bobby, Shelly and their daughter Becky about her abusive relationship with Steven, taking place in Norma's iconic diner (now the flagship store to a franchise of dubious quality) – the dialogue is suddenly interrupted when a bullet flies through the window, sending customers scrambling for cover. Running to investigate, Bobby discovers that the gun was accidentally fired by a child in a nearby car, whose parents can offer only incoherent and ineffectual platitudes. When Bobby moves to placate the driver of another car, who has been honking incessantly, he encounters an enraged woman screaming about her own sick child, who emerges from the shadows vomiting and convulsing, in a chain of increasingly incongruous and unnerving events to which the diegesis never returns.

Such scenes, and there are many, are noteworthy not just for the ways in which they trace ongoing alterations in the social fabric of America. What they express, indeed, is a collapse in epistemic authority which is characteristic of informatically mediated capitalism globally. This situation is exemplified in the series' dislocation of its own narrative reliability, and a consistent tendency to problematise modes of spectatorship predicated on a desire for resolution or revelation. While the season two finale left audiences with all manner of unanswered questions – Will Dale Cooper escape the Black Lodge? Did Audrey survive the explosion in the bank? Will Donna accept Ben Horne as her father? – season three quickly subverts any expectation that these questions might ever be satisfactorily answered, compulsively adding new characters, situations and mysteries which frustrate any possible epistemic satisfaction. In this context, as Matthew Ellis and Tyler Theus have observed, the series exemplifies 'a certain tendency [...] not to *extend* the original narrative, but to show that, in some sense, we as spectators have failed to understand just how enigmatic it always was'.[48] And indeed, when Lynch and Frost do ultimately 'resolve' key narrative arcs, they foreground the absurd unreality of any such 'resolution' – as when the series' antagonist is unceremoniously punched into screensaver oblivion by Freddie Sykes' magic green glove.

This near-complete eschewal of an already fragile mode of narrativisation is tied as much to the material conditions of the series' production as it is to broader (and related) changes in thought and sensibility. The series' status as a special televisual 'event' – distributed via subscription streaming service Showtime and as such quarantined from immediate commercial imperatives – granted Lynch and Frost significant creative freedoms, allowing them to intensify tendencies towards incommensurability and non-communication which were often restrained during the first two series.[49] At the same time, these inscrutable aspects of the show's diegesis dovetail with a broader climate of epistemic collapse, and a contemporary politics of misinformation, disinformation and conspiracy theories – schematised not only in the figure of Dr Jacoby (who has become a nativist conspiracy podcaster), but the penultimate episode's digital 'deep fake', which sees a 56-year-old MacLachlan time-travel to rescue an incompossibly unaged Laura Palmer. In our terms, we might observe that the series' structure articulates the *exhaustion* of a set of long-standing conventions for the sensible ordering of images, radically increasing their quotient of unthinkability, or capacity for *information*.

Again, Lynch's approach is noteworthy in its refusal to greet these developments as stultifying or restrictive. This collapse at the level of both reliable semantic information and sensory-motor narrative allows for a proliferation of obscure and disjunctively related images, far in excess of the pure 'opsigns' which characterised the first two seasons (the traffic light, the windswept trees, the waterfall beneath the Great Northern). A characteristic sequence features an employee sweeping the floor of the Roadhouse, dimly lit by neon signs and soundtracked by Booker T. & the M.G.'s, in a single shot which serves no narrative purpose and lasts over two minutes. At one point we spend nearly three minutes watching Laura Palmer's mother (Grace Zabriskie) herself watching TV – smoking, getting up and going into the kitchen to find more booze, while all we hear is an endlessly looped snippet from an old boxing match on television. Another sequence, which runs at over five minutes, uses digital special effects to restage the first testing of the atom bomb at White Sands, New Mexico – with the camera appearing to enter into the demented, particulate atmosphere of the expanding mushroom cloud in an extended visual study of the microphysics of evil.

Such images once more substitute pure perceptual intensities for purposive sensory-motor movements, returning to the disinterested visuality of the cinematic time-image. But more than this, in their radically disparate styles, subjects and techniques, they suggest the polyvocality of multiple-source image platforms like TikTok, UbuWeb or YouTube – connected as they are by an inscrutable, irrational and frequently sinister logic. Indeed, like *Inland Empire*, the connections which characterise *The Return* are fundamentally *disjunctive* – with improbable links and rapid, inexplicable cuts articulating a bizarre and consistently 'noisy' assemblage. The phenomenal experience of this hyperlinked image-space is nevertheless strangely familiar, replicating as it does the incongruous psychedelics of channel surfing or the Kafkaesque absurdity of intranets. Far from enacting a transcendent critique of these 'non-artistic' image-worlds, Lynch inhabits and accentuates them, proliferating their irrational connections across the vast dilation of the multi-episode soap opera – itself already tending towards incompossibility and illogic.[50]

This fundamentally 'problematic' connectivity stems once more from an experimental approach to post-production, with significant work taking place in the editing room to complicate the series' semantic and communicative dimensions. A characteristic technique saw Lynch and editor Duwayne Dunham organise scenes according to colour-coded index cards which stood for the different characters and locations. Dunham and Lynch would

> look at the board and say, "we haven't seen any green for a while. We're away for a long time, and we've got a little bit here and a whole bunch

over here. And you can just look at [the board] and say, what if we broke that up a little bit more?"[51]

And this approach, which subordinates all-too-human concerns like those of narrative to an operation we might call *algorithmic*, is characteristic of a consistent tendency of *The Return* to treat its images not as semantically meaningful but as information in the technical or ontogenetic sense of pure, a-signifying data.

Indeed a gradual withdrawal of Lynch the *auteur*, in favour of Lynch as *manipulator of data*, has been obliquely traced in critical commentary, albeit in terms of its paradoxical character. Jonathan Foltz, in an oft-cited essay, has suggested that *The Return* exemplifies Lynch's 'late style', a term he takes from Adorno, indicating a moment when the artist, confronted with the imminence of death, 'abandon[s] the very conceit of expression itself' in favour of an impersonal exploration of unadulterated conventions, tropes and mechanisms.[52] For Adorno, writing on Beethoven:

> The power of subjectivity in the late works of art is the irascible gesture with which it takes leave of the works themselves. It breaks their bonds, not in order to express itself, but in order, expressionless, to cast off the appearance of art.[53]

In this context, Adorno claims, 'the conventions [...] are no longer penetrated and mastered by subjectivity, but simply left to stand', in a movement which makes the later works 'catastrophes'.[54] And indeed, *The Return* is a kind of catastrophe – in the Greek sense of both end and overturning – marking as it does the exhaustion of any possibility that art might 'communicate', and the movement of Lynch's own disappearance into a realm of mysterious algorithms.

Entering Post-media Society

As I suggested in the previous chapter, I believe that this disappearance has broader implications, linked as it is to a generalised erosion of interiority and self-identity precipitated first by mechanical, and now digital reproducibility.[55] And this development need not be greeted as categorically baleful or unwelcome, if we understand the human 'subject' as always already linked to problematic modes of *subjection to* a particular social order. If Lynch's complex affirmation of digitality constitutes a kind of art, while paradoxically effacing the privileged figure of the artist as creator or communicator, then it perhaps suggests broader vectors of potential creativity and resistance – a *becoming-digital* we might think without lapsing into the Newspeak of Silicon Valley. A thought adequate to these developments, I claim, requires the continued interrogation of certain long-standing philosophical prejudices. Chief among these is an idea of aesthetic production as the exclusive remit of certain classes or individuals, and of art as an immaculate, quasi-religious experience beyond all vulgar apprehension. This is often how Deleuze appears to understand it, and this understanding leads to a denigration of forms of creative social individuation ('jolly people gossiping') which enact a more subtle and collective erosion of hegemonic axioms of production.

Part of what makes a return to the televisual image so fertile in this space is the way in which it helps us to articulate this presupposition, which is ultimately the site of what we once might have called *class antagonism*. Indeed, the categorical hostility of much so-called 'Continental' thought to cybernetic concepts and digital techniques is perhaps also meaningfully viewed in terms of this apparently antiquated notion. What makes Lynch's own work so compelling from this point of view is not only its deferral of a certain intentionality on the part of the artist to algorithmic and aleatory processes. Lynch's practice is also noteworthy for its emphasis on the intellect and creativity of *viewers*, who are not only invited to take part in a consistent co-creation of the significance of his images, but to identify with an artistic practice which is itself built out of an aberrant and creative form of 'viewing'. This destabilisation of traditional distinctions between the artist and his 'public' is particularly clear in the case of *Twin Peaks* fandom, which, as a number of commentators have observed,[56] takes in a bewildering array of creative and collective forms of amateur cultural production – from semiotically dense memes to a constellation of discussion boards, fan fiction and podcasts.

This compulsive co-creativity on the part of viewers stems, undoubtedly, from the fact that *Twin Peaks* is *addictive*, constructed as it is in keeping with many of the standard mechanisms of dividual episodic television. But whereas digi-mediatic addiction usually takes the form of a passivity associated with viewers being transformed into informatic nodes or 'receivers', the show's high *tension* of information – which is to say, its quotient of unthinkability – frequently transforms the injunction to consume into a compulsive creativity. And this, I'd like to suggest, indicates a danger inherent to forms of social engineering which depend upon both the massive dissemination of aesthetic materials and the production of subjectivity. Indeed, if – following Bergson and Deleuze – we understand subjectivity in terms of a particular capacity for *framing* (*cadrage*), with an attendant sense of virtuality afforded through mechanisms of *cutting* (*découpage*), editing (*montage*) and (why not?) *hyperlinking* – then subjectivity is always marginally dangerous, given the potentials for creativity and self-transcendence implied by this assemblage.

At the same time, broadcasting, or the extension of control networks, always implies the insertion of a foreign content (information) into a situation which has at least some degree of metastability. Lou Reed once sang about a girl whose life is saved when she happens upon a radio station playing rock'n'roll,[57] and we might extend this model to account for a universe of bedroom samplers and TikTok surrealists, or indeed a teenager who encounters *2001* (1968) on TV one night and determines to become a philosopher. These are the everyday events characteristic of societies which produce and disseminate masses of information, and as such potential encounters with the unthinkable, or outside. And while control algorithms are ceaselessly honed to better target information and as such reduce its unpredictability or tension, this proliferation is always simultaneously unfolding new and potentially volatile milieux, particularly those we might map throughout the worlds of decolonisation and capitalism's various 'peripheries'.[58]

This massive dissemination is accompanied by a vast multiplication of technical objects allowing for the amateur production of texts, sounds and images, the site of a new kind of pop art, or perhaps a pop philosophy.[59] As Deleuze and Guattari write, in a passage we have already encountered:

> machinic enslavement abounds in undecidable propositions and movements that, far from being a domain of knowledge reserved for sworn specialists, provides so many weapons for the becoming of everybody/everything, becoming radio, becoming electronic, becoming molecular... Every struggle is a function of all of these undecidable propositions and constructs *revolutionary connections* in opposition to the *conjugation of the axiomatic*.[60]

And Guattari in particular is persistent in his claim that capital is always producing mediatic techniques which might precipitate these revolutionary becomings. From his successful therapeutic application of video and tape recorders[61] to his involvement in the pirate radio stations associated with Italian Autonomia,[62] Guattari had direct and immediate experiences of these techniques as liberatory and transformative, in ways which hegemonic media operators must work ceaselessly to repress or render unthinkable.

For Guattari, the key ethico-aesthetic task is that of circumventing or short-circuiting the powers which *mediate* this revolutionary potential, 'conjugating' it in terms of hegemonic axioms of production. This task is eminently achievable, given that information and communication technologies are 'nothing other than hyperdeveloped and hyperconcentrated forms of certain aspects of human subjectivity and, let us emphasise, precisely not those aspects that polarise humans into relations of domination and power'.[63] If the terms here are familiar, it's perhaps because they echo a famous claim of Walter Benjamin's, *'that the [following] concepts which are introduced into the theory of art [...] are completely useless for the purposes of fascism'*;[64] and indeed, what Guattari and Benjamin share is a conviction oriented by their abiding Marxism – that technological reproducibility is always at least potentially revolutionary, releasing disruptive social forces which both fascist war machines and capitalist 'apparatuses of capture' must work ceaselessly to reterritorialise.

For Benjamin, a thought proper to mechanical reproducibility will be impervious to fascism precisely inasmuch as it will demystify the auratic aesthetics and archaic 'cult value' which guarantee fascism's successful libidinal investment. Mechanically reproduced images demystify not only by virtue of the way in which they show us how things *really are* – we might think of smartphone footage of extra-judicial killings, as much as Bazin's neo-realist 'fact images' – but also and especially because they *'change [...] the relation of the masses to art'*,[65] turning the masses *en masse* into writers, aesthetes and photographers.[66] Mechanical reproducibility thus opens up the potentials of an image produced by *just anyone*, and this seismic shift – as much political as aesthetic – is still only just being grasped by philosophy as we confront the image in the age of its *informatic reproducibility*.

While Deleuze remains largely uninterested in these developments, or at least deeply cynical about them, Guattari's work, as we have said, is characterised by an increasing attention to the creative possibilities of informatic technologies, sketching a 'post-media' society which might redeploy their energies contra dominant mass-mediatic techniques of infantilisation and homogeneity. For Guattari, these technologies' increasing miniaturisation and personalisation, combined with their capacity to open up 'creative mutant Universes' through heterodox semiotic investments, suggest that they might be put to genuinely creative and emancipatory uses – provided they are 'plugged-in' to pressing minoritarian struggles, including those related to 'irreversible ecological catastrophe', 'famine' and 'the mass-mediatic pollution of subjectivity'.[67]

This last factor is key, and signals the profound ambiguity of their deployment thus far, which has seen them pressed into the service of anything but creative, emancipatory or 'resingularising' endeavours. The problem, for Guattari, is the same as that confronted by Deleuze in his own thought on the image – that of *belief*, and a lack of belief in the world's capacity to change, exemplified in various strands of 'postmodernity'.[68] But the transition from a postmodern to a post-media society is possible, provided we are able to resist this prevailing climate of resignation and despair, *becoming active* in our affirmation of the creative potentials immanent to the images which surround us.

Lynch's 'late style', I've suggested, is significant in its embodiment of this ethical stance, and a determination to see new techniques of the image as not simply or strictly impoverishing vocabularies in thought and creation. This approach, which accords with Deleuze's own account of noesis – as the creative affirmation of the catastrophe of an encounter – seems more prescient than ever as we confront a barrage of digital images that is incessant, exhaustive and global. Certainly these images, like television, are the vehicles of control – the site of great stupidity, banality, vulgarity and worse. The injunction to 'co-create' is just as often the route to an insomniac overconsumption as it is a singular and genuine invention. But we must always 'start where we are', exploring the bleakest terrains for the signs of creativity, escape and resistance – *belief in the world* can mean nothing other than this. Or, as Deleuze remarks, in conversation with Gilbert Cabasso and Fabrice Revault d'Allonnes:

> All forms of creativity, including any creativity that might be possible in television [...] face a common enemy. Once again it's a cerebral matter: the brain's the hidden side of all circuits, and these can allow the most basic conditioned reflexes to prevail, as well as leaving room for more creative tracings, less 'probable' links. (N, 61)

Notes

1. Quoted in R. Brody, *Everything is Cinema: The Working Life of Jean-Luc Godard* (New York: Metropolitan Books, 2008), p. 330, translation slightly modified.
2. See, primarily, the articles 'Postmodern Deadlock and Post-Media Transition' and 'Entering the Post-Media Era', in F. Guattari, *Soft Subversions: Texts and Interviews 1977–1985*, trans. C. Wiener and E. Wittman (Los Angeles: Semiotext(e), 2009), pp. 291–306.
3. See T. W. Adorno, 'How to Look at Television', *The Quarterly of Film Radio and Television*, 8(3) (1954), pp. 213–35; T. Nannicelli, *Appreciating the Art of Television: A Philosophical Perspective* (New York: Routledge, 2017), p. 1.
4. Raymond Williams, who, alongside Marshall McLuhan, is perhaps the most influential early theorist of television as a medium, characterises its evolution to include commercials thus: 'What is being offered is not, in older terms, a programme of discrete units with particular insertions, but a planned flow, in which the true series is not the published sequence of programme items but this sequence transformed by the inclusion of another kind of sequence, so that these sequences together compose the real flow, the real "broadcasting."' R. Williams, *Television: Technology and Cultural Form*, ed. E. Williams (London: Routledge, 2003), p. 91.
5. T. Gerken, 'Young Watch Almost Seven Times Less TV than Over-65s – Ofcom', *BBC News*, 17 August 2022, https://www.bbc.com/news/technology-62506041.
6. B. Stiegler, *Symbolic Misery – vol. 1: The Hyperindustrial Epoch*, trans. B. Norman (Cambridge: Polity, 2014), p. 4.
7. Deleuze and Guattari, *Anti-Oedipus*, p. 10.
8. F. Guattari, *Schizoanalytic Cartographies*, trans. A. Goffey (London: Bloomsbury, 2013), p. 15.
9. Ibid.
10. L. Engell, *Thinking Through Television* (Amsterdam: Amsterdam University Press, 2019), p. 18.
11. See N. Carroll, *A Philosophy of Mass Art* (Oxford: Oxford University Press, 1998).
12. It should be noted that this situation has arguably changed since the end of the twentieth century, which has seen the consolidation of television studies as a serious academic discipline, alongside a proliferation of philosophical works in dialogue with TV. Paradigmatic of this new climate is the Blackwell Philosophy and Pop Culture series, which stretches to over 60 titles and includes the likes of *Family Guy and Philosophy*, *Lost and Philosophy*, *Mad Men and Philosophy* and *Arrested Development and Philosophy*, to name just a few. While I

don't claim to have read the series in its entirety, its approach often appears to be that of using the TV show in question *illustratively*, in order to introduce traditionally philosophical content in an accessible and engaging way. This is by no means a problem, but doesn't necessarily amount to a theorisation of the televisual medium and its effects in their specificity, and perhaps does not escape the substance of Carroll's charges.

13 G. Deleuze and C. Parnet, *Dialogues*, trans. H. Tomlinson and B. Habberjam (New York: Columbia University Press, 1987), p. 4.
14 See, for instance, R. Scruton, 'Photography and Representation', *Critical Inquiry*, 7(3) (1981), pp. 577–603.
15 In the context of a discussion of Deleuze's account of thought, for instance, Alain Badiou claims that 'contrary to all egalitarian or "communitarian" norms, Deleuze's conception of thought is profoundly aristocratic. Thought only exists in a hierarchised space. This is because, for individuals to attain the point where they are seized by their preindividual determination and, thus, by the power of the One-All – of which they are, at the start, only meagre local configurations – they have to go beyond their limits and endure the transfixion and disintegration of their actuality by infinite virtuality, which is actuality's veritable being.' A. Badiou, *Deleuze: The Clamour of Being*, trans. L. Burchill (Minneapolis, MN: University of Minnesota Press, 2000), p. 12. Leaving aside the specifics of Badiou's vocabulary here, he does touch upon an important tension present in Deleuze's work. His account of thought as rare, and as frequently implicated with the experience of a certain type of (bourgeois) aesthetic object, renders his philosophy at least apparently or explicitly elitist, in ways that need to be interrogated. Badiou's thought, it should be acknowledged, fares little better on this front.
16 Deleuze, *Bergsonism*, p. 98.
17 Deleuze characterises Beckett's increasing intolerance towards language thus: 'It is not only that words lie; they are so burdened with calculations and significations, with intentions and personal memories, with old habits that cement them together, that one can scarcely bore into the surface before it closes up again. It sticks together. It imprisons and suffocates us' (CC, 173). Indeed it is only via recourse to the *image*, claims Deleuze, be it optical or sonic, that we might commence the task of 'boring holes' in language to 'reveal what lurks beneath it...' (CC, 172).
18 See, for instance, S. Cavell, 'The Fact of Television', *Daedalus*, 111(4), 'Print Culture and Video Culture' (1982), pp. 75–96.
19 The fact that episodic television is produced in accordance with a 'feedback loop' comprised of ratings figures and an attendant advertising revenue – to which producers must be ceaselessly attentive – is well

known. 'Jumping the shark', the situation in which a TV series seeks to mitigate falling audience share by injecting a sudden, gimmicky 'event' (the phenomenon is named for an episode of the series *Happy Days* in which Albert 'Fonzie' Fonzarelli jumps over a shark while water-skiing, in complete discontinuity with the show's diegetic parameters to that point), is emblematic of this situation.

20 McLuhan's distinctions are as famous for their ability to confuse as anything else, and I don't propose a neat comparison here. Suffice it to say that the idea of television as a 'cool' medium in its relative discursive passivity is persuasive enough, provided we understand it as contributing to a highly sophisticated mechanism for the engineering of desire and calibration of subjectivity of which it comprises only a component. See M. McLuhan, *Understanding Media: The Extensions of Man* (Cambridge, MA: MIT Press, 1994).

21 See F. Fukuyama, 'The End of History?', *The National Interest*, 16 (summer 1989), pp. 2–18.

22 Animation, indeed, affords unique powers in this space, and *The Simpsons*' opening 'couch gag' – which sees the characters traverse a series of possible, but increasingly improbable events in order to arrive at their couch and watch the television: sitting down only for the couch to collapse in season one, being tipped off the couch by burglars in season three, negotiating a complex, M. C. Escher-style environment with multiple staircases to reach the couch in season six – serves as a blueprint for the absurd multiverses of *Futurama* (1999–) and later *Rick and Morty* (2013–), where the capacity to traverse Leibnizian incompossibility opens only onto a worst possible world of *ressentiment* and alcoholism.

23 Adorno characterises televisual identification thus: 'The stories teach their readers that one has to be "realistic," that one has to give up romantic ideas, that one has to adjust oneself at any price, and that nothing more can be expected of any individual. The perennial middle-class conflict between individuality and society has been reduced to a dim memory, and the message is invariably that of identification with the *status quo*.' Adorno, 'How to Look at Television', p. 220.

24 The broad conditions of the second so-called 'Golden Age of Television' are, as Angelo Restivo notes, '"what everyone already knows by now": immersive technologies that allow for greater engagement with audio-visual sensorium; diversification of viewing practices; new modes of dissemination of product; loosening of restrictions on content; increased economic viability of niche audiences – in short, all those elements that characterise the post network era.' A. Restivo, *Breaking Bad and Cinematic Television* (Durham, NC: Duke University Press, 2019), p. 4.

25 The first so-called 'Golden Age', which characterises American broadcast television from the late 1940s to the early 1960s, was marked

by innovative and often highly artistic content, including telecasts of ballets and symphonic works, alongside teleplays and 'anthology' series like *The Philco Television Playhouse* and *The United States Steel Hour*. Its demise has been convincingly traced to increased network reach and the need for a broader, trans-demographic appeal in programming. See J. Baughman, '"Show Business in the Living Room": Management Expectations for American Television, 1947–58', *Business and Economic History*, 26(2) (1997), pp. 718–29.

26 See the discussion in J. Mittell, 'The Qualities of Complexity: Vast Versus Dense Seriality in Contemporary Television', in J. Jacobs and S. Peacock (eds), *Television Aesthetics and Style* (London: Bloomsbury, 2013), pp. 45–56.

27 *The One Thousand and One Nights*, for instance, compiled during the Islamic Golden Age, is in many ways the quintessential serial-narrative production.

28 Indeed, the temporal disturbances that characterise *The Sopranos* bear a more than cursory resemblance to the 'sheets' and 'crystals' of time which Deleuze locates in the likes of Welles' *Citizen Kane*. The narrative 'present' of the series is consistently displaced: not only through Tony's prodigious therapeutic search for the singular events that instigated his own vectors of violence and self-loathing, but in the repeated motif of dementia, which for both Livia and Junior marks a flight from the imperatives of sensory-motor situations into a pure realm of crystalline indiscernibility.

29 Though this, it should be said, was already an admirably heterodox move in an age dominated by what David Bordwell and Noël Carroll would later call 'S.L.A.B. theory', that is, film theory rooted in the concepts of Saussure, Lacan, Althusser and Barthes. Deleuze also rejects such sociological-linguistically oriented approaches to the cinematic 'sign', albeit for altogether different reasons. See D. Bordwell and N. Carroll (eds), *Post-Theory: Reconstructing Film Studies* (Madison, WI: University of Wisconsin Press, 1996).

30 See P. Virilio, *Speed and Politics*, trans. M. Polizzotti (Los Angeles: Semiotext(e), 2006).

31 A. Galloway, *Laruelle: Against the Digital* (Minneapolis, MN: University of Minnesota Press, 2014), p. 69.

32 Ibid.

33 D. Broe, *Birth of the Binge: Serial TV and the End of Leisure* (Detroit, MI: Wayne State University Press, 2019), p. 245.

34 Ibid.

35 See, for instance, the discussion in B. Stiegler, *Acting Out*, trans. D. Barison, D. Ross and P. Crogan (Stanford, CA: Stanford University Press, 2009), pp. 55–65.

36 B. Stiegler, *Symbolic Misery – vol. 2: The Katastrophē of the Sensible*, trans. B. Norman (Cambridge: Polity, 2015), p. 19.

37. M. Proust, 'Letter to Camille Vettard – 5th October 1922', *The American Reader*, https://theamericanreader.com/5-october-1922-marcel-proust-to-camille-vettard/.
38. H. S. Thompson, *Fear and Loathing in Las Vegas* (London: Harper Collins, 1998), p. 190.
39. D. Foster Wallace, *A Supposedly Fun Thing I'll Never Do Again: Essays and Arguments* (New York: Back Bay Books, 2009), p. 352.
40. R. Loyd, 'Television Review: Stars in their Eyes in "Hollywood Heights"', *The Los Angeles Times*, 18 June 2012, https://www.latimes.com/entertainment/tv/la-xpm-2012-jun-18-la-et-hollywood-heights-20120618-story.html.
41. As Julie Grossman and Will Scheibel explain, the show's success was as much the result of ABC's effective pre-premiere marketing of it as a televisual 'event' as it was the so-called 'water cooler effect' with which it is frequently associated: 'ABC actually presold the series as a television milestone... When the two-hour pilot aired at 9:00 p.m. EST, an increasing number of viewers turned in every half hour, reaching a total audience of around thirty-five million (a 33 percent market share, or a third of the people watching television from 9:00 to 11:00 p.m.).' J. Grossman and W. Scheibel, *Twin Peaks*, (Detroit, MI: Wayne State University Press, 2020), p. 13.
42. D. Lynch, *Lynch on Lynch*, ed. C. Rodley (New York: Farrar, Straus and Giroux, 2005), p. 163.
43. Ibid., p. 165.
44. Ibid.
45. The show's ratings famously plummeted after the mystery was solved and Laura Palmer's killer was revealed part way through season two. As Lynch explains: 'The way we pitched this thing was as a murder mystery but that murder mystery was to eventually become the background story ... this they did *not* like. They did *not* like that. And they forced us to, you know, get to Laura's killer. It wasn't really their fault. People just got a bug in them that they wanted to know who killed Laura Palmer. Calling out for it. And one thing led to another, and the pressure was just so great that the murder mystery couldn't be just a background thing anymore. The progress towards it, but never getting there, was what made us know all the people in Twin Peaks: how they all surrounded Laura and intermingled. All the mysteries. But it wasn't meant to be. It just couldn't happen that way.' Ibid., p. 180.
46. Ibid., p. 176.
47. D. Lim, *David Lynch: The Man from Another Place* (New York: Amazon Icon Series, 2015), p. 98.
48. M. Ellis and T. Theus, 'Is it Happening Again? Twin Peaks and "The Return" of History', in A. Sanna (ed.), *Critical Essays on Twin Peaks: The Return* (Cham: Palgrave Macmillan (Springer Nature), 2019), p. 25.

49 See J. Fallis and T. Kyle King, 'Lucy Finally Understands How Cellphones Work: Ambiguous Digital Technologies in *Twin Peaks: The Return* and Its Fan Communities', in Sanna (ed.), *Critical Essays on Twin Peaks: The Return*, p. 56.
50 The incompossibilities of the soap opera in its garden variety are well known. We might think not only of actors replaced without comment and characters back from the dead, but of evil twins, medical miracles and children who age overnight – the terms of an aberrant yet self-replicant logic upon which Lynch and Frost draw liberally.
51 Quoted in Fallis and King, 'Lucy Finally Understands How Cellphones Work', p. 59.
52 J. Foltz, 'David Lynch's Late Style', *The LA Review of Books*, 12 November 2017, https://lareviewofbooks.org/article/david-lynchs-late-style/.
53 T. W. Adorno, 'Late Style in Beethoven', in *Essays on Music*, ed. R. Leppert (Berkeley, CA: University of California Press, 2002), p. 566.
54 Ibid., pp. 566–7.
55 Lynch's deferral to algorithmic or aleatory methods is in many ways contiguous with ongoing developments in artistic practice since the advent of photography, and its displacement of the figure of the artist as expressing some privileged inner life or 'feeling'. In this context, we might think not only of Arp's aleatory collages or Duchamp's 'readymades', but Gysin and Burroughs's 'cut-ups', Hendrix's feedback, and Aphex Twin's drum machines – each of which responds to the facts of mechanical reproducibility by deferring certain aspects of intentionality on the part of the artist to algorithmic and/or impersonal machinic systems, which as such 'co-create' the image.
56 See H. Jenkins, '"Do You Enjoy Making the Rest of us Feel Stupid?": alt.tv.twinpeaks, the Trickster Author and Viewer Mastery', in D. Lavery (ed.), *Full of Secrets: Critical Approaches to Twin Peaks*, (Detroit, MI: Wayne State University Press, 1995), pp. 51–69; M. Waugh, '"Make Sense of It": Cult and Complex TV Fandoms, Post-Truth Discourse and an Excess of Meaning in *Twin Peaks: Season 3*', *Critical Studies in Television*, 0(0) (2022), pp. 1–19.
57 The Velvet Underground, 'Rock & Roll', *Loaded*, Atlantic Records, 1970.
58 For more on this theme, and in particular the possibilities afforded by digital film-making, see W. Brown, *Non-Cinema: Global Digital Film-making and the Multitude* (London: Bloomsbury, 2018).
59 In the context of his work on what he calls 'Black Atlantic Futurism', Kodwo Eshun offers up one of the most pleasing accounts of a movement according to which ever more conceptually dense materials are encoded by the mass-produced artefacts of popular culture, engendering new and heterodox forms of embodied 'knowing': 'Producers are

already pop theorists: Breakbeat producer Sonz of a Loop da Loop Era's term skratchadelia, instrumental HipHop producer DJ Krush's idea of turntabilixation, virtualizer George Clinton's studio science of mixadelics, all these conceptechnics are used to excite theory to travel at the speed of thought, as sonic theorist Kool Keith suggested in 1987.' K. Eshun, *More Brilliant Than the Sun: Adventures in Sonic Fiction* (London: Quartet, 1998), p. 00[-004]. Eshun's claim that hypomnesic technologies not only capture and recombine space and time but certain ideas and attitudes towards them – remixing them in a form that acts directly upon the nervous system of the twenty-first-century listener or dancer – offers an alluring model of just what a 'pop philosophy' might look like.

60 Deleuze and Guattari, *A Thousand Plateaus*, p. 473.
61 See Guattari's commentary on the therapeutic uses of both tape recorders and film in 'Monograph on R.A.', in F. Guattari, *Psychoanalysis and Transversality: Texts and Interviews 1955–1971*, trans. A. Hodges (South Pasadena, CA: Semiotext(e), 2003), pp. 36–41.
62 See the discussion in M. Goddard, 'Guattari and Berardi and the Post-Media Era', in C. Apprich, J. Berry Slater, A. Iles and O. Lerone Schultz (eds), *Provocative Alloys: A Post-Media Anthology* (Berlin: Mute Books, 2013), pp. 44–61.
63 Guattari, *Schizoanalytic Cartographies*, p. 2.
64 Benjamin, 'Work of Art', p. 20.
65 Ibid., p. 36.
66 Genesis P-Orridge, founder of the industrial group Throbbing Gristle, articulates this situation well: 'Basically the power in this world rests with the people who have access to the most information and also control that information [...] These [information] systems are very expensive and cumbersome, requiring capital equipment which can't be utilised the whole time. So to cover costs and keep equipment running, these systems have been made available to the rest of us to keep them financially viable. That's why you can get access to cable TV, even the mail, Polaroids too, and video... They develop these systems for their own reasons, but they are so expensive they have to mass produce them to finance them. So we all get easier and easier ways to multiply our ideas and information, it's a parallel progression.' Quoted in T. Bey William Bailey, *Micro Bionic: Radical Electronic Music and Sound Art in the 21st Century* (Belsona Books, 2012), p. 24.
67 See Guattari, *Schizoanalytic Cartographies*, p. 42.
68 See ibid., pp. 36–42.

Conclusion: The Digital Outside

I began by suggesting that my goal was to place Deleuze's cinematic philosophy in dialogue with contemporary digital media, a move which I claimed might help us to better understand both digital media and Deleuze's thought. We saw that Deleuze, in his works from the 1980s and 1990s, was wary of the digitisation of the image, suggesting that new, 'electric' and 'numerical' images no longer have an 'out-of-field', eschewing visual experimentation in favour of information processing, in a development linked to the emergence of societies of control. In this context, we undertook to understand the contours and limitations of Deleuze's concept of information, proposing a turn to information theory itself in search of a new kind of outside which might be immanent to the digital image.

To this end, in Chapter 1 we attempted a cartography of the outside, tracing it through the works of Blanchot, Foucault and Deleuze. We saw that for Blanchot, the outside is the condition of literature, an impersonal space we might glimpse not only through the materiality of language, but through an operation whereby the author gives up saying 'I', becoming an effect of literature itself. We then saw Foucault take up this idea to posit the outside in ontological terms, as 'the hiding place of all being' – an absolute exteriority irreducible to interested discursive categories like 'truth', 'falsehood' and 'prophecy'. We saw Deleuze draw on this conception in his own work on Foucault, suggesting that the Nietzschean figure of the 'overman' might emerge from formal compounds between the human and various material and pre-individual forces from 'outside'.

We then linked these claims to Deleuze's account of noesis, and his critique of a 'dogmatic image of thought' animating Western philosophy. The dogmatic image raises a set of postulates to the level of philosophical principles, taking a reactive and conservative model of recognition for the totality of thought itself. This model, claims Deleuze, is ultimately un-philosophical, failing to realise philosophy's project of breaking with *doxa* and effecting new modes of thought and of life. In order to achieve this latter task, philosophical thought must rather be *creative*, and it's for this reason that we saw Deleuze evoke Kant's aesthetic philosophy, in particular the experience of the sublime. In this context, we saw Deleuze suggest that thought is not recognition or representation, but rather a state of shock or bewilderment – the result of an encounter with a 'sign' which impels us into the creation of new ideas or concepts. We saw that this encounter is, as such, double: a confrontation not only with the unthought as external object, but also with thought's fundamental 'impower', or the impossibility of thinking in any preordained way.

Attendant to this account, we saw Deleuze's delineation of three 'syntheses' of time. First, a contraction of temporality such as constitutes habitual repetition in the present. Second, the synthesis which serves as the condition for the first – the past in general – into which different presents 'pass', and which acts as virtual reservoir for counter-actualisations. Finally, we saw that the third synthesis – of the future and of freedom – constitutes not only a serial distribution of past, present and future, but also sees the subject 'split' in time, a function of its encounter with an event which requires it to become *other than it is*. The third synthesis thus calls for an ethics of affirmation, such as sees the subject embrace those very forces which precipitate its splitting, drawing on materials from 'outside' in order to become an *author* or *agent* of the future. In this way, we saw that Deleuze's noetic philosophy calls not just for a renovation of thought, but of the very identity of the thinker, who must self-problematise in a radical, reflexive movement of creation. We saw, moreover, that Deleuze remains sceptical about philosophy's ability to stage such noetic 'encounters', profoundly implicated as it is with the dogmatic model of recognition and representation. For this reason, in *Difference and Repetition*, Deleuze suggests that philosophy might seek encounters with the arts of cinema, theatre, literature and painting, which confront philosophy with new and 'unthinkable' compositions of sensible materials, as such renewing its own expressive potentials.

In this context, albeit some fifteen years later, we saw Deleuze articulate his long-standing interest in cinema, exploring its images through a series of 'commentaries' on Bergson's temporal philosophy. Here we saw Deleuze claim that cinema is uniquely placed to produce images of the virtuality which is obscured by thought's habitual or 'dogmatic' exercise. This is because the cinematic image delineates both a frame and an *out-of-frame*, provoking a thought of the virtual, qualitatively evolving 'whole' within which the image is

Conclusion

situated. We saw that this 'whole', however, disappears in post-war cinema, giving way to an 'outside' of thought and of the image. Whereas the classical cinema of the movement-image deployed the whole as a context for the unfurling trajectories of narrative, the collapse of what Deleuze calls the 'sensory-motor schema' sees this movement-image replaced by a pure, inhuman time-image. The time-image is the site of a new experience of temporality, no longer tethered to the sensory-motor interests of narrative or action. In this context, the virtual and actual sides of the image tend towards indiscernibility, producing crystalline formations like those we mapped through Chris Marker's *La Jetée*. Such images, which are *unthinkable* from the perspective of conditioned sensory-motor response, are as such *problematic*, producing and provoking *a thought from outside* which dislocates habitual mentation.

In Chapter 3 I argued that Deleuze conceives of this development as political, inasmuch as contact with the outside of thought provokes us to rethink our relations with any preordained or predetermined 'world'. I suggested that Deleuze's brief remarks around the relation between capital and cinema – its 'time–money conspiracy' – accord with an idiosyncratic Marxism we might trace throughout his work, alone and with Guattari, according to which the productive forces which might lead to an overthrow of capital must be conceived as immanent to capitalist production itself. This claim oriented my subsequent determination to uncover those forces which might resist informatic 'control' *within* the very images produced by information and communications techniques. I further argued that Deleuze's postulation of a contemporary situation in which 'the people are missing', and in which we have lost our 'belief in the world', is connected to his earlier account of thought and its encounter with the outside. It is only in the context of a movement beyond the pre-distributed categories of a sensory-motor *status quo* – by plunging into the hitherto unthought, and the virtual singularities which allow actualised states to become other than they are – that we might begin to create new peoples and new forms of life, *believing in the world* as a place we might meaningfully alter and inhabit. Again, the genesis of this creativity lies in an encounter with unthinkable forces and materials – here conceived in terms of the 'intolerable' situations of the post-war world, which outstrip all sensory-motor mechanism.

In Chapter 4 we returned to the contemporary problem of the digital, and the protracted critique of information which emerges across Deleuze's later works. I explored Gregory Flaxman's use of James Cameron's *Avatar* to extend some of the claims made by Deleuze around new 'electronic' and 'numerical' images. Flaxman, we saw, argues that *Avatar* is emblematic of a 'new idea of cinema' which embraces a spectacular, hyper-representational form, using powerful new techniques for the fabrication of images to unwittingly destroy the out-of-frame or outside. The contemporary cinematic image thus becomes 'overdetermined', both in terms of algorithmic manipulation and capital, in a model according to which all content '*must be represented*'. I drew from Flaxman's argument one key claim, that these new techniques eschew the cinematic shot in favour of an immersive data space which treats the image as information. I then broadened my discussion to trace the concept of information itself throughout Deleuze's later work, particularly as it emerges in the final chapter of *Cinema II*, and in the lecture 'What is the Creative Act?', where Deleuze identifies information with control, and an operation according to which we are '[told] what we are supposed to believe'.

In this context, I suggested that Deleuze appears to link what Luciano Floridi describes as *semantic information* – which is to say, meaningful or 'informative' data – to information in its technical sense as quantitative, statistically measurable uncertainty. I argued that this linkage might, however, obscure certain philosophically significant dimensions of information conceived in these latter terms. In this context, I turned to probabilistic, statistical and technical accounts of information emerging from communications and cybernetic theory. In particular, I explored some of the implications of Shannon and Weaver's 'Mathematical Theory of Communication', according to which information must be untethered from any semantic criteria, instead becoming the measure of uncertainty removed in the context of a probability space distribution.

But this ostensibly non-semantic approach, I claimed, is rendered problematic by Shannon and Weaver's distinction between *wanted* and *unwanted* uncertainty, which reintroduces certain interested semantic criteria. Shannon's work, indeed, is dedicated to reducing the presence of unwanted empirically derived 'uncertainties' – what he calls *noise* – throughout information transmission systems. This distinction, I suggested, obscures a radically a-semantic approach to information, conceived as an entropic production of differences at the fundamentally ontological level. According to this latter model, *noise is also information*, a fabric of differences taken up

Conclusion

and transmitted as data by an information system. I suggested that according to this latter conception, uncertainty might no longer be indexed to the possible – and to a reduction of data deficit – but to a kind of productive disparity which might form the condition for radically unforeseen signals. It is in these latter terms that we saw Simondon approach information as an ontogenetic category – the 'event' whereby a foreign content enters a hitherto stable situation, as such rendering it metastable. This metastability, which takes the form of an energetic disparity in need of resolution, becomes the site of a *process of individuation*, with the system's incompatibilities resolved through a progressive transduction of the milieu, as in the case of crystallisation.

As such, it appeared as though information, conceived both technically and ontogenetically, need not *necessarily* be implicated in conservative operations of control. Rather, if we affirm the presence of noise in information systems, we might conceive of these systems as producing new individuals beyond the pre-distributed terms of the 'neutral' MTC model. In this context, we turned to the idea of noise as it emerges in the context of aesthetics, tracing a genealogical filiation whereby, as in information theory, the term designates a certain 'failure to communicate'. Whereas in information theory, however, this 'failure' is a problem to be overcome, in the context of art – as we saw with reference to the likes of Russolo, Cage and Eco – it is valorised as the very condition for the production of new forms: the disordered, entropic and undetermined materiality which constitutes the 'outside' to a given artistic systematisation.

Equipped with this productive model of information, we returned to the digital cinema, and to a discussion of 'noise' as it appears in Lynch's *Inland Empire*. Here, I argued that at various registers Lynch interposes aleatory, impersonal and 'noisy' presences, such as co-determine the content of the image. In using a cheap hand-held camera which struggles to keep up with the empirical demands of the shoot, in deploying consumer editing technology such as imperfectly renders and juxtaposes the images, and in using widely available image manipulation software in order to achieve the film's thoroughly unbelievable special effects, Lynch foregrounds the materiality of the digital in such a way as to draw our attention to its impersonal and irreducible technical presence. I identified these dimensions of Lynch's film not only with certain aspects of Blanchot's literary 'outside', but also with the noetic model which Deleuze advances across *Difference and Repetition* and the two *Cinema* volumes.

But the outside, as I've claimed, has dimensions in excess of these purely technical and aesthetic functions. It is also political, which is to say it marks the site of an event whereby the present becomes problematic, and our thinking must reach for virtual potentials with which it might synthesise the new – in thought, and as such in life. And *Inland Empire*, I argued, likewise advances a 'political' problematisation of the actual present, drawing our attention to the economic and cultural forces which produce certain highly interested flows of information. In its dark portrait of Hollywood as a site for the communication of imperatives towards performance and (gendered) subjectivation, the film advances a kind of immanent critique not only of contemporary film production, but of a whole ecology of digital techniques which participate in the construction of the twenty-first-century 'dividual'.

This 'critique' is nevertheless both *productive* and *affirmative*, simultaneously sketching out modes of life which deploy these techniques in new and potentially resistant ways. In Nikki/Sue's simultaneous confrontation with, and embrace of, her structuration through the film's malevolent digital image-space, I argued that we catch a glimpse of an affirmative ethics of the encounter, such as resonates with Deleuze's own account of thought and the outside. In what I dubbed Nikki/Sue's *becoming-digital*, we encountered a model of contemporary subjectivity which, while structured through the networks of control and info-capital, might nevertheless embrace their ruinous productivity, redeploying these energies in the creation of genuinely new forms of life.

In Chapter 7 we extended this account into a discussion of the televisual image, as a means of ascertaining its significance for the contemporary ecology of digital images *tout court*. While Deleuze is broadly hostile to TV, which he feels also transmits the imperatives of control, I suggested that the televisual assemblage constitutes a more complex and multivalent proposition, offering up unthinkable materials in a variety of ways. In producing what I called *exhaustion-images* – images which, like the time-image, eschew purposive movement in favour of isolated and aimless 'situations' – I suggested that the televisual assemblage is perhaps expressing problems in both thought and life which Deleuze tends to associate with cinema exclusively. At the same time, I suggested that the products of the so-called 'Golden Age' of television remain preoccupied with impersonal, material forces, such as dislocate forms of cognition derived from the sensory-motor schema. In this context, I turned to Lynch's

Conclusion

televisual works, suggesting that their quotient of 'unthinkability' stems as much from a material 'return of the repressed', combined with certain potentials of the televisual image itself, as from Lynch's own particular artistry.

In this way, I've tried to problematise an elitist tendency on the part of aesthetic philosophy, such as Deleuze occasionally inherits. A reading of the televisual image as both symptomatic and unthinkable, combined with an account of its displacement of the privileged figure of the artist, pointed to broader vectors of aesthetic production which increasingly characterise information and control societies generally. In this context, I turned to the work of Deleuze's collaborator, Félix Guattari, in order to draw out some of the ways in which these societies are always menaced by the forms of creativity and self-reference which they depend upon and engender. I suggested that what Guattari calls 'post-media society' might still be imagined, provided we are able to adopt the affirmative ethics which I traced across the works of Deleuze and Lynch, embracing new techniques of power in terms of their disruptive and as-yet-unthinkable potentials. As such, we arrived once more at the question of *belief*, and the ethical imperative of inculcating a belief in the world's capacity to become other than it is, such as is menaced by a prevailing sense of anxiety, despair and disaffection.

Indeed, it's this latter exigency that has informed my own approach throughout this book, in which I've tried to greet the vast proliferation of control techniques in a spirit of affirmation distinct, I hope, from serene acquiescence. Anybody who has been involved in the teaching of young people over the last several years will appreciate the pressing need for this kind of playfulness, and a sense that singular experiences of creativity, intelligence and joy are still capable of being imagined. In this context, what I've tried to indicate are a series of ambiguities immanent to the assemblage comprised by Deleuze's philosophy and the current trajectory of the image. On the one hand, Deleuze's account of thought as rare and intensive bristles against popular narratives of ever-more streamlined artificial 'intelligences' which interpolate us through the digital image. On the other, his deployment of the image itself as an intensive composition of forces and materials enables us to explore it as a site of genuine contestation and creativity. The fertility of Deleuze's contribution is to render a tension between these two 'sides' or potentials of the image explicit, prompting us to realise the necessity of continued intervention.

An ambiguous situation, after all, is one which is not yet decided, and which as such requires something from us, be it a thought or an action. The success of a currently hegemonic configuration of powers depends upon its foreclosure of just this realisation, and a domestication of thought which makes the precipitation of real events appear to be 'impossible'. Part of Deleuze's singular value is to indicate that impossibility is itself a site of potential resistance and creation, expressing as it does the exhaustion of a predetermined sensory-motor schema. And beyond predetermination lies the undetermined, the unthinkable, *the outside* – that errant point where conditioned reflex fails, and thought itself can at last begin.

Bibliography

Adorno, T. W., 'How to Look at Television', *The Quarterly of Film Radio and Television*, 8(3) (1954), pp. 213–35.
— 'Late Style in Beethoven', in *Essays on Music*, ed. R. Leppert (Berkeley, CA: University of California Press, 2002), pp. 564–8.
— *Minima Moralia: Reflections on a Damaged Life*, trans. E. F. N. Jephcott (London: Verso, 2005).
— *Prisms*, trans. S. Weber and S. Weber (Cambridge MA: MIT Press, 1988).
Ansell-Pearson, K., *Deleuze and Philosophy: The Difference Engineer* (London: Routledge, 2002).
— *Germinal Life: The Difference and Repetition of Deleuze* (London: Routledge, 1999).
— 'The Reality of the Virtual: Bergson and Deleuze', *Modern Language Notes*, 120(5) (2005), pp. 1112–27.
Arnheim, R., *Film as Art* (Berkeley, CA: University of California Press, 1957).
Artaud, A., 'There's an Anguish', in *Artaud Anthology*, ed. J. Hirschman (San Francisco: City Lights, 1965), pp. 31–2.
Badiou, A., *Deleuze – The Clamour of Being*, trans. L. Burchill (Minneapolis, MN: University of Minnesota Press, 2000).
— *Logics of Worlds: Being and Event, 2*, trans. A. Toscano (London: Continuum, 2009).
Bailey, T. B. W., *Micro Bionic: Radical Electronic Music and Sound Art in the 21st Century* (Belsona Books, 2012).
Balbi, G., and Magaudda, P., *A History of Digital Media: An Intermedia and Global Perspective* (New York: Routledge, 2018).
Ballard, S., 'Information, Noise, et al.', in M. Nunes (ed.), *Error: Glitch, Noise and Jam in New Media Cultures* (New York: Continuum, 2011), pp. 59–79.
Bardin, A., *Epistemology and Political Philosophy in Gilbert Simondon: Individuation, Technics, Social Systems* (Dordrecht: Springer, 2015).
Bateson, G., *Steps to an Ecology of Mind* (New York: Ballantine Books, 1978).
Baudrillard, J., *In the Shadow of the Silent Majorities ... or the End of the Social*, trans. P. Foss, P. Patton and J. Johnston (New York: Semiotext(e), 1983).

Baughman, J., '"Show Business in the Living Room": Management Expectations for American Television, 1947–58', *Business and Economic History*, 26(2) (1997), pp. 718–29.

Bazin, A., *What is Cinema? – Vol. I*, trans. H. Gray (Berkeley, CA: University of California Press, 1967).

— *What is Cinema? – Vol. II*, trans. H. Gray (Berkeley, CA: University of California Press, 2005).

Beckman, F., 'Introduction: Control of What?', in F. Beckman (ed.), *Control Culture: Foucault and Deleuze after Discipline* (Edinburgh: Edinburgh University Press, 2018), pp. 1–19.

Belgrad, D., *The Culture of Feedback: Ecological Thinking in Seventies America* (Chicago: University of Chicago Press, 2019).

Benjamin, W., 'The Work of Art in the Age of its Technological Reproducibility', in *The Work of Art in the Age of its Technological Reproducibility and Other Writings on Media*, ed. M. W. Jennings, B. Doherty and T. Levin (Cambridge MA: The Belknap Press of Harvard University Press, 2008), pp. 19–55.

Berardi, F., *The Uprising: On Poetry and Finance* (Los Angeles: Semiotext(e) Interventions, 2012).

Bergson, H., *Creative Evolution*, trans. A. Mitchell (Mineola, NY: Dover, 1998).

— *The Creative Mind: An Introduction to Metaphysics*, trans. M. L. Andison (Mineola, NY: Dover, 2007).

— *Matter and Memory*, trans. N. M. Paul and W. S. Palmer (New York: Zone Books, 2005).

— *Mind – Energy: Lectures and Essays*, trans. H. W. Carr (Westport, CT: Greenwood Press, 1975).

— *Time and Free Will: An Essay on the Immediate Data of Consciousness*, trans. F. I. Pogson (Mineola, NY: Dover, 2001).

Bignall S., and Patton P. (eds), *Deleuze and the Postcolonial* (Edinburgh: Edinburgh University Press, 2010).

Blanchot, M., *The Book to Come*, trans. C. Mandell (Stanford, CA: Stanford University Press, 2003).

— *Faux Pas*, trans. C. Mandell (Stanford, CA: Stanford University Press, 2001).

— *The Space of Literature*, trans. A. Smock (Lincoln, NE: University of Nebraska Press, 1982).

— *The Work of Fire*, trans. C. Mandell (Stanford, CA: Stanford University Press, 1995).

Bogue, R., *Deleuze on Cinema* (New York: Routledge, 2003).

Bordwell, D., 'A Case for Cognitivism', *Iris: A Journal of Theory on Image and Sound*, 9 (1989), pp. 11–33.

Bordwell D., and Carroll, N. (eds), *Post-Theory: Reconstructing Film Studies* (Madison, WI: University of Wisconsin Press, 1996).

Bibliography

Boundas, C. V., 'Virtual/Virtuality', in A. Parr (ed.), *The Deleuze Dictionary – Revised Edition* (Edinburgh: Edinburgh University Press, 2010), pp. 300–2.

Bowden, S., '"Becoming Equal to the Act": The Temporality of Action and Agential Responsibility', in R. Braidotti and S. Bignall (eds), *Posthuman Ecologies: Complexity and Process after Deleuze* (Lanham, MD: Rowman and Littlefield, 2019).

— *The Priority of Events: Deleuze's Logic of Sense* (Edinburgh: Edinburgh University Press, 2011).

Brody, R., *Everything is Cinema: The Working Life of Jean-Luc Godard* (New York: Metropolitan Books, 2008).

Broe, D., *Birth of the Binge: Serial TV and the End of Leisure* (Detroit, MI: Wayne State University Press, 2019).

Brown, W., *Non-Cinema: Global Digital Film-making and the Multitude* (London: Bloomsbury, 2018).

Buchanan, I., 'Introduction: Five Theses of Actually Existing Schizoanalysis of Cinema', in I. Buchanan and P. MacCormack (eds), *Deleuze and the Schizoanalysis of Cinema*, (London: Continuum, 2008).

Buchanan I. and Parr A. (eds), *Deleuze and the Contemporary World* (Edinburgh: Edinburgh University Press, 2006).

Cage, J., *A Year from Monday: New Lectures and Writings by John Cage* (Middletown, CT: Wesleyan University Press, 1967).

Carr, N., *The Shallows: What the Internet is Doing to Our Brains* (New York: W.W. Norton, 2010).

Carroll, N., *Mystifying Movies: Fads and Fallacies in Contemporary Film Theory* (New York: Columbia University Press, 1988).

— *A Philosophy of Mass Art* (Oxford: Oxford University Press, 1998).

Castells, M., *The Rise of the Network Society (2nd Edition)* (Chichester: Wiley-Blackwell, 2010).

Cavell, S., 'The Fact of Television', *Daedalus*, 111(4), 'Print Culture and Video Culture' (1982), pp. 75–96.

Chabon, M., 'David Lynch's Night Truths', *The Paris Review*, 20 March 2018, https://www.theparisreview.org/blog/2018/03/20/david-lynchs-night-truths/

Chaplin, T., *Turning on the Mind: French Philosophers on Television* (Chicago: University of Chicago Press, 2009).

Clisby, D., 'Intensity in Context: Thermodynamics and Transcendental Philosophy', *Deleuze and Guattari Studies*, 11(2) (2017), pp. 240–58.

Colebrook, C., 'Review of P. Pisters (2012) *The Neuro-Image: A Deleuzian-Film Philosophy of Digital Screen Culture*', *Deleuze and Guattari Studies*, 8(1) (2014), pp. 147–53.

— *Understanding Deleuze* (London: Allen and Unwin, 2002).

Colman, F., *Deleuze and Cinema: The Film Concepts* (Oxford: Berg, 2001).

Conley, V., 'Order-Word', in A. Parr (ed.), *The Deleuze Dictionary – Revised Edition* (Edinburgh: Edinburgh University Press, 2010), pp. 198–9.

Critchley, S., and Webster, J., 'What is the Hole Inside the Hole: On David Lynch's Inland Empire', *Bedeutung*, 3, 'Life and Death', http://www.bedeutung.co.uk/magazine/issues/3-life-death/critchley-webster-lynch-empire/

Croombs, M., '*La jetée* in Historical Time: Torture, Visuality, Displacement', *Cinema Journal*, 56(2) (2017), pp. 25–45.

Dawtrey, A., 'Lynch Invades an Empire', *Variety*, 11 May 2005, http://variety.com/2005/film/markets-festivals/lynch-invades-an-empire-1117922566

Deamer, D., *Deleuze's Cinema Books: Three Introductions to the Taxonomy of Images* (Edinburgh: Edinburgh University Press, 2016).

Deleuze, G., *Bergsonism*, trans. H. Tomlinson and B. Habberjam (New York: Zone Books, 1991).

— *Cinema I: The Movement-Image*, trans. H. Tomlinson and B. Habberjam (London: Bloomsbury, 2013).

— *Cinema II: The Time-Image*, trans. H. Tomlinson and R. Galeta (London: Bloomsbury, 2013).

— *Desert Islands and Other Texts: 1953–1974*, ed. D. Lapoujade, trans. M. Taormina (Los Angeles: Semiotext(e), 2004).

— *Difference and Repetition*, trans. P. Patton (New York: Columbia University Press, 1994).

— *Empiricism and Subjectivity: An Essay on Hume's Theory of Human Nature*, trans. C. V. Boundas (New York: Columbia University Press, 1991).

— *Essays Critical and Clinical*, trans. D. W. Smith and M. A. Greco (Minneapolis, MN: University of Minnesota Press, 1997).

— *Expressionism in Philosophy: Spinoza*, trans. M. Joughin (New York: Zone Books, 2005).

— *Foucault*, trans. S. Hand (Minneapolis, MN: University of Minnesota Press, 1988).

— *Francis Bacon: The Logic of Sensation*, trans. D. Smith (London: Continuum, 2003).

— *Kant's Critical Philosophy: The Doctrine of the Faculties*, trans. H. Tomlinson and B. Habberjam (London: Athlone Press, 1984).

— *The Logic of Sense*, trans. M. Lester and C. Stivale, ed. C.V. Boundas (London: Athlone Press, 1990).

— 'Lucretius and Naturalism', trans. J. C. Bly, in A. Greenstine and R. Johnson (eds), *Contemporary Encounters with Ancient Metaphysics* (Edinburgh: Edinburgh University Press, 2017), pp. 245–53.

— *Negotiations, 1972–1990*, trans. M. Joughin (New York: Columbia University Press, 1995).

— *Nietzsche and Philosophy*, trans. H. Tomlinson (London: Continuum, 2002).

— 'Postscript on the Societies of Control', *October*, 59 (1992), pp. 3–7.

Bibliography

— *Proust and Signs*, trans. R. Howard (Minneapolis, MN: University of Minnesota Press, 2000).
— *Spinoza: Practical Philosophy*, trans. R. Hurley (San Francisco: City Lights, 1988).
— *Two Regimes of Madness, Texts and Interviews 1975–1995*, ed. D. Lapoujade, trans. A. Hodges and M. Taormina (New York: Semiotext(e), 2006).
Deleuze, G., and Guattari, F., *Anti-Oedipus*, trans. R. Hurley, M. Seem and H. Lane (Minneapolis, MN: University of Minnesota Press, 2000).
— *Kafka: Toward a Minor Literature*, trans. D. Polan (Minneapolis, MN: University of Minnesota Press, 2003).
— *A Thousand Plateaus: Capitalism and Schizophrenia*, trans B. Massumi (Minneapolis, MN: University of Minnesota Press, 2009).
— *What is Philosophy?*, trans. H. Tomlinson and G. Burchill (London: Verso, 1994).
Deleuze, G., and McMuhan, M., 'The Brain is the Screen: Interview with Gilles Deleuze on "The Time-Image"', *Discourse: Journal for Theoretical Studies in Media and Culture*, 20(3) (1998), pp. 47–55.
Deleuze, G., and Parnet, C., *Dialogues*, trans. H. Tomlinson and B. Habberjam (New York: Columbia University Press, 1987).
Descartes, R., *A Discourse on the Method of Correctly Conducting One's Reason and Seeking Truth in the Sciences*, trans. I. Maclean (Oxford: Oxford University Press, 2006).
Dosse, F., *Gilles Deleuze and Félix Guattari: Intersecting Lives*, trans. D. Glassman (New York: Columbia University Press, 2010).
Ebert, R., 'Armageddon', *RogerEbert.com*, 1 July 1998, https://www.rogerebert.com/reviews/armageddon-1998
Eco, U., *The Open Work*, trans A. Cancogni (Cambridge, MA: Harvard University Press, 1989).
Eisenstein, S., *Film Form: Essays in Film Theory*, trans. J. Leyda (New York: Harvest and Harcourt Brace Jovanovich, 1977).
Ellis, M., and Theus, T., 'Is it Happening Again? *Twin Peaks* and "*The Return*" of History', in A. Sanna (ed.), *Critical Essays on Twin Peaks: The Return* (Cham: Palgrave Macmillan, 2019), pp. 23–36.
Engell, L., *Thinking Through Television* (Amsterdam: Amsterdam University Press, 2019).
Engels, F., and Marx, K., *The Communist Manifesto*, trans. S. Moore (London: Penguin, 2002).
Eshun, K., *More Brilliant Than the Sun: Adventures in Sonic Fiction* (London: Quartet, 1998).
Fallis, J., and King, T. K., 'Lucy Finally Understands How Cellphones Work: Ambiguous Digital Technologies in *Twin Peaks: The Return* and Its Fan Communities', in A. Sanna (ed.), *Critical Essays on Twin Peaks: The Return* (Cham: Palgrave Macmillan, 2019), pp. 53–68.

Faucher, K., *Metastasis and Metastability: A Deleuzian Approach to Information* (Rotterdam: Sense Publishers, 2013).

Faure, É., 'Vocation du Cinéma', in *Fonction du Cinema, De la cinéplastique à son destin social (1921–1937)* (Paris: Éditions d'Histoire et de d'Art, Librairie Plon, 1954).

Fisher, M., *Capitalist Realism: Is There No Alternative?* (Alresford: Zero Books, 2009).

Flaxman, G., 'Cinema in the Age of Control', in F. Beckman (ed.), *Control Culture: Foucault and Deleuze after Discipline* (Edinburgh: Edinburgh University Press, 2018), pp. 121–40.

— 'Cinema Year Zero', in G. Flaxman (ed.), *The Brain is the Screen: Deleuze and the Philosophy of Cinema* (Minneapolis, MN: University of Minnesota Press, 2000), pp. 87–108.

— *Gilles Deleuze and the Fabulation of Philosophy: Powers of the False, Volume I* (Minneapolis, MN: University of Minnesota Press, 2012).

— 'Out of Field: The Future of Film Studies', *Angelaki: Journal of the Theoretical Humanities*, 17(4) (2012), pp. 119–37.

Floridi, L., *Information: A Very Short Introduction* (Oxford: Oxford University Press, 2010).

— *The Philosophy of Information* (Oxford: Oxford University Press, 2011).

— 'Semantic Conceptions of Information', in *Stanford Encyclopedia of Philosophy* (summer 2019 edition), ed. E. N. Zalta, https://plato.stanford.edu/archives/sum2019/entries/information-semantic/

Foltz, J., 'David Lynch's Late Style', *The LA Review of Books*, 12 November 2017, https://lareviewofbooks.org/article/david-lynchs-late-style/

Foster Wallace, D., *A Supposedly Fun Thing I'll Never Do Again: Essays and Arguments* (New York: Back Bay Books, 2009).

Fóti, V., *Vision's Invisibles: Philosophical Explorations* (New York: State University of New York Press, 2003).

Foucault, M., *Discipline and Punish – The Birth of the Prison*, trans. A. Sheridan (New York: Vintage, 1995).

— *Manet and the Object of Painting*, trans. M. Barr (London: Tate Publishing, 2009).

— 'Maurice Blanchot: The Thought from Outside', in M. Blanchot and M. Foucault, *Foucault / Blanchot*, trans. B. Massumi and J. Mehlman (New York: Zone Books, 1987), pp. 7–60.

— *The Order of Things: An Archaeology of the Human Sciences*, trans. A. Sheridan (Abingdon: Routledge, 2005).

Fridman, L., interview with Mark Zuckerberg, 'Mark Zuckerberg: Meta, Instagram and the Metaverse', *Lex Fridman Podcast*, 27 February 2022, https://www.youtube.com/watch?v=5zOHSysMmH0

Fuller, M., 'Art Methodologies in Media Ecology', in S. O'Sullivan and S. Zepke (eds), *Deleuze, Guattari and the Production of the New* (London: Continuum, 2008), pp. 45–55.

Bibliography

Fukuyama, 'The End of History?', *The National Interest*, 16 (summer 1989), pp. 2–18.
Galloway, A. R., *Laruelle: Against the Digital* (Minneapolis, MN: University of Minnesota Press, 2014).
— *Protocol: How Control Exists After Decentralization* (Cambridge, MA: MIT Press, 2004).
Galloway, A. R., and Thacker, E., *The Exploit: A Theory of Networks* (Minneapolis, MN: University of Minnesota Press, 2007).
Gammack, J., Hobbs, V., and Pigott, D., *The Book of Informatics* (Melbourne: Thompson, 2007).
Gaudreault, A., and Marion, P., *The End of Cinema? A Medium in Crisis in the Digital Age*, trans. T. Barnard (New York: Columbia University Press, 2015).
Gerken, T., 'Young Watch Almost Seven Times Less TV than Over-65s – Ofcom', *BBC News*, 17 August 2022, https://www.bbc.com/news/technology-62506041
Goddard, M., 'Guattari and Berardi and the Post-Media Era', in C. Apprich, J. Berry Slater, A. Iles and O. Lerone Schultz (eds), *Provocative Alloys: A Post-Media Anthology* (Berlin: Mute Books, 2013), pp. 44–61.
Gomery, D., *The Coming of Sound – A History* (Abingdon: Routledge, 2005).
Groenstad, A., 'Back to Bazin? Filmicity in the Age of the Digital Image', *Popular Culture Review*, 13(2) (2002), pp. 11–23.
Grossman, J., and Scheibel, W., *Twin Peaks* (Detroit, MI: Wayne State University Press, 2020).
Guattari, F., *Chaosmosis: An Ethico-Aesthetic Paradigm*, trans. P. Bains and J. Pefanis (Indianapolis, IN: Indiana University Press, 1995).
— *The Machinic Unconscious: Essays in Schizoanalysis*, trans. T. Adkins (Los Angeles: Semiotext(e), 2011).
— *Molecular Revolution: Psychiatry and Politics*, trans. R. Sheed (London: Penguin, 1984).
— *Psychoanalysis and Transversality: Texts and Interviews 1955–1971*, trans. A. Hodges (South Pasadena, CA: Semiotext(e), 2003).
— *Schizoanalytic Cartographies*, trans. A. Goffey (London: Bloomsbury, 2013).
— *Soft Subversions: Texts and Interviews 1977–1985*, trans. C. Wiener and E. Wittman (Los Angeles: Semiotext(e), 2009).
Haas, U., and Large, W., *Maurice Blanchot* (London: Routledge, 2001).
Hadjioannou, M., 'In Search of Lost Reality: Waltzing with Bashir', in D. Martin-Jones and W. Brown (eds), *Deleuze and Film* (Edinburgh: Edinburgh University Press, 2012), pp. 104–20.
Harper, T., and Savat, D. (eds), *Media After Deleuze* (London: Bloomsbury, 2016).
Heidegger, M., *Off the Beaten Track*, trans. J. Young and K. Haynes (Cambridge: Cambridge University Press, 2002).

— 'Traditional Language and Technical Language', trans. W. T. Gregory, *Journal of Philosophical Research*, 23 (1998), pp. 129–45.

Hill, L., *Blanchot: Extreme Contemporary* (London: Routledge, 1997).

Hoberman, J., and Rosenbaum, J., *Midnight Movies* (Cambridge, MA: Da Capo, 1991).

Holland, E. W., *Deleuze and Guattari's Anti-Oedipus: Introduction to Schizoanalysis* (London: Routledge, 2001).

Horning, R., and Ulman, A., 'Perpetual Provisional Selves: A Conversation about Authenticity and Social Media', *Rhizome*, 11 December 2014, https://rhizome.org/editorial/2014/dec/11/rob-horning-and-amalia-ulman/

Idato, M., 'David Lynch on the Return of *Twin Peaks* and Why He Will Never Make Another Film', *Sydney Morning Herald*, 16 April 2007 (updated 5 May 2017), http://www.smh.com.au/entertainment/tv-and-radio/david-lynch-on-the-return-of-twin-peaks-and-why-he-will-never-make-another-film-20170416-gvlr60.html

Jameson, F., *Postmodernism, or The Cultural Logic of Late Capitalism* (London: Verso, 1991).

Jenkins, H., '"Do You Enjoy Making the Rest of us Feel Stupid?": alt.tv.twinpeaks, the Trickster Author and Viewer Mastery', in D. Lavery (ed.), *Full of Secrets: Critical Approaches to Twin Peaks* (Detroit, MI: Wayne State University Press, 1995), pp. 51–69.

Kadner, N., 'Lynch Goes Digital with Inland Empire', *American Cinematographer*, 88(4) (2007), https://theasc.com/ac_magazine/April2007/PostFocus/page1.html

Kahn, D., *Noise, Water, Meat: A History of Sound in the Arts* (Cambridge, MA: MIT Press, 2001).

Kant, I., *Critique of Judgement*, trans. W. S. Pluhar (Indianapolis, IN: Hackett, 1987).

— *Critique of Pure Reason*, ed. M. Weigelt, trans. M. Weigelt and M. Muller (London: Penguin, 2007).

Kaplan, C., *Questions of Travel: Postmodern Discourses of Displacement* (Durham, NC: Duke University Press, 1996).

Krapp, P., *Noise Channels: Glitch and Error in Digital Culture* (Minneapolis, MN: University of Minnesota Press, Minneapolis, 2011).

Land, N., 'Circuitries', in R. Mackay and A. Avanessian (eds), *The Accelerationist Reader* (Falmouth: Urbanomic, 2014), pp. 251–74.

Lapoujade, D., *Aberrant Movements: The Philosophy of Gilles Deleuze*, trans J. D. Jordan (South Pasadena, CA: Semiotext(e), 2017).

Leibniz, G. W., *Discourse on Metaphysics*, trans. G. Rodriguez-Pereyra (Oxford: Oxford University Press, 2020).

Lim, D., *David Lynch: The Man from Another Place* (New York: Amazon Icon Series, 2015).

Loyd, R., 'Television Review: Stars in their Eyes in "Hollywood Heights,"' *The Los Angeles Times*, 18 June 2012, https://www.latimes.

com/entertainment/tv/la-xpm-2012-jun-18-la-et-hollywood-heights-20120618-story.html

Lynch, D., *Catching the Big Fish: Meditation, Consciousness and Creativity* (New York: Tarcher Perigee, 2016).

— *Lynch on Lynch*, ed. C. Rodley (New York: Farrar, Straus and Giroux, 2005).

Lyotard, J. F., *The Inhuman: Reflections on Time*, trans. G. Bennington and R. Bowlby (Stanford, CA: Stanford University Press, 1991).

— *The Postmodern Condition: A Report on Knowledge*, trans. G. Bennington and B. Massumi (Minneapolis, MN: University of Minnesota Press, 1984).

— 'The Sublime and the Avant-Garde', in C. Cazeau (ed.), *The Continental Aesthetics Reader – 2nd Edition* (New York: Routledge, 2017), pp. 585–97.

Manovich, L., *The Language of New Media* (Cambridge, MA: MIT Press, 2001).

Marrati, P., *Gilles Deleuze: Cinema and Philosophy*, trans. A. Hartz (Baltimore, MD: Johns Hopkins University Press, 2008).

Marshall, C., 'David Lynch Made a Disturbing Web Sitcom Called "Rabbits": It's Now Used by Psychologists to Induce a Sense of Existential Crisis in Research Subjects', *Open Culture*, 30 May 2018, http://www.openculture.com/2018/05/david-lynch-made-a-disturbing-web-sitcom-called-rabbits.html

Marx, K., *Capital: A Critique of Political Economy – Volume One*, trans. B. Fowkes (London: Penguin, 1982).

— *The Poverty of Philosophy: Answer to the Philosophy of Poverty by M. Proudhon*, trans. French Institute of Marxism-Leninism (Paris: Progress, 1955).

Maxford, H., *The A-Z of Hitchcock* (London: Batsford, 2002).

McLuhan, M., *Understanding Media: The Extensions of Man* (Cambridge, MA: MIT Press, 1994).

McGowan, T., *The Impossible David Lynch* (New York: Columbia University Press, 2007).

Metz, C., *Film Language: A Semiotics of the Cinema*, trans. M. Taylor (Chicago: University of Chicago Press, 1991).

Mittell, J., 'The Qualities of Complexity: Vast Versus Dense Seriality in Contemporary Television', in J. Jacobs and S. Peacock (eds), *Television Aesthetics and Style* (London: Bloomsbury, 2013), pp. 45–56.

Mulvey, L., 'Visual Pleasure and Narrative Cinema', *Screen*, 16(3) (1975), pp. 6–18.

Münsterberg, H., *The Photoplay – A Psychological Study* (New York: D. Appleton and Co., 1916).

Nealon, J. T., '"The Path is for Your Steps Alone": Popular Music, Neoliberalism and Biopolitics', in F. Beckman (ed.), *Control Culture:*

Foucault and Deleuze after Discipline (Edinburgh: Edinburgh University Press, 2018), pp. 101–20.

Negarestani, R., 'Death as a Perversion: Openness and Germinal Death', in J. Johnson (ed.), *Dark Trajectories: Politics of the Outside* (Creative Commons, 2013), pp. 55–79.

Negri, A., *The Savage Anomaly: The Power of Spinoza's Metaphysics and Politics*, trans. M. Hardt (Minneapolis, MN: University of Minnesota Press, 1991).

Newman, S., 'Politics in the Age of Control', in M. Poster and D. Savat (eds), *Deleuze and New Technology* (Edinburgh: Edinburgh University Press, 2009), pp. 104–24.

Niedland, J., *David Lynch* (Urbana, IL: University of Illinois Press, 2012).

Novikov, D. A., *Cybernetics: From Past to Future* (Cham: Springer, 2016).

Nunes, M., 'Error, Noise, and Potential: The Outside of Purpose', in M. Nunes (ed.), *Error: Glitch, Noise and Jam in New Media Cultures* (New York: Continuum, 2011), pp. 3–26.

Olkowski, D., *Gilles Deleuze and the Ruin of Representation* (Berkeley, CA: University of California Press, 1999).

O'Sullivan, S., and Zepke, S. (eds), *Deleuze, Guattari and the Production of the New* (London: Continuum, 2008).

Panofsky, E., 'Style and Medium in Motion Pictures', in *Three Essays on Style*, ed. I. Lavin (Cambridge, MA: MIT Press, 1995), pp. 91–129.

Patton, P., 'Philosophy and Control', in F. Beckman (ed.), *Control Culture: Foucault and Deleuze after Discipline* (Edinburgh: Edinburgh University Press, 2018), pp. 193–210.

Pierce, J. R., *An Introduction to Information Theory: Symbols, Signals and Noise (Second Edition)* (New York: Dover, 1980).

Pisters, P., *The Neuro-Image: A Deleuzian Film-Philosophy of Digital Screen Culture* (Stanford, CA: Stanford University Press, 2012).

Poster, M., 'Afterword', in M. Poster and D. Savat (eds), *Deleuze and New Technology* (Edinburgh: Edinburgh University Press, 2009), pp. 258–62.

Prigogine, I., and Stengers, I., *Order out of Chaos: Man's New Dialogue with Nature* (Toronto: Bantam Books, 1984).

Prince, S., *Digital Visual Effects in Cinema: The Seduction of Reality* (New Brunswick, NJ: Rutgers University Press, 2012).

Proust, M., *In Search of Lost Time: Volume I – Swann's Way*, trans. C. K. Scott Moncrieff and T. Kilmartin (New York: The Modern Library, 1992).

— 'Letter to Camille Vettard – 5th October 1922', *The American Reader*, https://theamericanreader.com/5-october-1922-marcel-proust-to-camille-vettard/

Rentschler, E., *The Ministry of Illusion: Nazi Cinema and Its Afterlife* (Cambridge, MA: Harvard University Press, 2002).

Bibliography

Restivo, A., *Breaking Bad and Cinematic Television* (Durham, NC: Duke University Press, 2019).
Rimbaud, A., *Complete Works, Selected Letters*, trans. W. Fowlie (Chicago: University of Chicago Press, 2005).
Rodowick, D. N., *Elegy for Theory* (Cambridge, MA: Harvard University Press, 2014).
— *Gilles Deleuze's Time Machine* (Durham, NC: Duke University Press, 1997).
— 'Introduction: What does Time Express?' in D. N. Rodowick (ed.), *Afterimages of Deleuze's Film Philosophy* (Minneapolis, MN: University of Minnesota Press, 2010), pp. xiii–xxiv.
— *The Virtual Life of Film* (Cambridge, MA: Harvard University Press, 2007).
Ropars-Wuilleumier, M., 'Image or Time? The Thought of the Outside in *The Time-Image* (Deleuze and Blanchot)', in D. N. Rodowick (ed.), *Afterimages of Gilles Deleuze's Film Philosophy* (Minneapolis, MN: University of Minnesota Press, 2010), pp. 15–30.
Rushton, R., *Cinema after Deleuze* (London: Continuum, 2012).
Russolo, L., 'The Art of Noise' (excerpts), trans. C. Tisdall, in U. Appollonio (ed.), *Futurist Manifestos* (London: Tate Publishing, 2009), pp. 74–87.
Ruyer, R., *La cybernétique et l'origine de l'information* (Paris: Éditions Flammarion, 1954).
Sauvagnargues, A., *Artmachines – Deleuze, Guattari, Simondon*, trans. S. Verderber and E. W. Holland (Edinburgh: Edinburgh University Press, 2016).
— *Deleuze and Art*, trans. S. Bankston (London: Bloomsbury, 2018).
Scruton, R., 'Photography and Representation', *Critical Inquiry*, 7(3) (1981), pp. 577–603.
Shannon, C., and Weaver, W., *The Mathematical Theory of Communication* (Urbana, IL: University of Illinois Press, 1964).
Sibertin-Blanc, G., *State and Politics: Deleuze and Guattari on Marx*, trans. A. Hodges (South Pasadena, CA: Semiotext(e), 2016).
Simondon, G., *Individuation in Light of Notions of Form and Information*, trans. T. Adkins (Minneapolis, MN: University of Minnesota Press, 2020).
— *On the Mode of Existence of Technical Objects*, trans. C. Malaspina and J. Rogove (Minneapolis, MN: Univocal, 2017).
Simpson, B., 'It's Our Act of Killing, Too', *The Nation*, 28 February 2014, https://www.thenation.com/article/archive/its-our-act-killing-too.
Sinnerbrink, R., *Cinematic Ethics: Exploring Ethical Experience Through Film* (Abingdon: Routledge, 2016).
— *New Philosophies of Film: Thinking Images* (London: Continuum, 2011).
Skakov, N., *The Cinema of Tarkovsky: Labyrinths of Space and Time* (London: I.B. Tauris, 2012).

Smith, D., and Protevi, J., 'Gilles Deleuze', in *The Stanford Encyclopedia of Philosophy* (spring 2018 edition), ed. E. N. Zalta, https://plato.stanford.edu/archives/spr2018/entries/deleuze/

Somers-Hall, H., *Deleuze's Difference and Repetition* (Edinburgh: Edinburgh University Press, 2013).

Spinoza, B., 'The Ethics', in *A Spinoza Reader: The Ethics and Other Works*, ed. and trans. E. Curley (Princeton, NJ: Princeton University Press, 1994), pp. 85–265.

— *Theological-Political Treatise*, ed. J. Israel, trans. M. Silverthorne and J. Israel (Cambridge: Cambridge University Press, 2007).

Spivak, G. C., 'Can the Subaltern Speak' (rev. edn), in R. Morris (ed.), *Can the Subaltern Speak? Reflections on the History of an Idea* (New York: Columbia University Press, 2010), pp. 21–78.

Sterritt, D., *The Films of Jean-Luc Godard: Seeing the Invisible* (Cambridge: Cambridge University Press, 1999).

Stiegler, B., *Acting Out*, trans. D. Barison, D. Ross and P. Crogan (Stanford, CA: Stanford University Press, 2009).

— *States of Shock: Stupidity and Knowledge in the Twenty-first Century*, trans. D. Ross (Cambridge: Polity, 2015).

— *Symbolic Misery – Vol. 1: The Hyperindustrial Epoch*, trans. B. Norman (Cambridge: Polity, 2014).

— *Symbolic Misery – Vol. 2: The Katastrophē of the Sensible*, trans. B. Norman (Cambridge: Polity, 2015).

— *Technics and Time, 1: The Fault of Epimetheus*, trans. R. Beardsworth and G. Collins (Stanford, CA: Stanford University Press, 1998).

Tampio, N., *Deleuze's Political Vision* (Lanham, MD: Rowman and Littlefield, 2015).

Tarkovsky, A., *Sculpting in Time: Reflections on the Cinema*, trans. K. Hunter-Blair (Austin, TX: University of Texas Press, 1989).

Thiele, K., '"To Believe in this World, As It Is": Immanence and the Quest for Political Activism', *Deleuze Studies*, 4 (2010), issue supplement – 'Deleuze and Political Activism', pp. 27–45.

Thomas, A. J., *Deleuze, Cinema and the Thought of the World* (Edinburgh: Edinburgh University Press, 2018).

Thompson, H. S., *Fear and Loathing in Las Vegas* (London: Harper Collins, 1998).

Toffler, A., *Future Shock* (New York: Bantam Books, 1971).

Virilio, P., *The Information Bomb*, trans. C. Turner (London: Verso, 2005).

— *Speed and Politics*, trans. M. Polizzotti (Los Angeles: Semiotext(e), 2006).

Voss, D., *Conditions of Thought: Deleuze and Transcendental Ideas* (Edinburgh: Edinburgh University Press, 2013).

— 'Deleuze's Third Synthesis of Time', *Deleuze Studies*, 8(1) (2013), pp. 194–216.

Bibliography

Wahl, J., *Vers le concret: Études d'histoire de la philosophie contemporaine* (Paris: J. Vrin, 1932).
Waugh, M., '"Make Sense of It": Cult and Complex TV Fandoms, Post-Truth Discourse and an Excess of Meaning in *Twin Peaks*: Season 3', *Critical Studies in Television*, 0(0) (2022), pp. 1–19.
Weber, M., *The Protestant Ethic and the Spirit of Capitalism*, trans. T. Parsons (London: Routledge, 2001).
Wiener, N., *Cybernetics: or Control and Communication in the Animal and the Machine* (Cambridge, MA: MIT Press, 1985).
— *The Human Use of Human Beings: Cybernetics and Society* (London: Free Association Books, 1989).
— 'A Scientist Rebels', *The Atlantic Monthly*, January 1947, p. 46.
Widder, N., *Political Theory After Deleuze* (London: Continuum, 2012).
Williams, J., *Gilles Deleuze's Difference and Repetition: A Critical Introduction and Guide* (Edinburgh: Edinburgh University Press, 2013).
Williams, R., *Television: Technology and Cultural Form*, ed. E. Williams (London: Routledge, 2003).
Woodward, A., *Lyotard and the Inhuman Condition: Reflections of Nihilism, Information and Art* (Edinburgh: Edinburgh University Press, 2016).
Zepke, S., '"A work of art does not contain the least bit of information": Deleuze and Guattari and Contemporary Art', in S. van Tuinen and S. Zepke (eds), *Art History after Deleuze and Guattari* (Leuven: Leuven University Press, 2017), pp. 237–54.
Žižek, S., *Organs Without Bodies: Deleuze and Consequences* (New York: Routledge, 2004).

Filmography

2001: A Space Odyssey (Stanley Kubrick, 1968)
8½ (Federico Fellini, 1963)
The Act of Killing (Joshua Oppenheimer, Christine Cyn and Anonymous, 2012)
Andrei Rublev (Andrei Tarkovsky, 1969)
Armageddon (Michael Bay, 1998)
Avatar (James Cameron, 2009)
L'Avventura (Michelangelo Antonioni, 1960)
Blue Velvet (David Lynch, 1986)
The Cabinet of Dr. Caligari (Robert Wiene, 1920)
Un Chien Andalou (Luis Buñuel, 1929)
Citizen Kane (Orson Welles, 1941)
Contempt (Jean-Luc Godard, 1963)
Daybreak (Marcel Carné, 1939)
Die Hard (John McTiernan, 1988)

Dog Star Man (Stan Brakhage, 1961–64)
Eraserhead (David Lynch, 1977)
Europe '51 (Roberto Rossellini, 1952)
La Femme du Gange (Marguerite Duras, 1974)
Fargo (Joel and Ethan Coen, 1996)
Germany, Year Zero (Roberto Rossellini, 1948)
Go! Go! Go! (Marie Menken, 1964)
Hitler: A Film from Germany (Hans Jürgen Syberberg, 1977)
Hostel (Eli Roth, 2005)
Inland Empire (David Lynch, 2006)
La Jetée (Chris Marker, 1962)
Jurassic Park (Steven Spielberg, 1993)
The Lady from Shanghai (Orson Welles, 1947)
Last Year at Marienbad (Alain Resnais, 1961)
Lights (Marie Menken, 1966)
Mothlight (Stan Brakhage, 1963)
No Country for Old Men (Joel and Ethan Coen, 2007)
Nosferatu (F. W. Murnau, 1922)
Passion (Jean-Luc Godard, 1982)
Persona (Ingmar Bergman, 1966)
Pierrot le Fou (Jean-Luc Godard, 1965)
Rear Window (Alfred Hitchcock, 1954)
Rope (Alfred Hitchcock, 1948)
Saw (James Wan, 2004)
The Shining (Stanley Kubrick, 1980)
Stalker (Andrei Tarkovsky, 1979)
Star Trek II: The Wrath of Khan (Nicholas Meyer, 1982)
Star Wars (George Lucas, 1977)
The State of Things (Wim Wenders, 1982)
The Structure of Crystals (Krysztof Zanussi, 1969)
Taxi Driver (Martin Scorsese, 1976)
Torn Curtain (Alfred Hitchcock, 1966)
Toy Story (John Lasseter, 1995)
Tron (Steven Lisberger, 1982)
Umberto D. (Vittorio de Sica, 1952)
Weekend (Jean-Luc Godard, 1968)
A Woman of Paris (Charles Chaplin, 1923)

Television

Breaking Bad (Vince Gilligan, 2008–13)
… but the clouds… (Samuel Beckett, 1977)
Curb Your Enthusiasm (Larry David, 2000–)
Fawlty Towers (John Cleese and Connie Booth, 1975–79)

Bibliography

Futurama (Matt Groening, 1999–)
Ghost Trio (Samuel Beckett, 1976)
Mad Men (Matthew Weiner, 2007–15)
The Office (Ricky Gervais and Stephen Merchant, 2001–03)
Peep Show (Jesse Armstrong and Sam Bain, 2003–15)
Quad (Samuel Beckett, 1981)
Rick and Morty (Justin Roiland and Dan Harmon, 2013–)
Seinfeld (Larry David and Jerry Seinfeld, 1989–98)
Sex and the City (Darren Star, 1998–2004)
The Simpsons (Matt Groening, 1989–)
The Sopranos (David Chase, 1999–2007)
Twin Peaks (Mark Frost and David Lynch, 1990–91)
Twin Peaks: The Return (Mark Frost and David Lynch, 2017)
The Wire (David Simon, 2002–08)

Other Works

Lucier, A., 'I am Sitting in a Room', New York, Lovely Music Ltd, 1981
Lynch, D., 'David Lynch Theatre', YouTube, 1 February 2020, https://www.youtube.com/c/davidlynchtheater
'Ontologist', 'I am Sitting in a Video Room 1000', YouTube, 28 May 2010, https://www.youtube.com/watch?v=8qKz5YW5J-U
Red Dead Redemption 2 (Rockstar Games, 2018)
The Velvet Underground, 'Rock & Roll', *Loaded*, Atlantic Records, 1970
World of War Craft (Blizzard Entertainment, 2004)

Index

8½ (Fellini), 80

action-image, 50–3, 84, 168, 209
Act of Killing, the (Oppenheimer, Cynn, Anonymous), 98–9
actual/actualisation, 32, 48, 55–62, 77, 144–5, 147, 149, 186, 189, 205, 233
Adorno, T., 79, 85, 165, 194n, 209, 219, 226n
affirmation, 33, 39n, 53, 68n, 189, 223, 232
Andrei Rublev (Tarkovsky), 87
Ansell-Pearson, K., 2, 55, 69n
Antonioni, M., 85
any-space-whatever, 85, 179, 205
Aristotle, 7, 37n, 142, 186, 197n
Armageddon (Bay), 81, 101n
Arnoux, A., 105
art, 5, 8, 19, 29, 34, 37n, 56, 66–7, 79, 83, 87, 94, 101n, 115, 124, 127, 130n, 148, 151–7, 160n, 175, 183, 186, 190–1, 195n, 197n, 198n, 199, 203, 219–20, 222, 235
Artaud, A., 22, 28–9, 53, 95, 152
Avatar (Cameron), 113, 234
L'Avventura (Antonioni), 85

Badiou, A., 74, 89, 225n
Bateson, G., 139–40, 159n
Bazin, A., 106, 110, 112, 130n
Bay, M., 81, 113
Beckett, S., 204–7, 225n

belief in the World, 74, 83, 86–8, 91–2, 128, 193, 223, 233
Benjamin, W., 9, 106, 222
Bergson, H., 32, 40–6, 48, 50, 53, 55–8, 60, 68n, 69n, 70n, 84, 97, 148–9, 161n, 205, 221
Berkeley, B., 93, 99
Blanchot, M., 9, 19–23, 25, 36n, 52–3, 164, 175–6, 231
Blue Velvet (Lynch), 179
Bogue, R., 13, 53–4
Bordwell, D., 52, 71n, 227n
Bowden, S., 31, 72
Brakhage, S., 157
...but the clouds... (Beckett), 205

Cage, J., 152
Cameron, J., 113
Carr, N., 6, 16n, 192
Carroll, N., 52, 71n, 203, 227n
capitalism, 10, 75, 77–9, 81–4, 95, 113–15, 120–2, 182, 187–8, 193, 200–2, 216, 221–2
capitalist realism, 84, 92
Chaplin, C., 1
Coen, J. & E., 70n
communication, 5–6, 7–8, 19–20, 23, 47, 117, 124, 127, 136–8, 141–2, 146, 148, 153, 155, 176, 181–2
control, 5–6, 75, 115, 118–23, 125–8, 134, 139–41, 164–5, 175, 182, 184–5, 187–8, 192–3, 200–1, 211–13, 221, 234–7

254

Index

Contempt (Godard), 80
crystal-image, 61–2, 66–7, 73n
Curb Your Enthusiasm (David), 207
cybernetics, 5, 119, 138–42, 144–7, 151, 158n

Dern, L., 172, 184–5
Die Hard (McTiernan), 51
different/ciation, 58–61
digital/digitisation, 3–6, 8, 10–12, 15n, 81, 105–14, 121, 137, 164–5, 172–6, 179, 180, 183–5, 188–94, 199–201, 211–13, 215–19, 220, 223, 231, 235–7
dividuality, 120–1, 187–8, 192, 197n, 235, 236

Eco, U., 152, 156–7, 163n
Eisenstein, S., 52, 87, 93, 99
Eraserhead (Lynch), 172
Eshun, K., 229–30n
Europe '51 (Rossellini), 96–7
exhaustion, 205–9, 210, 217

Faure, É., 86–7
Fawlty Towers (Cleese, Booth), 207–8
feedback, 5, 139–40, 215
Fellini, F., 80
Fisher, M., 84
Fisher, R., 135–6
Flaxman, G., 10, 44, 109–14, 126, 130n, 234
Floridi, L., 7, 116, 135, 137–8, 162n
Foucault, M., 9, 15n, 23–4, 118–19, 123, 231
frame/framing, 1, 42–3, 46–50, 53, 111–12, 114, 176, 232
Fukuyama, F., 208
Fuller, M., 190, 198n

Galloway, A., 12, 211
Germany, Year Zero (Rossellini), 54, 96
Ghost Trio (Beckett), 205
Godard, J.L., 53, 71n, 80, 204
Guattari, F., 46, 75–6, 77, 81, 83, 132n, 182, 201–2, 221–3, 237

Heidegger, M., 19, 116–17
Hegel, G.W.F., 22
Hitchcock, A., 49, 70n
Hitler: A Film from Germany (Syberberg), 126–7
Holland, E., 82–3
Hume, D., 86

image, 3–5, 26, 40–4, 46, 53, 56, 68n, 108, 126, 202, 204–5, 237
immanence, 43–4, 68n, 89–91
impossibility, 74, 85, 95, 238; *see also* the intolerable
incompossibility, 186–7, 197n
indexicality, 106, 109, 110–11, 184
individuation, 57–8, 60, 62, 65, 142–6, 177, 192, 235
information, 5–6, 11, 46, 113, 114–18, 120–2, 126–8, 134–42, 144–8, 149–52, 156–7, 164–5, 169–71, 174, 176, 182, 184–5, 191, 192, 193–4, 219, 221, 234–5
  Deleuze and, 5–6, 11, 46, 109, 115, 117–18, 122, 124, 126–8
  semantic, 7–8, 11, 135, 149–50, 151, 168–70, 234
  Simondon and, 141–2, 144–6, 235
Inland Empire (Lynch), 12, 164–81, 183–9, 191–4, 199, 235–6
Instagram, 191, 197n
intensity, 59–60

255

intolerable, the, 95–7, 183, 189, 233; *see also* impossibility

Jetée, La (Marker), 62–7, 233
Jurassic Park (Spielberg), 107

Kafka, F., 20–1, 93–4
Kant, I., 27, 29, 30, 38n
Kubrick, S., 2, 130n

Lang, F., 125
Lapoujade, D., 97, 178
Last Year at Marienbad (Resnais), 2
Leibniz, G.W., 186, 197n
literature, 9, 18–22, 52, 176, 210, 231
Lucas, G., 107
Lucier, A., 155–6
Lynch, D., 164, 168, 171–3, 175, 177–81, 183–4, 195n, 212–15, 217–19, 220, 223, 229n 235
Lyotard, J.F., 6, 16n, 85, 116, 153

Manovich, L., 108, 129n
Marker, C., 62–6
Marrati, P., 10
Marx, K., 81, 101n, 102n, 182, 196n
Mathematical Theory of Communication, 7–8, 136–8, 148–50, 153, 170, 234–5
McLuhan, M., 207, 226n
media, 3, 5, 6, 10, 105–8, 111–14, 125, 129n, 133n, 137, 157, 173, 175, 180, 183–4, 190–1, 200–1, 212, 221–3; *see also* social media, digitisation
memory, 29–30, 32, 56–8
Menken, M., 157
metastability, 142, 144, 146, 235
minority cinema, 91–5
movement-image, 44, 45–6, 50, 51, 56, 79, 80, 99, 176, 233
multiplicity, 59

Negri, A., 88, 90
Nietzsche, F., 25, 33–4, 43, 186, 231
noise, 8, 11, 148–57, 164, 176, 177–8, 179, 191, 192, 193–4, 211, 234, 235

Office, the (Gervais, Merchant), 208
Oppenheimer, Joshua, 98
out-of-Field, 47–8, 50, 109, 111, 176
outside, the, 2–3, 9, 20–5, 40, 52, 54, 67, 92, 95, 109, 111, 114–15, 124, 164–5, 175–6, 178, 183, 189–91, 193, 206–7, 211, 212, 221, 231, 233, 235–6, 238; *see also* the unthought
overman, 25, 192–3, 231

Panofsky, E., 86
Passion (Godard), 80
Patton, P., 121
Peep Show (Armstrong, Bain), 207–8
philosophy, 2–3, 4, 14, 16n, 17n, 26–7, 34, 41–2, 45–6, 48, 63, 115–16, 166, 183, 203, 221, 222, 231, 232
Pisters, P., 14
Plato, 41, 42, 43
politics, 5, 10, 51–2, 65, 74–8, 85–6, 91, 95, 97–9, 101n, 106, 117, 121, 160n, 178, 222, 236
possibility, 100, 138, 148–9, 205–7
post-media, 222–3
Proust, M., 56–7

Quad (Beckett), 205–6, 207

Rammellzee, 94
Rear Window (Hitchcock), 49

Index

Red Dead Redemption 2 (Rockstar), 112
Resnais, A., 2
Riefenstahl, L., 99
Rodowick, D.N., 14, 108
Ropars-Wuilleumier, M., 25
Rossellini, R., 54, 96
Russolo, L., 154–5

Sauvagnargues, A., 28, 43, 66, 69n, 73n
Scorsese, M., 85
Seinfeld (Seinfeld, David), 207
sensory-motor system, 32, 53–4, 55, 62, 65, 84–6, 91, 96–7, 125, 206, 233
Sex and the City (Star), 207
Shannon, C., 7, 134, 135, 136–8, 148–51, 234
Shining, the (Kubrick), 2, 130n
Sica, V. de, 96
sign, 27–8, 46–7, 63, 64, 232
Simondon, G., 14, 58, 62, 141–7, 148, 159n, 160n, 161n, 176, 212, 235
Simpsons, the (Groening), 208–9, 226n
Sinnerbrink, R., 104n, 164, 165, 195n
social media, 187, 191
Sopranos, the (Chase), 210, 227n
Spielberg, S., 107
Spinoza, B., 43, 88–91, 103n
Spivak, G.C., 103n
split subject, 30–1, 147, 185, 187–8
Stalker (Tarkovsky), 88
Star Trek II: The Wrath of Khan (Meyer), 107
Star Wars (Lucas), 107
Stiegler, B., 6, 14, 16n, 201, 212
State of Things, the (Wenders), 80
subjectivity/subjectivation, 31, 33, 56, 66, 119, 165, 188, 192, 201–2, 221, 236

sublime, the, 27, 29, 37–8n, 153, 200, 231–2
Syberberg, H., 126–27

Tarkovsky, A., 64, 87–88
Taxi Driver (Scorsese), 85
television, 79, 105, 112, 124–6, 133n, 191, 200–1, 202–5, 207–11, 213–15, 220, 223, 224n, 226n, 236
Thiele, K., 91
Thompson, H.S., 213
thought, 2–3, 4–5, 6, 22–4, 25–6, 31, 33, 43, 61, 67, 76–7, 86, 89, 95, 114, 140, 143, 147–8, 171, 183, 206, 231–2, 233, 237–8
  and cinema, 45, 49, 52–5, 76, 190, 232
  dogmatic Image of, 9, 26–8, 30, 33, 34, 46, 231–2
  without an Image, 29, 35, 61, 170; *see also* the outside
time, 44, 48, 50, 55, 57–8, 63–4, 67, 79–81, 85, 100, 186, 188, 206, 232
  three Syntheses of, 30–4, 86, 147, 232
time-image, 32, 51–2, 55, 62, 79, 80, 85, 91, 99, 100, 178, 186, 188, 206, 233
Toy Story (Lasseter), 107
transcendental illusion, 27, 60–1
transduction, 143–4, 146–8, 161n, 171, 176, 235
Tron (Lisberger), 107
Twin Peaks (Lynch, Frost), 180, 213, 214–19, 220, 228n

Umberto D. (de Sica), 96
unthought, the, 2, 5, 9, 28, 52, 76, 91, 114, 170, 232, 233; *see also* the outside

257

Virilio, P., 211
virtual/virtuality, 1, 10, 21, 32, 48, 55–63, 65–6, 77, 100, 124, 132, 142, 147, 149, 186, 188, 189–90, 193, 205, 207, 232–3, 236

Wahl, J., 36n
Weaver, W., 7, 135–6, 148–50, 170
Wenders, W., 80
whole, the, 9, 40–1, 43, 48–50, 52–3, 55, 62, 74, 99, 124, 134, 232–3
Widder, N., 43
Wiener, N., 119, 131n, 139–41, 179, 159n
Williams, R., 224n
Woman of Paris, A (Chaplin), 1
Woodward, A., 115–16
World of Warcraft (Blizzard), 112

Žižek, S., 74, 76, 84

EU representative:
Easy Access System Europe
Mustamäe tee 50, 10621 Tallinn, Estonia
Gpsr.requests@easproject.com

www.ingramcontent.com/pod-product-compliance
Lightning Source LLC
Chambersburg PA
CBHW070321240426
43671CB00013BA/2330